RECONCEPTUALISING PENALITY

Reconceptualising Penality
A Comparative Perspective on Punitiveness in Ireland, Scotland and New Zealand

CLAIRE HAMILTON
Queen's University Belfast, UK

Routledge
Taylor & Francis Group
LONDON AND NEW YORK

First published 2014 by Ashgate Publishing

2 Park Square, Milton Park, Abingdon, Oxfordshire OX14 4RN
52 Vanderbilt Avenue, New York, NY 10017

Routledge is an imprint of the Taylor & Francis Group, an informa business

First issued in paperback 2020

British Library Cataloguing in Publication Data
A catalogue record for this book is available from the British Library

The Library of Congress has cataloged the printed edition as follows:
Hamilton, Claire (Barrister)
Reconceptualising penality : a comparative perspective on punitiveness in Ireland, Scotland and New Zealand / by Claire Hamilton.
pages cm. -- (Advances in criminology)
Includes bibliographical references and index.
ISBN 978-1-4094-6316-0 (hardback)
1. Punishment – Ireland. 2. Punishment – Scotland. 3. Punishment – New Zealand. 4. Criminal justice, Administration of – Ireland. 5. Criminal justice, Administration of – Scotland. 6. Criminal justice, Administration of – New Zealand. I. Title.
HV9650.3.H36 2014
364.601–dc23

2014004286

ISBN 978-1-4094-6316-0 (hbk)
ISBN 978-0-367-60050-1 (pbk)

Contents

List of Figures

List of Tables

List of Cases

Napier v. Scottish Ministers [2005] SC 229 OH
R v. Belcher [2007] 1 NZLR 507
Hirst v. UK (No. 2) (2006) 42 EHRR 41
Vintner and others v. UK, European Court of Human Rights, Grand Chamber, 9th July 2013

List of Abbreviations

ACT	Association of Consumers and Taxpayers: New Zealand political party
ACYA	Action for Children and Youth Aotearoa (New Zealand)
AMS	Additional Member System: voting system which combines first-past-the-post with an element of proportional representation
ASBO	Anti-Social Behaviour Order
CAT	United Nations Committee Against Torture
CBD	Central Business District
CHS	Children's Hearing System
CJSW	Criminal Justice Social Work service: Scottish equivalent to the probation services
CIR	Citizen Initiated Referendum
CPT	European Committee for the Prevention of Torture and Inhuman and Degrading Treatment and Punishment
DPP	Director of Public Prosecutions (UK)
ECHR	European Convention for Human Rights and Fundamental Freedoms
ED	Executive Director
ESO	Extended Supervision Order
FGC	Family Group Conference
FF	Fianna Fáil: Lit. 'soldiers of destiny', centre-right Irish political party
FG	Fine Gael: Lit. 'family of the Gael', centre-right Irish political party
ICCPR	International Covenant on Civil and Political Rights
ICPS	International Centre for Prison Studies
ICVS	International Crime Victimisation Survey
INLA	Irish National Liberation Army, republican paramilitary group
IOM	Integrated Offender Management
MMP	Mixed Member Proportional: voting system which combines first-past-the-post with an element of proportional representation
NATO	North Atlantic Treaty Organization
NGO	Non-Governmental Organisation
NYC	New York City
NYPD	New York Police Department
NZ	New Zealand
OECD	Organisation for Economic Cooperation and Development
OLR	Order for Lifelong Restriction: Scottish incapacitative order
PD	Preventative detention: New Zealand order akin to a life sentence
PULSE	Police Using Leading Systems Effectively: electronic crime recording system used by the Gardaí

RMA	Risk Management Authority
SCC	Special Criminal Court
SNP	Scottish National Party
SPS	Scottish Prison Service
SST	Sensible Sentencing Trust: New Zealand victims' rights group
TD	Teachta Dála, Member of the Irish Parliament
UNCRC	United Nations Covenant on the Rights of the Child
UNCS	United Nations Crime Survey
UNICEF	United Nations Children's Fund (formerly United Nations Children's Emergency Fund)
ZTP	Zero Tolerance Policing

Foreword

I was delighted to be invited to write the foreword to this fine book.

Claire Hamilton is one of an emergent generation of international scholars whose research challenges core paradigms within criminology, criminal law and the sociology of punishment. I first became familiar with her work when I was asked to examine her doctoral thesis and I have followed her career with interest ever since. The viva voce was a memorable occasion not least for the liveliness of the intellectual conversation which ensued and her superb defence. It was also memorable because of the complexity of examination arrangements occasioned by the eruption of Eyjafjallajökull (Indeed, the grounding of flights because of the density of volcanic ash and the ensuing travel chaos provide a neat metaphor for a central theme of her book, namely how local and global influences can intersect in challenging ways!).

This book is of particular significance because it is empirically grounded, comparative in orientation, and because of the contribution which it makes to theory building. In *Reconceptualising Penality*, Claire argues for an approach to theory building based on analytical pluralism – an approach which acknowledges the impact of globalised influences and pressures on penal policy but, crucially, lays emphasis on the dynamics of particularity – recognising the greater significance (in her words the 'potency') of localised/cultural factors. Analytical pluralism is conceived as requiring both synchronic and diachronic modes of research and the empirical focus of her work takes in a 30-year sweep of history across three small-scale jurisdictions: Ireland, Scotland and New Zealand. This alone makes for a compelling read.

The argument in the book is framed by a critical examination of the ways in which the concept of punitiveness has been deployed in the broader sociological literature on punishment, highlighting inconsistencies in its interpretation and operationalisation across a broad spectrum of research. A core contribution of the book is the manner in which a more nuanced concept of punitiveness is evolved and applied to the three selected jurisdictions. For Claire, the punitiveness or otherwise of a particular jurisdiction requires careful calibration of process and culture across seven key dimensions (from policing through to the death penalty), taking into account factors such as the age of criminal responsibility, compliance with human rights imperatives, and the number of police complaints. The book will generate some debate with regard to the measure of punitiveness used and the method of scoring jurisdictions. However, it makes the very important point that the complexities of the real world should never be understated just so that theory attains a degree of 'elegance'; a devastating comment on some of the most influential and discipline-shaping theories which currently abound.

Claire concludes the book by stating that 'there is a need to better understand the present before we begin to contemplate the future'. In her careful exegesis of penal developments and her critical engagement with both theory and method, Claire reminds us of the need for greater reflexivity with regard to the concepts which we utilise to interrogate contemporary practice and the need to embrace more openly the multilayered and multilevelled terrain within which such scholarship is conducted. This important book will be of interest to theorists of penal change, those who wish to evolve stronger synergies between legal and criminological research, as well as those who have committed to supporting penal reform. On contemplating the future of comparative scholarship, it is clear that the discipline is in safe hands.

Lesley McAra
Professor of Penology
Dean, School of Law
University of Edinburgh
December 2013

Acknowledgements

I have incurred many debts in the long gestation of this book, first as a doctoral researcher and then in converting the thesis to a book. I must first of all extend my thanks to my contacts and interviewees across all three jurisdictions for providing me with the empirical data on which to base my conclusions. Specifically, I would like to thank the following for their considerable assistance with the collection and interpretation of statistical data: Venetia Haynes and Martin McNicoll in Prison Statistics, Scotland; Ann Tocher, Police Powers, Performance and Resources Division, Scotland; John Bole, General Manager, New Zealand Department of Corrections; Rufus Eames, New Zealand Police; Su-Wuen Ong, New Zealand Ministry of Justice and Seamus Beirne, Corporate Affairs, the Irish Prison Service.

Advancing arguments about jurisdictions which are not one's own can be a risky business and I owe a debt of gratitude to Dr Nessa Lynch, Dr Brian Easton and Dr Liz Campbell for their guidance in this regard. Closer to home I would like to extend my sincere thanks to Dr Barry Vaughan, Professor Shane Kilcommins and Professor Chris Whelan for taking the time to review my material so closely and for their insightful comments.

The research could not have been completed without the strong support of my supervisor, Professor Ian O'Donnell who was always available for guidance and continually challenged me to do better. I am also indebted to my former employers, Dublin Institute of Technology, for their financial support and for the many other ways in which they facilitated this research. Within DIT, David Forde in Mountjoy Square Library deserves a special mention for his kind assistance with my many and varied inter-library loan requests. Thanks also to Jane D'Arcy for her great assistance with interview transcription.

Special words of thanks must also go to the examiners of my thesis, Professor Lesley McAra and Dr Aogan Mulcahy. Their encouragement and highly constructive criticism played no small part in ensuring that the research was published as a book and I am particularly grateful to Lesley for taking the time out of a very busy schedule to write the foreword. Professor David Nelken, series editor of the Advances in Criminology Series, was also a great source of encouragement and I am grateful to both him and Alison Kirk in Ashgate Publishing for their faith in the project from the beginning.

Final, and deepest, thanks must go as always to my wonderful family for their support, particularly my husband Brendan.

Chapter 1
'Theory is not its own justification': Testing the Punitiveness Thesis

Criminology and the 'Punitive Obsession'

We live in an age of pessimism about punishment. While accounts as to the origins and contours of the 'punitive turn' in contemporary penal policies vary considerably, those surveying the criminological (and indeed sociological) literature in recent years would be left in little doubt as to the dystopian nature of the prognosis. Beginning in the 1990s, the unprecedented punitiveness of the United States, and England and Wales to a lesser degree, became a 'hot topic' among criminologists. Scholarly debate ensued on the forms this 'new punitiveness' had taken, its genesis and the inevitability of further increases in harshness. Its most obvious manifestation has been in the US where the eightfold rise in the use of imprisonment since the 1970s has resulted in it now having the highest rate of incarceration in the world. Mandatory sentencing laws, boot camps, supermax prisons, parole release restrictions, community notification laws and paedophile registers, among other developments, have also been cited as signifiers of the punitive turn. Pratt et al. (2005: xiii) authors of *The New Punitiveness*, identify the common thread underlying many of these policies as the return to 'emotive and destructive themes of sovereign punishment'. For them, what is 'new' about the 'new punitiveness' is its abandonment of the modernist imperatives of productive, restrained and rational punishment.

Punitive turn theorists aim to describe and explain these developments through reliance on a number of different reference frames. Importantly, despite the obvious connection in many people's minds, none of these involve crime as decades of criminological research have long since decoupled crime from punishment.[1] Kicking off the debate in the early 1990s, American criminologists Feeley and Simon (1992, 1994) drew attention to a new penological focus on risk management and the identification and management of unruly groups. This is achieved, they argue, by employing actuarial and managerialist techniques, promoting concerns with cost-effectiveness, efficiency and outputs. As criminal justice becomes an increasingly administrative system, the social purposes of punishment such as offender reintegration receive less emphasis, with much greater prominence given to social protection through incapacitation. Garland (2001), on the other hand, situates developments at the level of state sovereignty and explains the state's

1 For a synopsis see Tonry (2007: 1–3).

volatile reaction to crime in recent years in terms of its relative powerlessness to control crime rates. The title of his landmark text, *The Culture of Control*, denotes two policy adaptations in the face of high crime rates, namely, an adaptive strategy characterised by diversification of crime control functions and a sovereign state strategy that stresses coercive control of offenders. Both Garland's and Feeley and Simon's accounts allude to a 'late' or 'post-' modernity and the displacement of strategies aimed at rehabilitation of the offender ('penal welfarism') with those oriented towards protection of the public. Other elaborations of the punitiveness thesis point the finger at neo-liberalism, whether through the forced increased reliance on the criminal justice system to contain problems created by the dismantling of the social state or through the exclusionary cultural attitudes which such policies foster towards offenders (Pratt 1996; Wacquant 2003, 2009; Cavadino and Dignan 2006).

More recently, sceptical voices have emerged questioning the extent of the transformation. A significant number of criminologists have warned against 'criminologies of catastrophe' (O'Malley 2000) and the 'dangers of dystopias' (Zedner 2002) which overstate the reach of the 'punitive turn' and its coherence. Those most pertinent to the instant analysis include criticisms relating to the inconsistent operationalisation and general ambiguity surrounding the punitiveness concept and comparative studies challenging its empirical generality. Matthews (2005), for one, has been scathing of the failure to define punitiveness, describing it as a 'thin and undertheorised' concept. The vagueness which surrounds it, he argues, often allows commentators writing in the area to categorise a wide range of developments under the broad rubric of the 'punitive turn'. Other critiques, colourfully characterised by Hallsworth and Lea (2008) as the 'it hasn't happened here' variety, remain concerned about the lack of attention given to distinctive cultural, historical, constitutional and political conditions in individual countries and the need for criminologists to search for generalisations which help explain national differences (Melossi 2001; Nelken 2005, 2006; Tonry 2007). Indeed, one such critique by Kilcommins et al. (2004) questions the applicability of Garland's work to Ireland, observing the absence of a post-war 'golden era' of penal welfarism, the current lack of a 'sustained commitment' to penal populism and the continued salience of clinical over actuarial judgment. These criticisms are important and urge caution in embracing grand theories or perspectives on punitiveness without detailed empirical substantiation. A tendency may be discerned within the punitive turn literature to focus on the discursive, with the strength of the empirical case often waning as the argument moves from certain states in the US towards other English-speaking jurisdictions (Daems 2008). As argued by Brown (2005: 42) 'theory is not its own justification and requires testing against an empirical or non-discursive dimension particular to time and place, or face rejection or modification. The danger cannot be ignored – as Tonry (2007: 1) has remarked of the cognate concept 'penal populism' – that punitiveness may exist solely or substantially 'as reflections in academics' minds of other academics' ideas'.

It is against this context that the research presented in this book aims to investigate the empirical basis for the putative advent of a 'new punitiveness'[2] in three small common law jurisdictions, namely, Ireland, Scotland and New Zealand. Given the tendency in much of the literature to treat punitiveness as a 'one size fits all' phenomenon extending from the US into Europe and beyond, it was considered important to view criminal justice as it operated 'from the periphery' (Aas 2012). What is unique to this study is the application across these countries of a multidimensional tool for measuring punitiveness that incorporates a range of variables reflective of the defendant's journey through the criminal justice system. Thus, instead of focusing exclusively on a state's use of prison at the 'back' end of the system, the test also aims to capture the punitiveness of the state at the 'front' end through the exercise, for example, of police powers or restrictions placed on procedural protections for suspects and defendants. It further incorporates (increasingly restrictive) post-release policies and practices following conviction or release from prison or what McAra (2011: 100) has referred to as 'the increasingly complex penal infrastructure *beyond the prison*' (emphasis added).

In investigating the punitiveness thesis in these jurisdictions, the study also debates the appropriate test to be employed when assessing punitiveness. Despite the critical importance of this question for criminology, and indeed broader conversations on punishment, issues relating to the appropriate definition and measurement of punitiveness remain largely under-examined.[3] The final part of the investigation involves a shift away from issues concerning definition and measurement towards the explanatory. Borrowing from Tonry's (2007) framework of the three candidate determinants of penal policy – risk, protective and non-factors – key influences on the direction of criminal justice policy in the three jurisdictions are discussed. Additionally, it is hoped to get a sense of the relative influence of the global and the local: do local factors and institutions merely exercise a mediating effect or do they rather constitute the *primary* determinants of crime control policy? What is the role of policy transfer?

The plea advanced by the book is, in essence, 'analytical pluralism' (Daems 2008). Drawing on empirical data gathered in the three jurisdictions, an argument is mounted for a much broader lens to be employed in measuring punitiveness; one which includes legal as well as criminological criteria and which accords sufficient weight to the important qualitative dimension to punishment concerning policy intentions and system ethos. Similarly, there is a need for analytical pluralism when it comes to identifying the determinants of a jurisdiction's criminal justice policies, such that macro and micro contexts

---

2 Punitiveness has been used to refer both to public attitudes towards punishment (see, e.g., Kury and Ferdinand 2008; Kury 2008) and state punitiveness. It should be noted that it is exclusively *state* punitiveness which forms the subject of this book.

3 The notable exception here is Kutateladze (2009).

are held simultaneously in focus.[4] While common trends such as an increasing preoccupation with risk, victims and expressive policies were evident in all three case studies, the similarities were not so great that we can talk of a monolithic 'culture of control'. Rather, the most powerful factors appeared to relate to *national* legal, institutional, political and demographic arrangements, with an important role also reserved for national culture and psyche. The continued potency of national culture in the determination of criminal justice policy in the three countries serves to further reinforce the culturalist accounts of penal affairs referred to above and, concomitantly, the need for a comparative literature which takes account of such nuance.

Deconstructing Punitiveness

If the focus of this book is to be on a holistic assessment of state criminal justice systems, the question remains as to which factors should be considered. It is to imprisonment rates that researchers look most frequently in drawing conclusions as to the punitiveness of nations usually accompanied by a select number of other variables such as the death penalty and mandatory sentencing. There are few who would contest the use of prison as a yardstick of punitiveness yet the measurement of the use of imprisonment is not as unproblematic as it might first appear. While imprisonment per 100,000 of a country's population is the most commonly used measure, it conflates remand prisoners and convicted prisoners, as well as sentencing and discretionary release practices. For this reason, remand and convicted prisoner rates should be examined separately, both in terms of the 'stock' (population) and 'flow' (entries) of offenders into the prisons. A further consideration is that imprisonment rates *simpliciter* fail to account for the influence of crime on the use of imprisonment. As Lynch (1988) puts it, the population 'at risk' of imprisonment is not the general population but those who engage in criminal behaviour and it is notable how studies which have adjusted imprisonment rates for crime have produced counter-intuitive results. Lynch's own research, for example, found that standardisation of crime rates across several Western democracies lessened the extreme differences in the use of incarceration between the US and other Western states and in some cases, they disappeared entirely. A final, and critical, aspect of severity in the use of imprisonment is penal intensity or sentence length, preferably disaggregated by type of offence (see further Kutateladze 2007b, 2009; Frost 2008).

While the various ways in which states can use imprisonment against suspects/offenders is important, as already noted, the research presented in this book looks beyond this measure to incorporate several other dimensions of the criminal justice system. In this regard, it has been influenced by a small yet growing literature pointing up the importance of including a wide variety of variables in

4 Jones and Newburn (2007) have made similar arguments in the cognate field of policy transfer.

an instrument aimed at measuring state punitiveness. Pease's (1994) examination of punitiveness, for example, included not only various measures on the use of imprisonment but also data on the number of arrests, prosecutions and convictions across a number of jurisdictions. While the main focus of his work was on prisons (specifically the need to relate imprisonment to crime), his efforts at analysing this broader range of measures represent important early efforts to better articulate and assess state punitiveness (see also Lynch 1988, 1995).

Some years later, Australian criminologist, Lyn Hinds (2005), has also drawn attention to the possibility of increased punitiveness in law enforcement or what she terms the 'front end' of the criminal justice system. In a comparison of punitiveness in the US, Australia and Europe, Hinds broadened the scope of her inquiry to include 'police rates' (the number of police employees per 1,000 population) and police expenditure as well as the conventional measure of imprisonment rates. Her findings suggest the existence of a 'crime control continuum', with Europe and Australia choosing to focus on social control at the 'front end' of the criminal justice system and states in the US (particularly the South) exhibiting a preference for custodial control or the 'back end' of the criminal justice system. Hinds's (2005) work (like that of Diana Gordon (1989) before her) points to the importance of taking a holistic view of a state's crime control policy together with the need to recognise that states exhibit different 'national signatures' in the way they deal with the problem of crime.

The point that states may be punitive in the way in which they *police* their populations in addition to the way in which they *sentence* them is one which carries particular significance for comparative research. Neapolitan (2001) has conducted research into cross-national differences in imprisonment rates and has found that aggressive street-level law enforcement has a negative association with imprisonment rates. His explanation for this (relying also on the finding that more civilised nations tend to have higher quality prisons) is that less developed nations may not have the resources to put into prison building in order to use prison extensively and tend to rely on coercive street law enforcement, corporal punishment and informal family and tribal responses to crime. If Neapolitan is correct in his assessment, then for the suspect/offender in these jurisdictions prison rates are not a particularly good indicator of punitiveness, neglecting as they do 'front end' law enforcement. The police are only one of many social control agents operating at this end of the system, of course, and researchers should also be sensitive to the activities of private security operators. As earlier research by Davis (1992) and others has argued, moves towards an increased use of private security may – coupled with the growing privatisation of public spaces – lead to new forms of social and spatial exclusion which are highly punitive in their effects.

Another important advance in this area has been made by Tonry (2007) in his seminal comparative text on punishment. Recognising the need for informed comparative analysis to move beyond the narrow measure of imprisonment rates, Tonry (2007) takes the unusual step of outlining a core set of measures that researchers of punitiveness should at a minimum incorporate. His definition is noteworthy as he adopts a broader system-wide approach which takes account of policy changes at the investigative and trial stages of the criminal process (see Table 1.1 for indices). In his view *procedures* are directly relevant to charges of punitiveness as both the UK and the US have witnessed systematically reduced procedural protections for defendants along with increases in imprisonment rates. These include weakened controls over police powers, weakened jury trial rights and the narrowing of exclusionary evidential rules.

Table 1.1 Tonry's indices of punitiveness

Measures of Punitiveness
Policies:
1. Capital punishment (authorisation)
2. Mandatory minimum sentence laws (enactment)
3. Laws increasing sentence lengths (enactment)
4. Pretrial/preventative detention (authorisation)
5. Prison alternatives (creation)
6. Juvenile waiver to adult courts (authorisation)
Practices:
1. Patterns of use of policies 1–7
2. Adult prison population and admission rates over time
(a) Disaggregated for pretrial and sentenced prisoners
(b) Disaggregated by offence for sentence lengths and admission rates
3. Juvenile institutional population and admission rates over time
(a) Disaggregated for pretrial and sentenced prisoners
(b) Disaggregated by offence for sentence lengths and admission rates
4. Procedures: Patterns of use of procedural protections

Source: Tonry (2007: 14).

While the above analyses represent clear improvements in the measurement of changes in punitiveness over time, they continue to focus on a number of select areas within the criminal justice system such as policing, imprisonment and juvenile justice. In an important critique of researcher selectivity in the measurement of punitiveness, Kutateladze (2007a, 2009) has argued for a radical reconceptualisation of the concept which reflects its multidimensional character and which incorporates a broader range of indices of criminal justice activity. The instrument of penal harshness which he developed to measure American punitiveness includes 44 variables categorised under the following headings: (i) Political and Symbolic Punishment (e.g. death penalty, 'three strikes' laws);

(ii) Incarceration; (iii) Punishing 'Immorality' (e.g. prostitution, gambling); (iv) Conditions of Confinement; and (v) Juvenile Justice. Applying these criteria to all of the US states and comparing the results with those obtained using a more limited number of criteria, he found that nearly all states changed their places on the punitiveness ladder with a significant number of states moving from a non-punitive category into a highly punitive one and vice versa.

Kutateladze draws heavily on the work of James Whitman (2003), a legal historian who conducted an examination of the relative harshness of North American and continental European systems. Whitman relies on a multiplicity of measures in his work, including those which gauge harshness in criminalisation and law enforcement as well as harshness in punishment. In total he identifies 10 different dimensions across these three areas (criminalisation, law enforcement, punishment) including factors such as the range of behaviour criminalised, the level at which such crimes are graded, flexibility in criminalisation and punishment, and the treatment of offenders in prison. The common thread running through the work of both Kutateladze and Whitman is that they recognise that sentencing occurs at the end of a lengthier process and is only one aspect of criminal justice policy. By the time at which the offender reaches the sentencing stage, s/he may have been arrested and detained by the police, interrogated, detained on remand, tried and/or arraigned. While technically the purpose of the earlier stages is not to punish but to determine guilt or innocence, the reality for the offender is much different. As first recognised by Malcolm Feeley (1979) in his book *The Process is the Punishment*, the distinction between the pretrial and sentencing stages (attendant on formal adjudication) is largely illusory for the offender. From his/her vantage point, punishment in the form of arrest, detention, prolonged pretrial custody, etc. begins prior to formal adjudication and this is becoming increasingly significant as the difference between 'accused' person and 'offender' is incrementally blurred (Brown 2008).

The broader conceptualisation of punitiveness in the current study – beginning at the moment of identifying a suspect to the point of this person's death – provides for a deeper understanding of the 'punitiveness' of the states under consideration. This requires attention to differences in police powers and practices as they relate to the identification of suspects and investigation of crime but also prison conditions and monitoring and restrictions following release from prison. While it is true that the use of multiple measures makes comparisons more complex and conclusions harder to draw, it is argued that the central aim of constructing a more accurate and realistic picture of the punitiveness of the three states in question should be prioritised over the elegance of the arguments presented. Taking the work of Lynch, Tonry, Kutateladze, Whitman and Hinds into consideration, the indices of punitiveness (clusters of variables) used for the purpose of the study are outlined in Table 1.2.

Table 1.2 Indices of punitiveness used in this study

Indices of punitiveness		Variables
A	Policing	Zero-tolerance policing, police expenditure, strength of police service, police powers, number of police complaints, strength of the private security sector.
B	Procedural protections for defendants	Right to silence, rule against double jeopardy, evidential exclusionary rules, use of civil law to control criminal behaviour, law relating to bail.
C	Use of imprisonment	Presumptive or mandatory sentences, use of alternatives to custody, imprisonment rates, convicted prisoner rates, prison admission rates, convicted prisoner admission rates, imprisonment rates using different types of crime as a base, length of prison sentences.
D	Juvenile justice	Age of criminal responsibility, compliance with human rights instruments, sanctions and alternatives to detention, detention rates.
E	Prison conditions	Respect for human rights, deaths in prison, size of institutions, overcrowding, rehabilitative programmes, medical services and food.
F	Post-release control	Sex/drug offender notification schemes, shaming schemes, post-release supervision, reintegration, and expungement of criminal records.
G	Death penalty	Date of abolition, date of last execution.

It is important to stress that the above test does not claim to advance the selected variables as objective phenomena which unproblematically reflect the 'real' world but rather as proxies for the punitiveness of the criminal justice system. Still less does it pretend to be an exhaustive measure of the punitiveness or harshness of a state towards its citizens. While convincing arguments may be made for the inclusion of broader mechanisms of social control in a test for state punitiveness (O'Sullivan and O'Donnell 2007, 2012) the inexhaustibility of the subject of social control necessitates some selectivity. In this case the compromise struck was a focus on the objects of criminal justice system only. The test does, however, have a number of advantages over those currently employed. The first of these concerns transparency and the fact that the definition and measurement of punitiveness is given much greater consideration than it is usually accorded. Secondly, in addressing the current bias towards 'back end' system outcomes, it seeks greater alignment of the punitiveness test with the experience of the offender.

Whom to Compare and Why?

Comparative research, even in a small number of jurisdictions, is valuable as it permits theories to be tested across political, social and cultural boundaries and also varied historical contexts (George and Bennett 2005). Manifestations of the 'punitive turn' have been observed to quite varying degrees in each of the three sample jurisdictions and it was precisely the range of experiences between and also within the criminal justice systems of each of these countries which made them such attractive prospects for exploration. The question of whom to compare with Ireland was informed by a number of considerations, one of them being population size. The suggestion in the literature (McAra 2005; Hutton 2005) that small countries may be more resistant to the transformative impulses sweeping the US and England and Wales is debatable, yet it was considered important that the jurisdictions selected were as similar as possible in order to be useful as case studies. Another criterion was similarity in terms of their political and legal arrangements. There would be little point in comparing, for example, a developing, non-democratic society with Ireland as any observed differences would immediately be attributed to such fundamental differences. For this reason the countries selected are English-speaking, Western democracies with liberal market economies. Another important commonality between the three is that they are all common law countries with similar legal cultures and a shared history with England and Wales.

While the countries selected were all similar enough to enable meaningful comparison, efforts were also made to include within the group jurisdictions with very different criminal justice policies and prison populations. Diversity in this regard was considered desirable for, as Cavadino and Dignan (2006) have argued, an understanding of both commonalities and discontinuities between countries and the reasons for them is required if we are to make sense of contemporary penality. Readers familiar with Ireland's criminal justice system will be aware of its low imprisonment rate by international standards (76 per 100,000 population in October 2007), affirming its early reputation as a country 'not obsessed by crime' (Adler 1983). However, the rate of increase in its prison population has also been very significant, particularly in the period 1996–2001, when Ireland outstripped her European neighbours (Kilcommins et al. 2004). A further twist in the tale is provided by research conducted by O'Donnell (2005) which shows that the convicted prisoner rate has remained constant in the period between 1994 and 2004 so that the volume of sentenced prisoners has remained the same. While on many fronts Ireland appears to have resisted punitive trends, such as towards formal risk assessment tools, there have also been periodic crime crises which have resulted in seismic changes in legal protections for defendants (Walsh 2002). Overall, however, there has not been a sustained commitment to 'penal populism' or penal punitiveness in the way that Garland and others describe and rehabilitation remains a core aim of both sentencing and probation practice.

Turning now to Scotland, preliminary analysis reveals some points of convergence and divergence between it and Ireland: while their imprisonment rates differ considerably, both jurisdictions demonstrate some form of resistance to the 'punitive turn' through their continued commitment to rehabilitative policies and progressive youth justice systems. Indeed, Scotland presents as something of a paradox in penal terms (Young 1996/97, 1997). On one index of punitiveness – imprisonment rates – it would appear quite punitive and indeed until the late 1990s its rate of imprisonment surpassed even that of England and Wales. A closer look, however, reveals a continued commitment to welfarism, not least through the distinctive system of youth justice operating in the form of the Children's Hearing System. McAra (1999: 372) has examined developments in three aspects of the Scottish penal system in the late 1990s (the role of social work, juvenile justice and the prison service) and has concluded that 'within all of the policy sites reviewed, core aspects of rehabilitation remain'.

The final comparator country, New Zealand, is often cited in the literature as a paradigmatic exemplar of the Anglophone drift towards punitiveness (if same exists) (Cavadino and Dignan 2006; Pratt 2007). The significant upward spiral of its prison population to reach 179 per 100,000 population in 2004 as well as the sustained commitment of its political parties to tough rhetoric on crime rest comfortably with this characterisation. In 1999 a Citizens Initiated Referendum was held where 92 per cent voted for greater emphasis on the needs of victims, and the imposition of minimum sentences and hard labour for all serious violent offences (Pratt and Clark 2005). The subsequent Sentencing, Parole and Victims Rights Acts in 2002 led to significant increases in penalties for murder and other serious violent and sexual offences and restricted parole for these groups of offenders. In terms of the overall characterisation of the New Zealand penal system, however, it is important to remember that the country is also well known for its pioneering approach to juvenile justice in the form of restorative family group conferencing (Morris and Maxwell 1993) and despite high levels of imprisonment there 'does not as yet appear to be any generalized state of "penal crisis"' (Cavadino and Dignan 2006: 88). As with Scotland, then, points of convergence and divergence emerge. Ireland's low imprisonment rate stands in sharp contrast to that of New Zealand's, which is one of the highest in the Western world. On the other hand, lenient youth justice policies represent affinities between all three countries and it is perhaps of some significance that New Zealand is a jurisdiction to which Irish policymakers sometimes look in penal matters (e.g. family conferencing in the Children Act 2001). Given the divergence *within* as well as *between* these jurisdictions, important questions may be posed as to the distinct form that the 'new punitiveness' has assumed in each and the factors behind such developments. While the 'culture of control' in Scotland and New Zealand may not be as 'diluted and distinct' as the Irish version (Kilcommins et al. 2004), nevertheless, significant counter-currents can be detected in both countries.

A Note on Methodology

Punitiveness in the three countries was examined over a 30-year period from 1976 to 2006 in the light of the fact that many commentators appear to have identified these decades as the period during which policies and practices have become more punitive (Garland 2001: 1–2). The year 2006 acts as the endpoint of the study given the difficulties anticipated in obtaining more recent data. Data were collected on the three jurisdictions using a multi-method approach involving examination of extensive quantitative data, interviews with key criminal justice stakeholders and documentary analysis. Raw data relating to policing (Index A), crime, the use of imprisonment (Index C) and the operation of juvenile justice (Index D) were first of all collected and then adjusted for population changes over the period. This was considered important as the population in both New Zealand and Ireland has increased significantly over the study period (Scotland's population has remained fairly static). A scoring system was then applied whereby each of the 34 variables identified in the Table 1.2 was given a score of 10, 20 or 30 denoting low or less than moderate punitiveness; moderate punitiveness; and more than moderate or high punitiveness. A score was awarded based on the punitiveness of the states at the end of 2006 but consideration was also given to how policies and practices had evolved over the 30 year study period. The scores for all the variables in each index were totalled and divided by the total number of variables to get overall punitiveness scores (OPSs) (Kutateladze 2009). Finally, a mean OPS score for all the indices (the sum of the OPSs for each index divided by 7) was calculated for each of the countries. The results for all three jurisdictions are presented and discussed in Chapter 7.

In addition to detailed analysis of statistical data relating to crime, imprisonment and police rates/expenditure, the conclusions reached in the book are based on interviews with key criminal justice stakeholders in each jurisdiction, including civil servants, academics, lawyers, politicians, crime editors and at least one current or former Minister for Justice. These interviews were conducted mostly during the course of an extended visit to the jurisdiction in question, an experience which was invaluable in itself for the light it shed on the justice system's 'ethos' or ideology.

A Brief Overview of the Book

The analysis begins in the next chapter with an outline of developments in the literature on penal transformation and the not insignificant criticisms which have been levelled at these accounts. Invoking Hallsworth and Lea's rather colourful (and indeed scathing) term for country case studies critiquing the punitive turn, the chapter then explores the geographical limits of the punitiveness phenomenon through a survey of research revealing cultural proclivities bearing on a country's punitive orientation. The final section in the chapter discusses what appear to be the most promising models outlining the factors explaining variations in punitiveness.

The following three chapters examine punitiveness in each of the countries between 1976 and 2006 both thematically (according to the indices outlined above) and chronologically. Thus, the sense of flow which is often gained by an account of punishment policies and practices over time is not lost to the necessity of examining each country using the seven indices outlined above. Briefly put, the case studies speak to the complexity of penality and militate against any conclusions which may be drawn on the basis of one indicator alone. Some support is derived for the 'new punitiveness' thesis in these countries given the general chilling of the political climate towards offenders since the mid 1990s and the pattern of increased legislative activity aimed at controlling violent and sexual offenders.

The final section of the book (Chapters 6–9) presents and analyses data on the three sample countries. Chapter 6 concentrates on what has been learned about the punitiveness of the countries under examination from the statistical data, supplemented in some instances by data from the interviews. In addition, attention is drawn to a number of issues concerning the empirical substantiation and measurement of the 'new punitiveness'. There is a need for qualitative as well as quantitative indices, for multiple rather than singular indices across the various sectors of the criminal justice system (juvenile justice, prisons, post-release restrictions, etc.), and for 'front end' as well as 'back end' indices. Greater precision is generally required in measuring the '*new*' punitiveness and choices relating to its measurement require justification.

Chapter 7 returns from the general to the specific and endeavours to draw some conclusions about changes in punishment in the three countries selected. Assessing punitiveness on the multidimensional test outlined above, all three case studies remain returned relatively 'moderate' penal scores despite their very different depictions in the literature. This finding is qualified somewhat by differences in the distribution of moderate-high scores across the indices indicating a more punitive approach gaining momentum across a number of different sectors of New Zealand's criminal justice system.

Leading on from this, the book moves to a discussion in Chapter 8 of the primary determinants of crime control strategies. Using Tonry's (2007) framework of risk, protective and non-factors, attention is drawn to the historical, institutional, legal and political conditions in the three countries which appear to explain the different paths taken in penal policy. It is argued that a number of risk factors are present in New Zealand such as a history of race relations and lack of trust in the political system which do not feature in Scotland and Ireland. Conversely, these jurisdictions benefit from several protective factors such as a robust and embedded legal culture which are not present to the same degree in New Zealand. Most significantly, the data highlight the crucial manner in which national culture or psyche interacts with other risk and protective factors in the three jurisdictions. The palpably different effects which similar legal and political arrangements had in all three comparator countries points to the need for close attention to the empirical object as well as the critical importance of different cultural settings and values.

Chapter 9 concludes the book with a discussion about the limitations of current approaches to assessing and understanding punitiveness. As noted, the argument developed in this book laments the dearth of attention in the literature to matters of definition and to the formulation of clear-cut social scientific criteria of punitiveness. It is only when criminologists finally embrace analytical pluralism in matters of both measurement and explanation that a satisfactory understanding of contemporary crime control may be achieved.

Chapter 2
'It hasn't happened here...': The Limits of the Punitiveness Thesis

Introduction

Explanations of the social roles of punishment within criminology have tended to focus on moral (Durkheim), economic (Marxist), cultural (Elias) or narrowly political (Foucault) explanations of punitiveness. More recently, however, a different type of analysis has emerged, one premised on the political economy of punitiveness, or more specifically, the influence of the newly dominant neo-liberal economic model, on the penal realm. A wide range of contemporary writers such as Garland (2001), Wacquant (2009), and Cavadino and Dignan (2006), all advance arguments linking (in various direct and indirect ways) the 'free market turn' (Downes 2011: 30) to its penological adjunct, 'the punitive turn'. It is the aim of this chapter to briefly set out these arguments, together with some of the other main accounts of the 'new penality'. As a major limitation of this literature is its tendency to over-homogenise, the second part of the chapter is devoted to analysis of explanations of trends in punitiveness which focus more on local variation or specificity, particularly the role of culture in mediating the effects of any putative 'late modern' punitiveness. This is followed by a third, related section outlining some of the best explanations for differences in penal severity among Western democracies developed in recent years.

The 'Punitive Turn'

The search for general explanations for the rise in punitiveness[1] or what Young has termed criminology's 'new problematic' began in earnest in the early 1990s. Tonry (2012) credits the tripling of US imprisonment rates between 1973 and 1990 together with the increased availability of data on the use of imprisonment with the spike in criminological interest in the causes and consequences of a putative growth in punitiveness. Certainly, the publication of Garland's influential *Culture of Control* (2001) acted as a major stimulus for discussion to the degree that the 'punitive turn' now represents one of the major debates within the sociology of

---

1 It is important to note that punitiveness for the purposes of the book is to be read as 'state punitiveness' and consideration is not therefore given to punitive attitudes among the public which more often takes the term 'punitivity' (see Kury 2009). Given their similar connotations, 'penality' is used interchangeably with 'punitiveness' throughout the book.

punishment today, particularly comparative work (Nelken 2011; Downes 2011). Suggestions by Loader (2010) to the effect that a change of mood towards 'penal moderation' can now be detected probably do not challenge this assertion given that recent comparative work (Loader cites Tonry 2007; Pratt 2008a, 2008b; Lacey 2008) emerged largely as part of the conversation begun by Garland and others. Thus, the discussion which follows in the latter parts of this chapter on the geographical limits of the penal state and its primary influences is prefaced by a brief, and necessarily selective, synopsis of the main accounts of penal transformation.

Early Beginnings

Debate as to the existence of a postmodern or 'new' penological era was initiated by the American criminologists, Malcolm Feeley and Jonathon Simon in the early 1990s. 'In a strikingly provocative and influential statement' (Sparks 2000: 131) they argued that a 'new penology' is in the ascendancy which does not concern itself with the punishment, deterrence or rehabilitation of individuals but rather with the identification and management of unruly groups. Within this new framework, the 'normalisation' (and individualisation) of offenders and their reintegration into society – the concerns of the old penology – are abandoned in favour of their categorisation and management. Reflecting 'the lowered expectations for the penal system that result from failures to accomplish more ambitious promises of the past' the goal of the system becomes 'managerial not transformative' (Feeley and Simon 1992: 452). Actuarial and managerialist techniques are employed to this end, promoting concerns with cost-effectiveness, efficiency and organisational outputs. Feeley and Simon's analysis paints a bleak picture of contemporary America in which the corrections system functions merely as a 'waste management system' for a permanent offender population or 'underclass'. Recidivism is no longer significant as a measure of success since offending among a chronically troublesome population is taken for granted.

Another early contributor to the debate is Bottoms (1995: 40) who puts forward the concept of 'populist punitiveness' as 'the notion of politicians tapping into, and using for their own purposes, what they believe to be the public's generally punitive stance'. As originally conceptualised by Bottoms the phenomenon coexisted alongside other, more established discourses such as human rights and managerialism, and was directed mostly at violent and sexual offenders. Writing over a decade later, Pratt (2007) argues that its successor, 'penal populism', now wields a more powerful influence and, further, is triggered by a wider range of deviant acts such as youth crime and anti-social behaviour. Thus, Bottoms' association of the concept with bifurcatory penal policies – a twin-track approach to crime following which governments simultaneously increase the penalties for serious offenders and decrease them for less serious offenders – no longer holds true. Another key difference is that, for Pratt, contemporary populism has become decidedly more 'bottom-up' in its orientation. Pratt speaks of a new axis of penal power where politicians act *in conjunction with* the people rather than *on their behalf.* Using the 2002 New Zealand general election as an example, he describes how victims' rights groups effectively led the 'law and order' campaign and were courted by MPs from all the main political parties. Pratt's idea of penal populism is thus intricately bound up with the democratisation of the penal sphere which has occurred in the last quarter of the twentieth century, a development well documented by Ryan (2003) and more recently Loader (2006).

Culture of Control

Garland incorporates arguments relating to both of the penal trends noted above into his landmark text on penal transformation, *The Culture of Control* (2001). His main achievement, however, lies in his masterful location of this approach within the broader framework of contemporary social and economic policy. In the book he argues that the increased punitiveness of the US and UK over the past three decades can be explained as a cultural adaptation to two social forces: first, the dramatic social changes witnessed by the citizens of late modernity over this period including economic crises, changes in family structure and the democratisation of social life and, secondly, the free market conservative politics adopted by successive governments (2001: x). This reconfigured social environment made crime much more likely while economic deregulation and neo-conservatism had by the 1980s resulted in a hardening of social divisions.

Faced with stubbornly high crime rates and the limitations of the criminal justice system to do anything about them, Garland sees the state's reaction as largely ambivalent in nature. He identifies two broad types of policies which can be characterised as an adaptive/preventative partnership strategy and an expressive/punitive segregation strategy. The first adaptive response promotes, as the name suggests, a pragmatic approach which seeks to face up to the predicament presented by high crime rates. On this account, various measures taken by the state in recent decades such as the privatisation of specific criminal justice functions; the diversion of minor offences from the system and the new managerialism which now pervades criminal justice agencies all form part of this overarching initiative. An important part of this project has also been the attempt to 'responsibilise' individuals within the community to exert their powers of informal social control and thereby to enhance crime control: 'property owners, residents, retailers, manufacturers, town planners, school authorities, transport managers, employers, parents, individual citizens … must all be made to recognise that they have a responsibility in this regard' (2001: 126).

The second more expressive strategy takes the form of both a *denial* of the limited power of the sovereign state to control crime and a type of '*acting out*' whereby 'the capacity to control future crime … is less important than their immediate ability to enact public sentiment, to provide an instant response, to function as a retaliatory measure that can stand as an achievement in itself' (2001: 133). He cites the American government's 'War on Drugs' as a classic example of a state dealing with its limitations through *denial*; a hugely costly undertaking (in both human and economic terms) which all the evidence suggested would not work. Similarly, policies such as Three Strikes, sexual predator statutes and paedophile registers should be understood in terms of the state *acting out* to denounce the crime and reassure the public that 'something will be done' about it. It is these two policy adaptations which together form, in Garland's view, the 'culture of control' which forms the title of the book. The punitive shift is thus described by Garland as cultural, rather than structural, in nature. Like the institutions of the welfare state itself, criminal justice agencies such as police and probation have not been dismantled but overlaid with a new political culture. Within this new culture, priorities are shifted away from rehabilitation ('welfarism') towards public protection and from a 'social' to an 'economic' style of reasoning.

Governing through Crime

Like Garland, Simon links a crisis of state governance to the current centrality of crime in political rationality. There are important differences between the two accounts, however. First, Simon does not share Garland's view as to the importance of high crime rates as an explanatory factor and, secondly, Simon presents his book purely as American study. In short, his argument is that crime has become the paradigmatic means of governing social conduct in the US with harmful consequences for the penal system and civil society. 'Governing through crime' occurs, he claims, not simply when people act in response to crime fears, but rather when crime is used to legitimate control of a broader range of social behaviours or indeed to legitimate interventions which have different motivations altogether. Instead of crime being the last response to various forms of resistance, it is the first response. Simon's book (2007) cites many examples of this strategy operating in the institutional sites of everyday life, including the education, domestic and employment spheres. Just as the family has become a 'nexus of crime' (with fears of domestic and sexual abuse and parents purchasing drug testing kits for their children), the educational system and workplace now increasingly borrow measures from the criminal law. While Simon devotes more of his efforts to the descriptive task of tracing the contours of this culture of control (he describes himself as providing a 'thick account' of the ways in which crime dominates contemporary life in America) than the intricacies of the 'why' question, he explains the phenomenon of 'governing through crime'[2] by reference to post-war crises in other modes of governance, most notably the welfare state or New Deal political order. His explanation for the selection of crime as a 'risk issue' on which to reconstruct government rests on the relative ease with which it could be mobilised in comparison with competing strategies.

2 Simon uses the 'governing through crime' term here in a broader sense of providing a framework for normative regulation rather than solely in terms of political opportunism in an era of fractionated politics (see Caplow and Simon 1999).

Simon thus convincingly relates what criminologists have termed the 'criminalisation of social policy' to the 'punitive turn'. For him, they form part of the same frame, one which 'we must map if we are to disentangle American democracy from its late modern relationship to crime' (2007: 16). In this crime-obsessed society, prison and its analogues such as immigration detention and gated communities act as the common denominator. To use Simon's words, 'mass imprisonment is the stable solution to the highly competitive political logic established by governing through crime' (2007: 159). Simon identifies three features of the criminal justice system in this new order: first, in line with the prevalent political rationality, prison is seen not as rehabilitative but rather as a waste management system charged with the simple task of containment (Feeley and Simon 1992, 1994). Second, the penal system is transformed into a system of 'mass imprisonment', in line with the expansionist logic of governing through crime; and finally, sentencing and parole decisions are hamstrung by the categorical logic of mass imprisonment which aims to 'substitute rigorous rules for the soft and untrustworthy judgment of judges and other governmental officials' (2007: 156).

Other Interpretations

While Garland paradoxically views the new punitiveness as a function of the sovereign state's weakness, there are others who *a contrario* view the carceral boom as an instrument of state repression. Writing in a neo-Marxist vein, Wacquant (2005) points to the highly disproportionate effect which mass imprisonment has had on the African American community in the US and argues that in the United States the prison has partly supplanted the urban ghetto as the main vehicle for control and containment of the black underclass. In his view, political elites since Nixon have seized upon the 'law and order' mantra, originally invoked by Southern politicians to defend segregation, as a means of controlling a black population which had shown itself capable of organised resistance in the 1960s. The 'war on drugs' launched by Reagan and continued by his successors, provides a prime example of how this law and order strategy, through its differential laws and enforcement, led to the 'punitive containment' of black urban neighbourhoods. In his later writing, Wacquant (2009) describes how the arrival of the 'penal state' in America is intimately bound up with the dismantling of the social state which accompanied neo-liberal government. In effect, poverty is criminalised so as to frighten people into submissive acceptance of the replacement of reliable wage-work with precarious labour. While the US is certainly Wacquant's primary reference point, his thesis extends beyond North America. Wacquant advances a similar argument in relation to those Western countries to which the neo-liberal ideology of submission to the free market has spread. He claims that the success of neo-liberalism as a 'transnational political project' (2009: 266) has set even countries such as France on a trajectory towards mass imprisonment, fuelled in part by the importation of US academic and expert knowledge about crime control.

Conversely, Cavadino and Dignan (2006) offer a fourfold typology of political economies (neo-liberal, conservative corporatist, social democratic and oriental corporatist) to help explain differences in penal systems. While they share Wacquant's views on the connections between the welfare and the penal state, they do not view neo-liberalism as a general political pattern within the Western world, but rather as a model which could characterise some countries' economies. The basic argument is that increased punitiveness is related to the individualistic and exclusionary cultural attitudes which neo-liberal policies foster. Nelken (2011: 14) summarises it thus:

> neo-liberal societies have the highest prison rates because they follow social and economic policies which lead to what they describe as exclusionary cultural attitudes towards our deviant and marginalised fellow citizens. On the other hand, Continental European corporatist societies and, even more, Scandinavian social democratic societies, are said to 'pursue more inclusive economic and social policies that give citizens more protection from unfettered market forces.' In their view, these latter societies see offenders as needing resocialisation which is the responsibility of community as a whole.

The idea of neo-liberal principles generating a culture of irresponsibility towards others is one which is shared by Reiner (2007), although his argument focuses heavily on the anomic (and hence criminogenic) effects of rising consumerism, increasing social inequality and social exclusion. Pratt (1996, 2002) too shares this 'bottom-up' approach to the neo-liberalism thesis but focuses less on its criminogenic effects than on the manner in which it affects penal politics. As we have seen, Pratt considers a different, more virulent form of penal populism to be in the ascendant, with a 'new axis of penal power' between the state and the general public as a 'key feature of the neo-liberal political programme' (2002: 181). While in *Punishment and Civilization* (2002) Pratt relied on Elias as a theoretical framework on which to advance claims about the 'decivilizing' of punishment and the 'new punitiveness', the shift from public indifference to intolerance central to understanding the broader argument is explained by Pratt by reference to *inter alia* 'the election of neo-liberal governments who were prepared to open up penal development to popular sentiments' (2002: 174). Indeed, the links between the two are best expressed by Bell (2011: 23) who argues that 'it is in the context of neoliberalism, otherwise known as "late modernity", that the "decivilisation process" described by Pratt makes most sense … helping to explain the development of a culture of "egotistical individualism" (Reiner 2007) which has facilitated the desire to exclude…'.

Critique

Without intruding too much on the arguments made in the next section, a number of comments can be made about the accounts laid out above. The first relates to the empirical basis for the punitiveness claim and the ambivalence of contemporary penality. Perhaps in their desire to bring order to a bewildering array of volatile and contradictory policies, criminologists have been unable to resist the temptation to ignore more inconvenient truths or what may be termed the 'temptation of elegance' (Goff 1983). In this relation criticisms include: the tendency among criminologists to reify 'punitiveness'; the idealised way in which such writers portray the post-war period; the extent to which continuities with the past are glossed over in favour of more exciting tendencies towards the exceptional and the excessive; the focus on rhetoric rather than empirical reality; and a failure to consider how 'resistance' by professionals within the criminal justice system has served to mitigate some of the harsher effects of the new penality. A second, related criticism concerns the geographically limited reach of the new phenomenon. Mandatory sentences, chain gangs, community sex offender notification schemes and boot camps have been cited by Simon (1995, 2007), Pratt (2002, 2005) and others as examples of 'get tough' policies, while for Garland (2001: 102) 'the term that best captures the New Right's ideal is that of "zero tolerance"'. With the notable exception of mandatory sentences, however, many of these are uniquely American innovations and do not permit of generalisation. As Daems (2008: 102) astutely observes in his study of Pratt's writing, 'the strength of his empirical case ... often decreases as he moves from (a particular state of) the US to those other English-speaking jurisdictions...'. Moreover, those policies which have been transferred to other jurisdictions tend to be honoured more at a symbolic than a practical level, possibly on account of the professional resistance referenced above (Jones and Newburn 2007).

As a final point, it can be strongly argued that there is a lack of conceptual clarity in the literature around 'punitiveness' or penal 'harshness' (although it is often referred to variously as 'toughness' or the 'get tough' movement, 'intolerance' or 'populist' policy-making). Matthews (2005: 178), for one, has been a fierce critic of the selectivity which comes with the failure to define punitiveness, describing it as a 'thin and under theorised' concept in much the same manner that Sparks (2001) has criticised penal populism. Certainly, the precise indices of the 'new punitiveness' is an issue meriting increased attention from those putting forward grand theories on punitiveness, enabling us to tell what is 'in' from what it 'out' (Daems 2008). Garland (2001), for example, refers to an array of policy developments but otherwise only relies on two graphs showing the rise in English/Welsh and American imprisonment rates. The failure to define may also result in a partiality of focus in terms of the aspects of punitiveness that are omitted. An often neglected feature of the 'new punitiveness', for example, has been the erosion of the due process rights of suspects and accused persons in an effort to increase the likelihood of conviction (Kilcommins et al. 2004; Campbell 2008). Clearly thus, if we are to illuminate rather than obscure our understanding of these issues, a broader criminology is required which takes account of the empirical as well as discourse analysis and which includes *all* aspects of the criminal justice system such as changes in criminal procedure.

The 'Cultural Turn'

The spatial limits of the new punitiveness have important implications for the arguments advanced above as they point up not only the fact that late modernity may be pushing us *towards* leniency as well as *away from it*, but also the historically contingent nature of current punitiveness even in those countries which have succumbed to it. Such 'cultural' accounts are necessarily less pessimistic than the literature of general explanation outlined above in that the 'punitive turn' can be understood less as a facet of late modernity and more as an embedded aspect of American (and perhaps English) exceptionalism (Nelken 2006). As observed by Garland himself (2011: 17), a 'cultural turn' has occurred in the sociology of punishment literature since the publication of *Culture of Control*. The change in emphasis signalled by this body of work arises out of a desire to explain not only convergence but also divergence in the field of penal policy, not least the cavernous differences in incarceration rates between the US and Europe.

One of the most well-known accounts in this vein is Savelsberg's (1999, 2002, 2004) study of the differences between punishment practices in Germany and the US. Savelsberg identifies two factors which have mediated the culture of control in Germany and produced a distinct reaction in the form of a steady imprisonment rate. First, the institutional arrangements in Germany or German model of bureaucracy ties decision-makers closely to the state apparatus while insulating them from public opinion. A second factor stems from the experience of the Nazi regime which led to a post-war secularisation of traditional Protestant concepts of rehabilitation and forgiveness (2002: 696). The German experience therefore supports the idea that institutional structures as well as 'foundation cultures' and major historical events, should be considered when we seek to explain variation in penal severity. In same manner, Savelsberg contends that the dispersed nature of governmental power and high level of accountability in the structure of American governance together with the influence of fundamentalist Protestant beliefs sheds some light on the stronger culture of control dominant in the US (see also Tonry 2009).

Melossi (2001) has expressed support for Savelsberg's ideas in his own work on the differences between the Italian and American cultures of punishment. Echoing Savelsberg (1999), he argues that religious beliefs are important influences on penal policy, not as strict 'determinants of punitive attitudes but [as] resources available within a cultural "toolkit"'. Religious traditions indirectly impact upon a state's punitiveness as part of a cultural vocabulary invoked in response to socioeconomic and political change. This is very far from determinism in that there are choices to be made in the state response to changing social and political conditions but these choices are limited. Thus, the US found itself emerging victoriously with a booming home economy from the Second World War and, moreover, as the only world superpower at the end of the 'Cold War'. This positive experience of violence and war 'would articulate quite nicely with the stern rigour of the most radical varieties of Protestantism' (2001: 417). On the other hand, the devastating effect of violence and concentrated power in the Second World War for Italy, 'articulate[d] quite nicely with the [Catholic] "indulgentist" tradition that ... has its roots in a long Italian history' (ibid.). Melossi sees a dynamic relationship between historical conditions and cultural vocabularies giving rise to certain unique features within a society in a given historical period. For him, 'punishment is deeply embedded in the national/cultural specificity of the environment which produces it' (2001: 407).

James Whitman's *Harsh Justice* (2003) represents yet another attempt to explain the 'widening divide' between the US and Europe. His focus differs from the previous authors in that it spans several centuries and indeed the burden of his argument is that the recent divergence between the two continents in terms of their relative harshness or leniency can be traced back to the foundation of the American republic. The rejection of Continental European status differentiation and the democratic ideal promoted in the US meant that Americans never systematically imprisoned political dissenters or debtors and consequently never felt the need to 'level-up' in terms of extending honourable punishment to all prisoners. The paradoxical effect of this democratisation of imprisonment was what Whitman terms 'equal opportunity degradation' and a desire to 'level-down' or reduce all offenders to a low status. In Europe, he argues, the traditions are very different. The collective memory of past status degradation and the tradition of honourable punishment have meant that egalitarianism takes on a 'levelling-up' dynamic so that all offenders are treated with a certain level of dignity. Salas (2005) has made similar claims about a European cultural heritage that curtails the right to punish, yet he also argues that this culture was strongly revitalised by the human rights framework put in place after the horrors of the Second World War.

The second explanatory factor identified by Whitman is the strong state institutions in place in Europe and the high level of autonomy which they enjoy. Like Savelsberg (2002), Whitman argues that state structures matter greatly in insulating penal policy from retributive sentiment, identifying 'tepid bureaucratic routinisation of criminal law' as 'an important barrier to the kind of overheated democratic retributivism that has come to America' (2003: 200). The organising concept which connects both degradation and state power is, he claims, 'authority' and it is the very different traditions of authority in Europe and the US which have led to their divergent trajectories of punishment.

Local case studies can also reveal much about the cultural constraints under which penal actors and institutions operate. Looking at the Scottish case, McAra has found evidence of continuity as well as change in key institutional sites such as the Children's Hearing System and penal policy, so that overall it would appear the traditional welfarist ethos has been renegotiated rather than replaced. She attributes this to the mediating effect of Scottish civic culture and also the prominent role played by a number of elite policy networks in Scottish penal policy. The significance of the role played by these elites is that they themselves were driven by penal welfarist imperatives, shored up by a civic culture which 'valorises community, public provision of welfare and mutual support' (2005: 294). The net effect is that the larger transformative processes described above are significantly constrained by local processes and values or, more specifically, 'self reflexive modes of communication' which allow the society in question to continually reconstruct the social world within their own terms. For McAra, therefore, a systems analytical approach is useful for the very fact that it permits analysis at the level of both the general and the local and cognisance can be taken of the interplay between the two. McAra's depiction of Scotland as a jurisdiction whose distinct cultural values have mitigated the effects of more punitive policies emanating from south of the border aligns it with other jurisdictions such as Canada and Finland who have maintained milder penal policies in an effort to distinguish themselves from more punitive neighbouring jurisdictions. Brodeur (2007: 72) describes this as 'self-definition by contrast' and gives the example of how Canada's core values such as pacifism (in contrast to its larger cousin's role in world policing) translate into less coercive measures in its penal system as well.

The salience of the local is once again to the forefront of several case studies contained in the recent edited anthology, *Travels of the Criminal Question* (2011). In particular, the final two chapters on policy transfer to Italy and Argentina powerfully support the argument that surface similarities often belie the mediating influence of local politico-cultural environments. Rossella Selmini's chapter relates how both British and French crime prevention strategies have been adopted and adapted at a local level in Italy to create a mixed model. While the influences may therefore be international, her work also draws attention to the importance of local actors: the institutional conflict among different levels of government in Italy, particularly the struggle of local authorities to acquire new competencies and responsibilities, remains, for her, 'the main factor influencing the shape and style of the policies developed in the last decade' (2011: 178). In a similar manner, local peculiarities such as public distrust of the police in Argentina have significantly altered cultural imports such as Neighbourhood Watch in that jurisdiction, prompting Sozzo to contemplate how 'cultural translation' can 'open a certain field of possibilities for the local translators' (2011: 210).

What are the implications of these culturalist critiques for the work of Garland and others? The importance of distinctive cultural, historical, constitutional and political conditions in individual countries may rather suggest a shift from a common '*culture* of control in contemporary *society* to *cultures* of control in contemporary *societies*' (Savelsberg, 2004: 707). Although the challenge to structuralist accounts would appear to be significant, there remain certain difficulties with the use of the concept of culture (or its close associates) as an explanatory variable which caution against overly deterministic cultural accounts at the nation state level. The first concerns the influence of culture over time. Nelken (2006) has criticised Whitman for a failure to properly articulate his *explanandum*, or more specifically the time period which he is seeking to account for. The greater divergence between Europe and the US over the last number of decades than in the previous centuries sits uneasily with the fact that historical memories should grow weaker, not stronger with time. What is missing is therefore greater detail on how the culture continues to wield an influence or 'an account of the mechanisms that transmit this cultural attitude through time, and reproduce it in the present' (Garland 2011: 37).

A related issue concerns the impact of globalisation and the illusion of a 'pure' national culture which is wholly distinctive and unmixed with that of others. In this regard, Garland (2011: 29) has written that in most advanced societies the 'contrasts between national cultures (or between local cultures within a nation) are now mostly a matter of degree and emphasis rather than mutually exclusive difference'. The extent to which Garland has overstated the argument on the dissolution of cultural difference here is worthy of debate. Nelken (2011), for example, has argued that accounts of the demise of the nation state may be overdrawn and Lacey (2008) is also at pains to argue that globalisation does not necessarily denote convergence. The effect of globalisation on national culture and identity remains an important point, however, and one which is acknowledged by most of the scholars cited above. Melossi (2011), for example, has expanded upon his (2001) arguments concerning the cultural embeddedness of punishment by considering neo-liberalism's 'elective affinities' in the context of penality, political economy and international relations. McAra's (2005) systems analytical approach operates at *both* a global and local level allowing for a more nuanced reading of culture and identity and her more recent writing also makes clear her preference for a multilevel analysis (McAra 2011). Similarly, Savelsberg (2011) agrees with Garland that, in light of the powerful effects of globalisation, studies which treat countries as autonomous units can no longer be justified. He goes on to say, however, that in line with the increasing recognition given to the local context in globalisation studies (described as the 'process turn'), comparative analyses remain crucial for the light they shed on the mediating role of local cultural conditions.

Both Garland (2011) and Nelken (2011) also raise the tricky issue of the appropriate unit of analysis: is it Continental Europe, the nation state or the region? The answer of course depends to a significant degree on what we are seeking to explain but in identifying key influences on penal policy it is impossible to ignore research highlighting significant differences within nation state territories themselves (Hughes and Edwards 2005; Muncie 2011). It would seem necessary, as others have done (Field and Nelken 2010), to reflect on the extent to which practices, and the cultural interpretations we place on them, assume a regional, national or even European flavour. Whatever the level of analysis, Muncie (2011) is correct to draw attention to the continued centrality of local actors and culture in realising the transnational, or indeed the national, 'on the ground'. As he observes, the simple fact that criminal justice will usually be 'done' by local actors rooted in national and local cultures (as evidenced in Sozzo and Selmini's empirical work discussed above), warns against generalising arguments inferring changes common to all Western societies. The next section consequently sets out some models which aim to explain developments from a different perspective to that adopted by Garland and others, namely, to search for generalisations which help explain national differences while also remaining alive to cultural and political values (Snacken and Dumortier 2012).

Punitiveness Risk and Protective Factors

Despite the wave of comparative research which (paradoxically) followed Garland's thesis, the debate on the key factors influencing punitiveness is far from settled (Nelken 2011). Significant progress has, however, been made; not in the form of 'neat, positivistic' formulae (Downes 2011: 37) but rather in the form of factors to which some causal weight can be attributed. The arguments of the three comparative theorists set out below all make significant advances in the effort to identify some of the pieces which make up the jigsaw of penality in advanced industrial societies. While clearly important work has been done by other authors, their work has been selected on the basis of: its impact on the field of comparative research; its comprehensiveness; and its sensitivity (to varying degrees) to national cultural differences.

Tonry

Borrowing from the work of Farrington and others on child delinquency, Tonry (2007) adopts a framework setting out risk and protective factors which increase or decrease the likelihood of punitiveness respectively (see Table 2.1). For Tonry, 'the most prominent national risk factors include conflict political systems, elected judges and prosecutors, particular forms of sensationalist journalism, Anglo-Saxon political cultures, and a predominant view that criminal justice policy falls appropriately within the province of public opinion and partisan politics' (2007: 17–18). The fact that the US and the UK share many of these characteristics forms, in Tonry's view, part of the explanation for their high prison populations and punitive policies. Conversely, the existence of protective factors such as 'consensus political systems, non-partisan judges and prosecutors, Francophonic political cultures, and a predominant view that criminal justice policy falls appropriately within the province of expert knowledge and professional expertise' (2007: 34) in many Continental European countries (and Canada) goes part of the way to explaining the milder penal policies in place there. Tonry rightly stresses the probabilistic and dynamic nature of his analytical model as risk/protective factors will inevitably interact with specific national features to make an outcome more or less likely; they are 'no more destinies for countries than for individuals'. A case in point is the Netherlands where, despite the existence of many protective factors and the absence of any shift at a policy level, penal practices since the 1970s have become significantly harsher (Downes 2007) (although this trend has been reversed more recently). Similarly, it is difficult to achieve a full understanding of the US's punitive zeal without reference to its own culture and history. Factors identified by Tonry in his later work (2009) concern the existence of a certain brand of Protestant fundamentalism, governmental structures and its particular history of race relations.

Table 2.1 Tonry's risk and protective factors

Risk factors	Protective factors
Conflict political systems	Consensus political systems
Elected judges and prosecutors	Non-partisan judges and prosecutors
Anglo-Saxon political cultures	Francophonic political culture
Public-led criminal justice policies	Expert-led criminal justice policies
High levels of income inequality	Low levels of income inequality
Weak social welfare systems	Generous social welfare systems
Low levels of trust in government and governmental institutions	High levels of trust in government and governmental institutions
Sensationalist journalism	

Lappi-Seppälä

Building on earlier work on Scandinavian 'exceptionalism', Lappi-Seppälä (2011, 2012) has put forward a sophisticated overview of the various contexts in which penal policy is formed based on the results of a large cross-national study covering 25 countries over the period 1980–2005. Analysing quantitative data on imprisonment and a range of potentially explanatory factors, strong correlations were observed between imprisonment rates and variables such as income inequality, welfare provision, political culture, social trust and legitimacy. Thus, his analysis suggests that the key drivers of penal policy in the national sphere are: social policy orientation and the strength of the welfare state (type may also be important); political culture (as defined by Lijphart's (1999) distinction between majoritarian and consensus democracies); levels of 'vertical' trust (in social and political institutions) and 'horizontal' trust in fellow citizens. As is evident from Figure 2.1, however, the role played by other factors is also acknowledged. Lappi-Seppälä identifies demographics (there is evidence that population heterogeneity correlates with imprisonment rates), judicial structures, legal cultures and the role of the media as factors which interact strongly with the core variables to reinforce or attenuate pressures towards punitiveness. Overall, Lappi-Seppälä paints an optimistic picture; although penal practices may be constrained by structural factors, it would seem they are not determined by them. In keeping with this probabilistic approach, Lappi-Seppälä is careful to emphasise the fluidity of his model. First, it is far from automatic or mechanical and, operates – like the risk/protective factor matrix examined above – to explain the shape of penal policies in advanced Western democracies only. Second, the model still allows room for individual agency in the form of politicians or experts, particularly in smaller jurisdictions. Third, room should be left for 'country-specific exceptionalism' and unforeseen contingencies which may change the course of events.

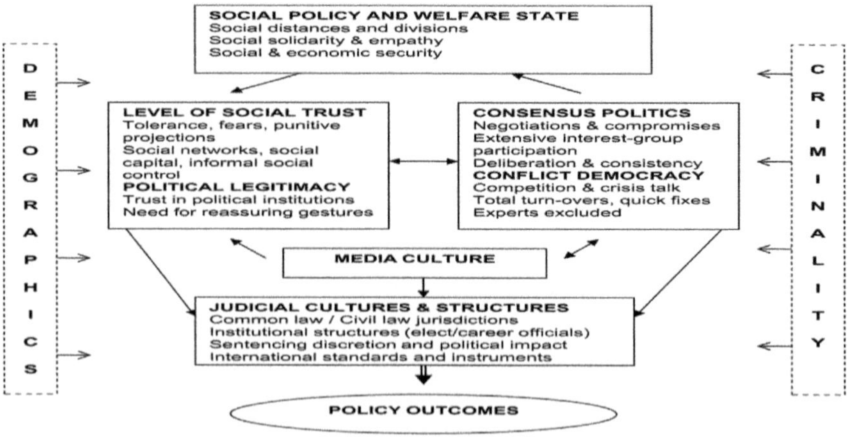

Figure 2.1 Penal policy and its social, political, economic and cultural contexts

Source: Lappi-Seppälä, 2012: 63.

Lacey

Nicola Lacey's *The Prisoner's Dilemma* (2008) turns attention to what Britain can learn from those Continental European countries pursuing a more moderate path in penal policy. Her work has two main strands, one socioeconomic and the other political. Building on the 'varieties of capitalism' literature, and particularly the arguments put forward by Cavadino and Dignan (2006) and others on political economy, Lacey draws a distinction between 'liberal' and 'co-ordinated' economies, with countries falling in the former category more likely to inflict harsher criminal penalties (Sparks 2011). As she argues 'liberal market systems more oriented to flexibility and mobility have turned inexorably to punishment as a means of managing an excluded population consistently excluded from the post-Fordist economy' while 'co-ordinated systems which favour long-term relationships – through investment in education and training, generous welfare benefits, long-term employment relationships – have been able to resist the powerfully excluding and stigmatising aspects of punishment' (2008: 109).

Lacey adds to this literature by relating political economy to the electoral arrangements and type of political culture in which criminal justice is embedded. In her view, political institutional structures are independently important factors which play an important role in reinforcing economic differences between countries. Institutional features of political systems, in other words, make or it more or less difficult for governments to respond in a punitive way to popular anxiety about crime fostered by economic inequality and insecurity. As with Lappi-Seppälä (2012) and Tonry (2007) when distinguishing between political cultures she chooses to adopt Lijphart's typology based on consensus and 'majoritarian' or 'conflict' democracies. The main distinctions between the two models can largely be derived from the terms themselves (Lappi-Seppälä 2008). Majoritarian democracies are based on a two-party, 'winner takes all' philosophy where the will of the majority dictates the choices that are made by policymakers. There is little incentive to compromise as the object is to oust the opposition from power and coalition government is rare. Consensus style democracies, on the other hand, seek to protect minorities and share power with as many views as possible being taken into account. Power is shared and dispersed in various ways such as: through coalitions or minority governments; stronger legislatures; interest group participation; and multiparty systems with proportional representation election systems. Lacey's contention in this regard is that the varying levels of accountability demanded by the need to negotiate with other groups within the political system itself impacts on the 'strength' (in the sense of policy-making autonomy) of the production regime. Her arguments as they subsequently relate to criminal justice policy are neatly encapsulated in the following excerpt:

> In liberal market economies with majoritarian electoral systems, particularly under conditions of relatively low trust in politicians, relatively low deference to the expertise of criminal justice professionals, and a weakening of the ideological divide between political parties ... the unmediated responsiveness of politics to popular opinion in the adversarial context of the two party system makes it harder for governments to resist a ratcheting up of penal severity (2008: 76).

Recent work by Green (2007, 2008, 2009) on political culture and penal policy similarly views Lijphart's dichotomy as a useful heuristic device in explaining a country's propensity to penal populism. He uses the concept of 'political culture' or 'ways of doing politics' to explain the contrasting reactions to two child-on-child homicides in Norway and England respectively in the early 1990s. While public reaction to the killing of 2-year-old James Bulger in England in 1993 was 'rhetorically demonstrative and punitive', responses to the killing of a young girl by three 6-year-old boys in Norway one year later were comparatively 'muted'. This is explained by Green by reference to a number of factors, including crime rates, differences in the ages of the killers, different cultural conceptions of childhood and the complex interaction of politics with the media. At its core, however, Green's argument concerns incentives to penal populism or the exploitation of crime for political gain based on the Lijphartian distinction between majoritarian and consensus democracy. The majoritarian style of English political culture meant that incentives to exploit the Bulger murder were considerable, while far fewer of these incentives faced Norwegian politicians owing to their consensus style of democracy.

Conclusion

There would appear to be a broad consensus among the detailed accounts set out above that penal variation can best be explained in terms of political economy, social trust and political structures, although this is not to dismiss the role played by judicial structures, legal and media cultures. For Tonry, Lacey and Green, in particular, it is the way that politics is conducted in a given jurisdiction that is the master variable, although one may strongly question whether all countries fit so neatly into Lijphart's binary categories. While these accounts are far from comprehensive delineations of penal dynamics in all Western jurisdictions (Cuneen 2010, for example, refers to the dearth of attention given to race relations and colonialism/post colonialism) they do nevertheless serve as a guide to some of the most critical influences at the level of the nation state. At the international level, globalisation may not be the homogenising force for convergence that it is sometimes contended to be, but in its various guises, both economic and legal, it certainly forms an increasingly influential backdrop to policy-making in nation states. That said, given the by now extensive research on the cultural embeddedness of penal matters, it is always prudent, as Downes contends (2011: 37) 'to leave room for explanation in some regards to be cast at the level of the local and the national'. The resilience of the cultural and the local in the face of any putative 'late modern' or neo-liberal penality reinforces their analytical salience and ultimately paints a more optimistic picture of the future than the ones presented at the beginning of this chapter.

Chapter 3
Ireland 1976–2006: Stagnation and Change

Introduction

Having briefly introduced the three countries under examination in the first chapter, it is the aim of the next three chapters to provide a more extensive review of crime and the criminal justice response to it in each of them for the period 1976–2006. Each of these chapters will fall into two parts: the first section traversing developments in criminal justice over the 30-year period, with a particular eye to a shift towards more punitive policies and the latter part assessing – in broad trajectory – punitiveness using the seven indices outlined in Chapter 1.

Criminal Justice in Ireland 1976–2006

Crime in Ireland changed dramatically over this period. Alongside increases in crime associated with urbanisation and industrialisation, the country witnessed the emergence of a drug culture and the growth of organised crime. The criminal justice response lagged behind somewhat but appeared to arrive with some gusto in June 1996 with the double murder of policeman Gerry McCabe and journalist Veronica Guerin. These events shocked the nation and saw 'law and order' rise to the very top of the political agenda. A nation once described by Adler (1983) as 'not obsessed with crime' rapidly shed its apathy in this area, although this level of concern does not appear to have endured. Reflecting the significance of these events for criminal justice in Ireland, the first part of this chapter is subdivided into three time periods, namely, 1976–95, 1996–97 and 1998–2006.

1976–95: A Nation Not Obsessed with Crime?

Ireland made a relatively 'late entry' as a crime conscious society with 'consensus emerg[ing] only in the mid-1970s that crime … has reached crisis proportions' (Rottman 1984: para. 1.1). Criminologist David Rottman (1980) carried out a study of Irish crime trends in the 1951–75 period and argued strongly that a decisive break with the past had occurred, primarily with regard to serious property offences: 'Between 1964 and 1975, the Garda statistics show a 4.3-fold increase in housebreaking, a 3.2-fold growth in shop-breaking, a 7.5-fold increase in the number of stolen motor vehicles, and an 11.4-fold rise in robberies'. As can be seen

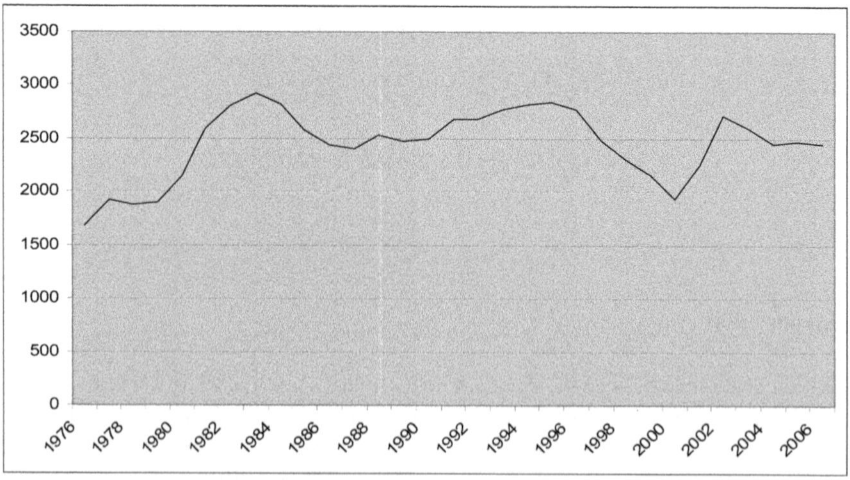

Figure 3.1 Indictable/Headline Crimes in Ireland per 100,000 population

Source: Annual Reports of An Garda Siochána, various years.

from Figure 3.1, this upward trend continued until 1983 when crime peaked and the critical threshold of 100,000 indictable crimes[1] was broken for the first time. The record number of indictable crimes recorded in 1983, however, marked a period of decline and between 1983 and 1987 the crime rate fell by 18 per cent (O'Donnell and O'Sullivan 2003: 44). Serious crime increased again in the early 1990s in tandem with growing concerns about urban crime and disorder, particularly crimes against tourists and acts committed by groups of intoxicated young males. In 1995, indictable crime culminated in a new high of 102,484 before once again declining. The peak in headline crime in 2000 is most likely a function of the change to a new Garda (police) recording system called PULSE (O'Donnell 2002).

Paradoxically, in light of the two crime peaks in 1983 and 1995, issues relating to crime did not significantly feature in the seven general elections from 1977 to 1992. Examination of party manifestos for these elections reveals that they were dominated by the poor economic conditions facing the state at the time such as high levels of unemployment and the growing numbers of young people forced to emigrate. Where crime is addressed, there appeared to be cross-party consensus that the best course of action to tackle crime was the review and updating of the criminal law; increased resourcing of the Gardaí; neighbourhood watch and community policing. Even where the issue of increased prison places is mentioned as a policy, it appears more *reactive* than *proactive*, cited more as a necessary step in increasing the ability of the system to cope with an increased flow of prisoners. Against this general background, however, it is possible to detect the political mood towards

1 For most of the period under examination crime statistics in Ireland were based on the legal distinction between indictable and non-indictable offences and were generally understood to refer to 'serious' and 'less serious' offences (CSO 2008).

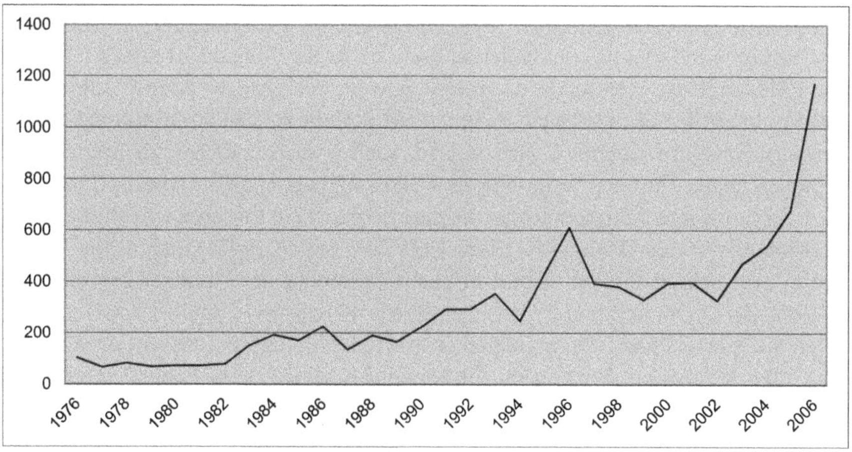

Figure 3.2 Number of hits for 'crime' in Dáil and Seanad debates
Source: http://debates.oireachtas.ie/.

crime hardening over time (see also Kilcommins et al. 2004). References to civil liberties and constitutional rights evident in the party manifestos of the late 1970s disappear in the later election programmes and specific policy proposals in the party programmes during the period were occasionally draconian such as Fianna Fáil's pledge in 1987 to introduce 20-year mandatory sentences without remission for drug traffickers. A search for 'crime' on the parliamentary debates online also appears to locate the politicisation of crime slightly earlier than 1996. As can be seen from Figure 3.2 interest in talking about crime among parliamentarians had been increasing steadily since 1990 and rapidly gathered pace after 1994.

The relative lack of interest in crime at a political level is supported by analysis conducted by Kilcommins et al. (2004: 132–41) on opinion polls covering general elections in this period. In marked contrast to other jurisdictions where the issue of crime became highly politicised in the 1980s, the authors found that 'in every general election between 1981 and 1992, the problem of crime was a low priority for voters' (2004: 136). O'Donnell (2008: 126) explains this lack of interest in terms of a historically low crime rate and a Department of Justice that was guarded and inward-looking: 'Add to this mix of low crime, secrecy and deficient sources of information, a public that was acutely concerned about emigration and unemployment, and it becomes clear why penal policy was a matter of little popular concern'.

Whatever the source of this indifference, it would be unfair to characterise the period as a time of unbroken complacency about criminal matters. The overspill in paramilitary violence relating to Northern Ireland contributed to the number of more serious crimes such as armed robberies and the increased use of firearms. Mulcahy (2002) notes that armed robberies increased from 12 at the start of 'The Troubles' in 1969 to 228 in 1979. Writing on the impact this had on everyday life in the Republic, Inglis (2003: 121) draws a comparison with the terrorist attacks in

America on 11 September 2001: 'Fear and suspicion were rampant, and a general feeling prevailed that the fundamental basis of society was under attack'. During the 1980s full use was made of special powers designed to control subversive activity in earlier decades such as extended periods of detention and use of the non-jury Special Criminal Court. Indeed, such powers increasingly came to be deployed against ordinary criminals as well (Vaughan and Kilcommins 2008).

Every now and then, moreover, the general inertia in this area was shattered by a 'crime crisis' (see O'Mahony 1996, 1998; O'Connell 1998), such as the 'moral panic' over sentencing for sexual offences following the Lavinia Kerwick case in 1992. As O'Donnell and O'Sullivan (2001: 49) observe, interest was soon lost when these crises had been managed or averted, although the institutional legacy was often legislation. Writing on the Lavinia Kerwick case, Fennell (1993: 12) describes the pattern of knee-jerk policymaking and band-aid solutions which are typical of the period:

> Here again the government has appeared to respond to public demands for actions with alacrity and relative ease. Schooled in the process of legislating a response, the government introduces and passes bills with a degree of ease and consensus which can only indicate that either the changes are long overdue, or warranted, or do not pose any fundamental problems for our collective consciences. The public – lulled into the security of law as a panacea for political reform – appears to be satiated by the legislative response. Few ask the awkward questions as to what other social, economic or political responses might be appropriate.

Walsh (2002: x) too has also identified the 1990s as a decade of frenetic legislative activity in the criminal justice arena: '[i]f the pace of legislative change in criminal justice matters from the establishment of the State to the end of the 1980s can be likened to a gentle breeze, that in the 1990s will have to be described as a hurricane which shows little sign of abating'. An examination of the relative number of criminal justice statutes enacted in the 1980s and 1990s would appear to confirm this: 12Acts were passed in the period 1980–89 compared to 27 in 1990–99. Further, many of these Acts were larger Acts dealing with more substantive areas of criminal procedure.

To conclude, while continuity characterised most of the period, there were some signs that things were beginning to change. An increased level of interest in crime as an item of political import can be detected through increased attention in the Dáil, the increasing pace of legislation in criminal justice matters and the production of policy papers such as *The Management of Offenders: A Five Year Plan* (Department of Justice, 1994). Viewed in this light, it may be argued that in the previous half-decade some of the foundations were laid for the events of the summer of 1996.

1996–97: Crime Gets Political?

At around 1pm on 26 June 1996, a white motorcycle pulled up alongside the car of investigative journalist, Veronica Guerin, while she was stationary at the traffic lights on the Naas dual carriageway in Dublin. The pillion passenger opened fire on the journalist, shooting her several times in the upper body. She was believed to have died instantly. Her killers were suspected to be among a group of major Dublin criminals who had been linked to illegal drugs trafficking and were reported to be led by a man named John Gilligan. Ms Guerin had written extensively about the activities of this criminal gang and had received several violent warnings to keep out of their affairs. Three weeks earlier on the 7 June policeman Jerry McCabe had been shot by the IRA during a robbery in Adare. Moreover, these two high-profile murders took place against a background of a spate of rural killings in areas which had previously been relatively untouched by crime (McCullagh 1999).

The period following the death of these two figures can be viewed as a watershed in Irish criminal justice policy. In sharp contrast to the low priority accorded crime in previous soundings, opinion polls now showed crime to be a key issue for the public. In 1997, an election year, 41 per cent of people polled indicated that 'crime, law and order or justice' should be the main issue on which the parties should fight the campaign. A further 88 per cent felt that the government was losing the fight against crime. As O'Donnell and O'Sullivan (2003: 48) note: 'These killings were defining moments in the debate about law and order in Ireland. They were the catalyst for a hardening in political attitudes. Crime control became a national priority and for a time it was almost as if a state of national emergency had been declared ... This was a textbook case of "moral panic"'.

The reaction of the political establishment to these murders was swift. Following intense media coverage of the crime issue, the Dáil was recalled from its summer recess for a special debate on crime on the 25 July. In a remarkably short space of time after the journalist's murder, the government of the day had met public concern with a £54 million 'anti-crime package', described by the *Bar Review* (1996: 5) as 'the most radical single package of alterations to Irish criminal law and procedure ever put together'. The basic principles underlying bail were to be revised, 7-day detention introduced for those charged with serious drugs offences, and a novel civil process introduced to facilitate the seizure of the proceeds of crime. In addition, the package provided for the recruitment of 400 extra Gardaí; the increased 'civilianization' of the force; more prison spaces; a new remand prison at Wheatfield; increased supervision of prisoners granted early release; and new powers to provide for the eviction of known drug dealers from housing estates. As O'Donnell and O'Sullivan (2001: 78) note, 'the response was swift, harsh, uncompromising and skewed towards punishment'.

The obvious public concern that a journalist could be the target of a contract killing in broad daylight on a public highway was doggedly exploited by Fianna Fáil in opposition. In 1996 the Justice portfolio was held by Nora Owen who was viewed by Fianna Fáil in opposition as the Achilles heel of the Fine Gael cabinet. The Fianna Fáil spokesperson on justice, John O'Donoghue, had been quick to grab the law and order platform and had famously declared 1995'the year of the criminal'. With an election looming in 1997, conditions were rife for intense party-political 'law and order' scaremongering and indeed this is precisely what unfolded in the period following the two murders. In the 12 months between the killings and the 1997 general election, O'Donoghue and his colleagues in the Fianna Fáil party defined the threat to law and order in the gravest possible terms: organised crime 'posed a threat to democracy' and the security of the state; intimidation was 'rife'; organised crime 'had a grip on the country' and we were in the midst of a 'crime wave' or 'epidemic' (Hamilton 2007). The shadow Minister promised to 'wage war on crime' and 'to give the streets of the country back to the Irish people'. His party's election manifesto contained promises on mandatory sentencing for those dealing in drugs over a certain value, reform of the bail laws to allow for preventative detention, extra Gardaí, 2,000 extra prison places and – the jewel in the crown of the opposition strategy – zero-tolerance policing.

The ill-defined and elastic concept of 'zero-tolerance' became a Fianna Fáil mantra in the 1997 election, with party supporters even wearing T-shirts emblazoned with the slogan. It was borrowed from New York where the policy had been accredited with success in restoring street safety (though not without some oversimplification, see Bowling 1999). In a theoretical sense, it drew heavily on Wilson and Kelling's (1982) idea of 'broken windows' whereby a neighbourhood is said to rapidly degenerate if small crimes are allowed to flourish. The party enlisted the help of John Timoney, the Irish-American deputy to New York police chief William Bratton, to help them draw up their programme for government. The concept, as outlined in an extract from the 1997 party manifesto below (Fianna Fáil 1997: 5), claims to effectively eliminate police discretion:

> Zero tolerance–no crime, and no victim of crime, is unimportant ... Fianna Fáil in government will operate a strategy of zero-tolerance, an approach that has produced impressive results elsewhere. This reflects the following principles:
>
> - No crime, no matter how small, is insignificant.
> - There is a definite connection between lesser and more serious crimes.
> - Tolerance of small crimes creates a climate where big crimes flourish.
> - Certain crimes will not be overlooked because they are not important.
> - Toleration of lesser crimes sends the wrong message to the law-abiding citizen that the Gardaí and the government are ineffective.
>
> Accordingly, we will overlook no crimes because they are not perceived to be important. Zero-tolerance means implementing the law of the land as it stands.

As noted by Bratton himself (1998: 42–3, cited in O'Donnell and O'Sullivan 2003: 51), zero-tolerance of all crimes, however minor, 'would be impossible to implement in a modern disorderly society'. Choices in the application of the criminal law are a necessary part of modern policing. Yet the vision held up by John O'Donoghue in the 1997 election was critical to refashioning Fianna

Fáil as the party of 'law and order'. As O'Donnell and O'Sullivan (2003: 49) note: '[John O'Donoghue] made law and order into a central part of political life by accentuating the differences between Fianna Fáil's hard line policies and what he portrayed as the ineffectual approach of the other political parties'. In the event, his strategy enjoyed dubious success. Fianna Fáil was returned to government in coalition with the Progressive Democrats and the support of several independent TDs. However, it appeared to be factors other than the politics of 'zero-tolerance' which resulted in the party's electoral gains (O'Donnell and O'Sullivan 2003: 51).

1998–2006: 'Volatile and Contradictory' Politics

The period following the events of 1996 witnessed a unprecedented fall in the crime rate such that between 1996 and 2000, 'recorded crime in Ireland dropped faster and further than in any other EU country' (Kilcommins et al. 2004: 92). Moreover, the wave of public concern which had swept the country during the election appeared to have dissipated. For example, in 1998 the chairman of the government-established National Crime Forum noted that 'perhaps one of the most surprising messages was the absence from the presentations to the Forum, oral and written, of any significant demands for dramatic reactions to crime from the authorities. We were presented with reasoned and balanced views, which saw crime as a real problem in the community, but not a crime crisis' (National Crime Forum 1998: 10). In 2001, only 14 per cent of those polled rated crime as one of the main issues in the upcoming election and polls in subsequent years confirmed that crime was once again off the electoral agenda (Kilcommins et al. 2004: 139). Lower crime levels and a calmer public mood, however, did not prevent the new Minister for Justice from delivering on his election promises with some gusto. Between 1996 and 2000, the Garda and Prison Votes were increased by 42 and 43 per cent respectively (O'Sullivan and O'Donnell 2003). Most significantly, in 1997 the Minister introduced proposals for a mandatory minimum sentence of 10 years for the offence of trafficking drugs worth over £10,000 (€13,000). While the legislation was drafted in such a way that the judge could disapply the sentence in exceptional circumstances (hence it is more correctly characterised as a presumptive sentence) the introduction of this legislation was nevertheless highly significant. There were few mandatory sentences in Ireland at the time (the most notable being the life sentence for murder) and calls for mandatory sentences had in the past been resisted on the grounds that the courts were in a better position to judge such matters. Another legacy of the period was the swelling prison population which leapt from 2,124 in 1995 to over 3,000 persons in 2000. As O'Donnell (2001: 166) has remarked 'this is a staggering rate of change' and one which put Ireland well ahead of its European neighbours (Kilcommins et al. 2004: 249–50). The sharp upwards spike in the prison population appears all the more dramatic when the number of prisoners per 1,000 recorded crimes and per 1,000 proceedings commenced is calculated: this figure more than doubled in the period spanning 1996–2001. As Kilcommins et al. (2004: 252) conclude:

'while it is too early to say if the politicisation of the law and order debate around the time of the 1997 general election had enduring consequences in terms of public apprehension, or even political rhetoric, it certainly marked a point of departure for the prison population'.

Against this background of falling crime rates/rising imprisonment rates, the trend towards ad hoc policymaking in Irish criminal justice continued. Periodic crises were met with predictably harsh, knee-jerk responses from the Minister and his department, while attempts at more considered measures floundered. A white paper on crime promised following the *Report of the National Crime Forum* (1998), for example, never materialised despite assurances to the contrary (O'Donnell 2008). By way of contrast, the bomb exploded by the Real IRA in Omagh in 1998 met with an immediate – and draconian – legislative response. As Vaughan and Kilcommins (2008: 80) note similar British legislation introduced at the same time was described by Lord Donaldson as a 'charter for internment dressed up to look like the result of criminal justice'. Similarly, the media furore which surrounded the deaths of two Gardaí in a tragic collision with teenage joyriders in April 2002 led to the construction of a new €10 million wing for 14–15-year-old offenders in St. Patrick's Institution. In the event, this complex was built but was never used for its planned purpose, illustrating perhaps a tendency for Irish politicians to adopt measures without subsequently following through on them.

The tone of the debate on criminal justice changed with the accession of Progressive Democrat Michael McDowell to the role of justice Minister in 2002. His combative personality (or what one politician termed 'Michael's irresistible urge to make enemies', *Sunday Tribune* 2007) combined with the Progressive Democrats' tough stance on crime paved the way for a more contested politics of law of order. The announcement in August 2004 that two new 'superprisons' were to be built in Cork and Dublin together with the publication of a controversial Criminal Justice Bill in 2004 made clear McDowell's intentions to initiate change. The Criminal Justice Bill originally started life as a bill to extend Garda powers but a significant number of amendments made after it was initiated extended its reach to matters as disparate as organised crime, sentencing and antisocial behaviour. Some of these policies clearly owed their origins to Anglo-American legislation such as the provisions to allow for the electronic tagging of offenders and antisocial behaviour orders. The Minister was contemptuous of those in civil society who disagreed with his policies describing them as 'pointy-headed intellectuals' who 'need to get out of their leafy suburbs'.[2] A similar approach was taken with constituencies or stakeholders within the system whose interests clashed with those of the Minister. During his term in office McDowell won a bitter battle with the prison officers to reduce their overtime bill and was also openly critical of the judiciary for their reluctance to impose the 'mandatory' 10-year sentence on drugs offenders. In March 2006, following public outrage at the killing of a young mother by an armed gang, the Minister called on the

2 Criminal Justice Bill 2004, Committee Stage Debate, Seanad Debates, 3 July 2006.

judiciary to 'make examples of' offenders and the Taoiseach also criticised what he described as 'excessively lenient' jail sentences for those convicted of serious crimes (*Irish Times* 2006).

Overall, it is fair to say that the political climate further hardened during the period 1998–2006; a product of two conservative Ministers for Justice, a number of 'crime crises' and an opposition party which now appeared increasingly willing to play the 'crime card'. This trend is particularly pointed in the period 2002–2006 during Michael McDowell's ministry, as evidenced by greatly increased attention to crime in the Dáil and the media. The lack of *sustained* attention to the crime issue, however, renders it unlikely that Irish penal politics has been transformed in the dramatic way that Garland (2001) and Simon (2007) describe. Moreover, as is often the case in Irish criminal justice, a number of contradictory currents can be detected. During this same period, a drug court and several restorative justice projects were established and a Children Act introduced which is widely regarded as progressive in nature (see section on juvenile justice below). It would appear that in Irish criminal justice a 'volatile and contradictory' set of impulses often jockey for position with one another (Kilcommins et al. 2004) and, as such, the messiness of the contemporary may defy simple characterisation.

Punitiveness in Ireland 1976–2006 by Index

As observed by Tonry (2007: 11), assessments of a country's punitiveness become more problematic and conclusions harder to draw when several indices are used. This statement applies *a fortiori* to Ireland which maintains low 'back-end' imprisonment rates, yet which in the last 20 years or so has introduced many reforms at the 'front end' of the system enhancing police powers and curtailing defendants' rights. Poor physical prison conditions and a recent overhaul of the youth justice system add further layers of complexity.

Index A: Policing

Writing on the drift towards increased 'front-end' punitiveness, Hinds (2005: 49) identifies three punitive policies in law enforcement: (i) 'zero-tolerance' policing, (ii) political rhetoric that emphasises law and order themes of more police and wider police powers and (iii) technologies such as private security companies that increasingly exclude targeted groups from public spaces. It is arguable that of these three policies, the first two are the most relevant to Ireland over the last number of decades, although to quite varying degrees. As discussed above, zero-tolerance enjoyed its brief period in the political sun in the 1997 general election campaign but its effects were short-lived. Proceedings taken against beggars and prostitutes increased markedly in the years following 1996 but then slowly fell off (Kilcommins et al. 2004: 216). Aside from this and an almost obligatory nod towards the idea in some Department of Justice strategy statements (1998, 2002), there has been very little evidence of zero-tolerance policing in practice. No mention was made of the policy in the 2002 Fianna Fáil manifesto.

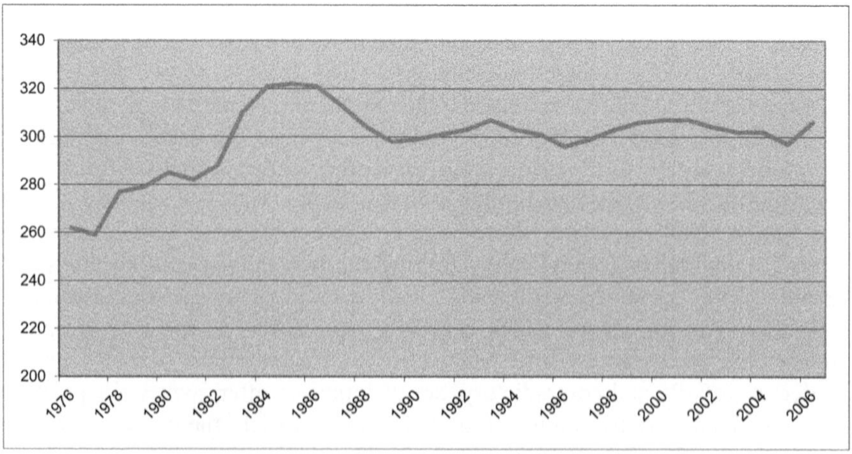

Figure 3.3 Police numbers in Ireland per 100,000 population

Source: Statistical Abstract of Ireland, An Garda Siochana Annual Reports.

On the second criterion, it is clear that calls for increased police powers gathered momentum in the early 1990s based on the idea that the balance of the criminal justice system had swung too far in favour of the accused (Walsh 2005a; Hamilton 2007). In this connection, Walsh (ibid.) has observed that there have been 27 major criminal justice enactments since the Criminal Justice Act 1984 enhancing the powers of the police and the prosecution. The 2006 Criminal Justice Act was particularly significant in this respect, more than doubling the maximum period of detention and providing for the Gardaí to issue search warrants to themselves in certain circumstances without the traditional safeguard of judicial supervision. Equally, it is clear that the Garda Síochána have benefited from increased resources over the period under examination. Police strength has increased significantly (from 8,449 in 1976 to 12,954 in 2006) but when account is taken of the rapidly rising population, the line in Figure 3.3 appears relatively flat. Particularly striking is the increase in police expenditure per head of population which has more than doubled between 1976 and 2006 in real terms (see Figure 3.4 in which prices are adjusted to 2008 levels).

It is difficult to comment on the third punitive policy identified by Hinds, namely, the increased use of private security in Ireland as a means of excluding certain groups from public places. This may appear less likely here than in large American (Davis 1992) or English (Coleman and Sim 2005) cities owing to the smaller, more dispersed nature of marginalised communities and suggestions that an Irish 'underclass' does not exist (O'Donnell and O'Sullivan 2003: 42).

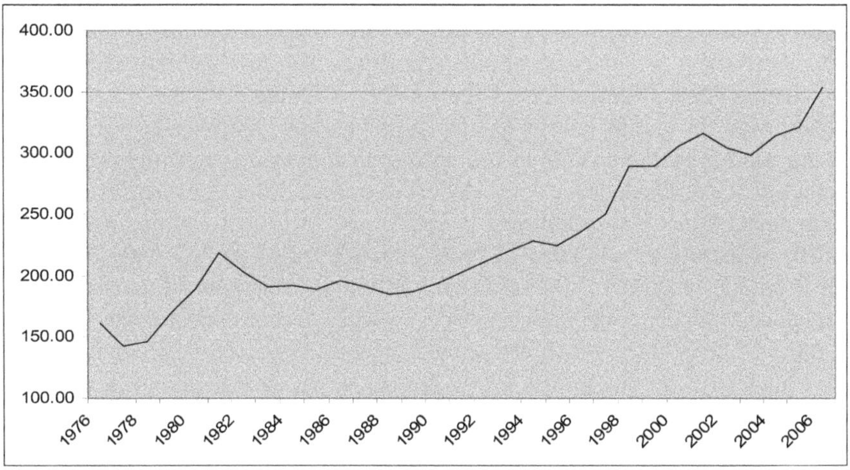

Figure 3.4 Net police expenditure (€s) per capita in Ireland

Source: Department of Finance (data request).

An alternative measure – though difficult to measure with any degree of precision – is growth in the private security industry. Writing in 1997, the Consultative Group on the Private Security Industry (1998) estimated the number of employees to be at most 10,900. Some years later the regulatory body established as a result of that report – the Private Security Authority (PSA) – noted in their 2005 Annual Report that the number approached 20,000 (2006: 7). If these estimates are accurate, the near doubling of the numbers employed in the industry in the space of eight years represents a startling rate of growth. This would indicate that in 2005 private security employees outnumbered Gardaí by a ratio of at least 1.6:1 (Garda Síochána 2005). When examining the relative strength of the public and private security sectors, however, it should be noted that the overlap between these two types of policing is probably greater in Ireland than in other jurisdictions, albeit impossible to quantify. Cases have come to light in the past of members of Gardaí working part-time as nightclub bouncers (*Irish Times* 2001) and it is generally known that off-duty and former Gardaí are employed in this area.

While it is clear that the above provides strong evidence for what has been termed the 'quiet revolution' in the private security industry (Stenning and Shearing 1980) it should also be noted that Ireland has been slow to privatise the role of the public police. This has not occurred at all save to the extent that a volunteer Garda Reserve force was established by Minister McDowell in 2006. Thus, despite the greater prevalence of commercial security in Ireland, there has not been, *contra* Garland (2001), a 'greater impetus towards contracting out and privatisation of police functions hitherto assumed by the state' (Kilcommins et al. 2004: 204).

Before leaving this section, some account should be given of the number of complaints made against the police over the period. As Hinds (2005) has acknowledged, police numbers and expenditure considered alone do not convey the punitiveness or otherwise of police practices and how they are experienced by communities. Examination of the number of complaints made against the police over the period may allow us to gain some insight into the 'weight' (King and McDermott 1995) of law enforcement as experienced by the general populace. Complaints have risen by 33 per cent since the Garda Síochána Complaints Board was established in 1987, from 1,015 to 1,350 in 2006, a level which appears low compared to other similarly sized jurisdictions (Scotland, for example, recorded 3,122 complaints in 2006). This may be at least partly explained by doubts over the independence of the Board itself and the very low number of complaints which are actually upheld, both factors which may well have hindered reporting (Walsh 2009). Further, cognisance should be taken of the differential manner in which policing is experienced by middle and working class communities in Ireland. In a recent report on the relationship between the Gardaí and marginalised communities, Mulcahy and O'Mahony (2005) observed the negative attitudes held by these communities towards the Gardaí and claimed that the travelling community is 'over policed and under protected'. A study carried out by the Institute of Criminology, University College Dublin for the National Crime Council (2003) also presented some evidence of class prejudice in policing practice (at least in relation to public order offences).

Index B: Procedural Protections for Defendants

As noted in the previous section, it is a by now familiar criticism of the criminal justice system in Ireland that it has swung off balance and that the rights of victims are neglected in favour of the accused. Substantiating the argument that Ireland is far too generous to her defendants, the Minister for Justice, Michael McDowell, stated in April 2003 that Ireland is 'the only member state of the EU in which individual citizens are guaranteed: the constitutional right to due process, to the exclusion of illegally obtained evidence, to trial by jury in all non-minor cases, to fair bail, to the presumption of innocence, to *habeas corpus*, and the right to have any law invalidated in the courts which conflicts with his or her rights and the right to have any of these rights altered except by referendum' (*Irish Times* 2003). While this statement is contestable, the Minister's strength of feeling on the issue was such that in 2006 he established an expert group (Balance in the Criminal Law Review Group 2007) to examine whether it was necessary to curtail a number of well-established protections for the defendant in order to restore the much vaunted notion of 'balance' in the system.

These direct attacks on the traditional rights of suspects and defendants have been accompanied by a trend towards the use of the civil law to regulate criminal activities, raising concerns that these provisions may deny due process protections to persons accused of substantive criminality. This was first evidenced by the introduction of the Proceeds of Crime Act in 1996 providing for a novel civil forfeiture procedure whereby applications can be made to the High Court to seize assets which are believed to constitute directly or indirectly the proceeds of crime. This was a new departure for law enforcement in Ireland, and indeed, Europe-wide. While the Offences Against the State Act 1985 authorises the freezing of bank accounts that are believed to be held on behalf of unlawful organisations and the disposal of moneys to the benefit of the Exchequer, the Act only applies to subversive crime. The 1996 Act applies to the proceeds of *all* kinds of crime. Constitutional challenges to the Act have been unsuccessful, yet many commentators maintain that the aims of the Act are punitive in nature (see, e.g., Meade 2000). As McCutcheon and Walsh (1999: 131) have noted in this regard, 'If a disciplinary charge of plagiarism against a student is "criminal in nature" is the case for the same conclusion not as compelling, if not more so, in criminal assets proceedings?' More recently, the introduction of civil orders controlling sex offenders (Sex Offenders Act 2001) and antisocial behaviour (Criminal Justice Act 2006) appear to have consolidated this trend. Both of these orders are hybrid in nature: they aim to control certain behaviours or risk groups through civil orders granted on the civil standard of proof but breach of the order is a criminal offence punishable by imprisonment. As with civil forfeiture, debate is ongoing as to whether the proceedings are in reality and in substance criminal in nature (Ashworth 2004; McDonald 2003; Hamilton 2007).

It had been said of the due process rights of an accused person in Ireland that they have a 'look but do not touch, touch but do not taste' feel about them (Kilcommins et al. 2004: 174). In a similar vein, Hamilton (2007) has argued that the dramatically altered criminal justice landscape in the period following the enactment of the Criminal Justice Act 1984 has meant that the realisation of the presumption of innocence in Irish criminal law falls far short of the rhetoric which surrounds it. The short period following the death of Veronica Guerin and Garda Jerry McCabe provided the context for many significant reforms such as revision of the law on bail (allowing it to be denied where there is a reasonable apprehension that the accused will reoffend), civil forfeiture under the Proceeds of Crime Act and the erosion of the rights to silence for those charged with serious drugs offences. Thus, the tangible benefits of the presumption in the form of the right to bail (Bail Act 1997), to remain silent (Criminal Justice (Drugs Trafficking) Act 1996) and even to remain free of punishment until a finding of guilt by a court (Proceeds of Crime Act 1996) are no longer available to the citizen in certain circumstances.

An important qualification to this argument is the continuing commitment of the Irish judiciary to due process values. This cannot be disregarded even it does coexist alongside an oftentimes overly deferential judicial approach (Hamilton 2007: 36–60). By way of illustration, Vaughan and Kilcommins (2008: 117–18) point to cases concerning alleged or actual sexual misconduct:

> The judgments in *Curtin* (the right to have unconstitutionally obtained evidence excluded), *CC* (the right not to be criminalised for mentally blameless conduct), *O'Donoghue* (the right to have evidence excluded because its positive probative value is outweighed by its prejudicial effect on the accused) and *WC* (the right to individuated justice) all demonstrate the continued resonance of accused rights,

> and their capacity to continue to compete for priority and act as a counterpoint to the supremacy of the paradigm of control.

Thus, while here also the field is contested, it can be strongly argued that the fundamental shift in state-accused relations represents one of the most crucial factors in the engendering of a culture of control in Ireland (Campbell 2008). This readiness to concede civil liberties in the last number of decades is perhaps a function of Ireland's history in that we have perhaps become desensitised to the erosion of our rights by the extreme measures adopted in the past to counter paramilitary activity (Kilcommins et al. 2004; Vaughan and Kilcommins 2008). In this respect it is certainly relevant that the right to silence was first eroded and the civil forfeiture procedure first introduced in the context of the struggle against subversive crime.

Index C: Use of Imprisonment

In comparative terms, Ireland's imprisonment rate of 72 per 100,000 in September 2006 is low (ICPS 2006). We are ranked near the bottom of the Council of Europe's table of prisoners and our detention rate is much closer to that of the Nordic countries such as Norway (66), Denmark (77) and Finland (75) than the UK (148) or even Germany (95). However, this does not provide a complete picture of the use of imprisonment in Ireland for a number of reasons outlined below.

First, it should be noted that the above only represents the 'stock' of prisoners on any given day. When the rate of prison entry or 'flow' of prisoners through the system is examined, Ireland appears in the midrange of the scale and the disparity between these two indices can be explained by the heavy reliance on short sentences of imprisonment in Ireland. According to Council of Europe statistics (2006 enquiry) (2008), Ireland's average term of imprisonment was 3.5 months, one of the shortest in Europe. Secondly, the picture looks dramatically different when our rates of imprisonment are correlated with our crime rates, arguably a more reliable indicator of 'punitiveness' than the rate of imprisonment per se (Lynch 1988, 1995). When expressed per 1,000 crimes our use of custody is three times higher than that of England and Wales and five times as high as Finland (Kilcommins et al. 2004). Third, a closer look at Irish sentencing practices suggests that judges use imprisonment heavily (O'Donnell 2001). Using figures from the Annual Reports on Prisons and Probation and Welfare data, O'Donnell (2004: 257) has shown that the ratio of immediate custody to probation and community service has been for many years consistently tipped in favour of imprisonment. In the 1980s, a defendant was two or three times more likely to receive a sentence of imprisonment than probation or community service. While the differential has considerably narrowed in recent years, the Comptroller and Auditor General's report (2004) observed that almost as many offenders are imprisoned each year as are supervised in the community (a ratio of 1.3:1 in favour of community supervision). An even gloomier picture is presented by recent statistics published by the Court Service (2004) which suggest that immediate imprisonment was more likely than probation and community service combined in both Limerick and Dublin in relation to road traffic offences and larceny. This was also true of assault and public order offences in Limerick. The profile of offenders committed to Irish prisons is also suggestive of an overreliance on custody: 79 per cent of committals in 2006 were for periods of imprisonment of one year or less and only 14.5 per cent of offenders were sentenced in respect of crimes involving violence (Irish Prison Service 2007). Thus, Ireland presents as a cautionary tale in terms of using a singular variable alone as a basis for drawing conclusions as to punitiveness: low imprisonment rates mask a higher rate of committals to prison and a heavy reliance on short terms of imprisonment.

A final important qualifier is that, as noted above, Ireland's imprisonment rate has significantly increased in recent years (in the period from 1997 to 2002 alone, it increased by over 30 per cent), albeit from a low base. While this may suggest an increase in the number of people sentenced to terms of imprisonment, O'Donnell (2005) has shown that this does not appear to be the case. The disparity between the daily average prison population over a 10-year period (2,133 in 1994 compared to 3,169 in 2004) disappears when adjustments are made for population increases, an increased number of those on remand or on immigration warrants and, most importantly, the decline in the use of temporary release over the period. Considered in the light of the sharp fall in the number of individuals committed to prison under sentence, this is strongly suggestive of an increase in the average term of imprisonment. O'Donnell (2004) observes that in 1981, 7 per cent of those committed to prison had received sentences of two years or more and this rose to 10 per cent in 1991 and to 13 per cent in 2005. The Annual Report of the Prison Service in 2005 (Irish Prison Service 2006: 11) has also referred to the 'general trend of longer sentences, which has been discerned in recent years'. Figure 3.5 illustrates the trends in the number of offenders entering prison who have received (i) life sentences, (ii) determinate sentences of two years imprisonment or more and (iii) determinate sentences of less than two years. 1976 is used as a base year in order to track changes in the number of shorter/longer sentences imposed over the period. While the number of sentences of less than two years has doubled, there has been a much more dramatic increase in the number of longer sentences imposed. Both the life sentence group and the group receiving fixed sentences of two years or more has increased by approximately 700 per cent. These figures should be treated with caution owing to the small numbers involved (hence the particularly volatile pattern of the life sentences) and the gaps in available data between 1995 and 2000. However, there is a clear upward trend in both categories. This may be attributable to an increase in the number of violent offences coming before the courts in the last number of years or a more punitive judiciary. As O'Malley (2006: 431) notes it is most likely a combination of these factors: there has been an increase in the number of persons sentenced for murder, serious sex offences and drug dealing in recent years and these offences attract heavy sentences. Additionally, the courts are under significant pressure to impose heavy sentences for s.15A drug dealing

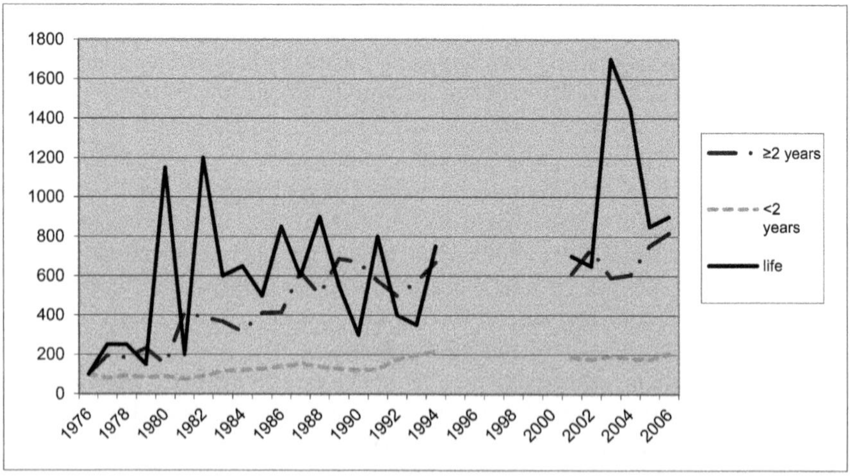

Figure 3.5 Number of offenders in Ireland receiving life sentences, determinate sentences of two years imprisonment or more and determinate sentences of less than two years, using 1976 as an index year

Source: O'Donnell et al. (2005); Irish Prison Service, Annual Reports 2004–2006.

offences (those over €13,000 value, discussed above) and for sex offences. Actual time served for both these categories of offender is also longer given that these offenders do not benefit from early release.

This leads us on to the complexity of determining actual sentence served in Ireland. While the chart shows that the length of sentences *imposed* may have increased somewhat in the last decade, it is important to note that this effect may be more pronounced if the average time *served* was charted (unfortunately this information is not available). As O'Donnell (2005: 58) has shown temporary release acted as an important safety valve for the state in the 1980s and 1990s and 'there was a poor relationship between the sentence of the court and time actually served'. The reduction in its use from the late 1990s onward is likely to have impacted considerably on the average time served. The effect is likely to have been all the greater with the introduction of the presumptive 10-year sentence for drug trafficking in 1999 given that, as noted, this cohort of offenders cannot be released early.

It is probable that this trend towards longer sentences will continue with the recent enactment of further presumptive and mandatory sentencing provisions in the Criminal Justice Act 2006. Presumptive sentences were created for certain firearms offences under the 2006 Act[3] and the Act also tightened up the

3 These are: possession of a firearm while taking a vehicle without authority (5 years;s.57, *Criminal Justice Act 2006*); use of a firearm to assist or aid an escape (10 years; s. 58 *Criminal Justice Act 2006*); possession of a firearm or ammunition in suspicious

provisions concerning the 10-year presumptive sentence for s.15A offenders so that this sentence *must* now be imposed on repeat offenders (in other words, a true mandatory provision).

Index D: Juvenile Justice

The area of juvenile justice raises distinct issues and as such merits separate consideration in any assessment of punitiveness (Tonry 2007; Kutateladze 2007b). For instance, the argument for rehabilitation over retribution is strongest in relation to young offenders owing to their developmental immaturity. There is also supposed global consensus on the need to promote the core principles of 'best interests' of the child, custody as a last resort, separation from adults and processes that respect the dignity of the child as evidenced by the large number of signatories to the UN Convention on the Rights of the Child (UNCRC). In his article on the 'punitive turn' in juvenile justice, Muncie (2008: 110) argues that in Western Europe and the US 'punitive values associated with retribution, incapacitation, individual responsibility and offender accountability have achieved a political legitimacy to the detriment of traditional principles of juvenile protection and support'. In attempting to marshall evidence of this trend he goes on to measure punitiveness through (a) the degree of compliance with international rights conventions and (b) comparative rates of juvenile custody.

Attempts to assess the punitiveness of the Irish juvenile justice system on these indices are immediately beset with difficulties owing to the lack of statistical data and empirical research. O'Dwyer (2002: 182) has described the information that is available as being 'usually outdated, partial, limited, not integrated, and poorly explained'. Fortunately, however, a number of key publications in recent years (Walsh 2005b; Kilkelly 2006) have made some insights into this area possible.

Turning to Muncie's (2008) indices concerning juvenile custody rates and children's rights compliance, it would appear that recently in Ireland there has been increased recognition (at least at a doctrinal level) of the rights of the child in the justice field. Many of the philosophies enshrined in the UNCRC and other international instruments have now been given statutory protection in a landmark piece of juvenile justice legislation, the Children Act 2001. Further, the appointment of an Ombudsman for Children and the publication of the National Children's Strategy have raised the profile of preventative work with children (Seymour 2006). Kilkelly (2006) has done much work in this area, carrying out an effective 'audit' of the various elements of the Irish criminal justice system in terms of its compliance with international human rights standards.

Her conclusions are mixed in that certain elements of the system appear to be functioning very well, while others fall far short of international norms. The

---

circumstances (5 years; s.59, *Criminal Justice Act 2006*); carrying a firearm with criminal intent (5 years; s.60 *Criminal Justice Act 2006*); shortening the barrel of a shotgun or rifle (5 years; s.65 *Criminal Justice Act 2006*).

Garda Diversion Programme would – on balance – appear to fall within the former category in that young people are being effectively diverted from the courts and prosecution. This programme has been running since 1963 and is frequently credited with significant success in reducing recidivism. Recent figures, for example, indicate that since its inception, 87.6 per cent of young people reached their eighteenth birthday without being prosecuted for a criminal offence (Garda Síochána 2002 cited in Seymour 2006: 128). This statistic should be treated with caution in light of the concerns expressed elsewhere about official measures of crime (O'Donnell and O'Sullivan 2003; Kilkelly 2006: 255) and the fact that the scheme does not appear to have impacted significantly on Ireland's overall rate of juvenile detention. Indeed, the recent decline in the number of young people committed to detention discussed below seems independent of the scheme. Nevertheless, as Kilkelly (2006: 255) writes 'the programme does appear to work in the interests of the young people who are engaged in it'. Kilkelly also reserves praise for the 'less celebrated' Children Detention Schools which provide a secure environment for children under the age of 16. She observes that the rights of children in these units are for the most part well protected and that children are afforded opportunities to address their various welfare and educational needs.

On the other side of the balance sheet, Kilkelly expressed concerns about the treatment of children in St. Patrick's Institution and the Children Court. While Ireland maintains a separate court system for those children under age 18 (17 prior to the enactment of the Children Act), this is beset by difficulties relating to poor communication, lack of coordination and delay. Generally the Court, despite the good intentions of individuals working within it, fails to recognise the particular needs of young people and operates in a manner more akin to the adult court (Kilkelly 2008). One aspect of the juvenile justice system which is wholly out of line with international standards is St. Patrick's Institution. This Dublin-based detention centre traditionally held young male offenders aged 16 to 21, in breach of the UNCRC and the International Covenant on Civil and Political Rights (ICCPR). St. Patrick's is described by Kilkelly as a 'punitive' institution, without a care or an educational ethos and with high levels of bullying and drug taking such that 'comparison with the international standards ... serves to fuel rather than quell ... anxiety' (2006: 259). It should also be noted that under Irish law it is possible for children as young as 15 to be detained in an adult prison where they are certified by the court as 'unruly and depraved'. In 2006, for example, three 15-year-old children were so detained (Irish Prison Service 2007).

Custody rates of juveniles in Ireland are very difficult to ascertain, primarily owing to the way the statistics are presented. With respect to prisons, in the Annual Reports up until 2005 attention is focused on those under 21 rather than those under 18 so that a definitive account of the juvenile rate of detention is not available. Separate data are available for St. Patrick's Institution (the main detention centre in the state) for the years 1976–94 and this can be broken down by age so that some indication of the juvenile detention rate can be derived for this period. Combined with information given on the number of committals to St

Patrick's in the Annual Reports on Prisons for 2001–2006 (no data for 1995–2000 are available), it is possible to compile a time series.

Figure 3.6 shows both the total numbers of those committed to St. Patrick's from 1976 to 2006 (the broken line) and the number of offenders under 18 committed to St. Patrick's from 1976 to 1994 (the solid line). As Walsh (2005b: 449) remarks, there is a clear upward trend in the total number of committals from 1976 to 1994 but this does not appear to hold true for the number of juveniles committed to St. Patrick's which has remained static for most of the period. While it is difficult to know what occurred in the period 1994–2006, if committals for juveniles followed the same trajectory as those for 16–21-year-olds then it is likely to have fallen considerably in the last number of years. Some indication is provided by the number of juvenile males committed to both prison and St. Patrick's in 2006 and 2007. As noted above this figure was recorded by the Irish Prison Service for the first time in 2006 and stands at 280 – considering that this also includes juveniles committed to prison it would appear to be a significant reduction on the 1994 figure of 380 juveniles committed to St. Patrick's. This would not appear to be an exceptional year given that it fell again in 2007 to 242.

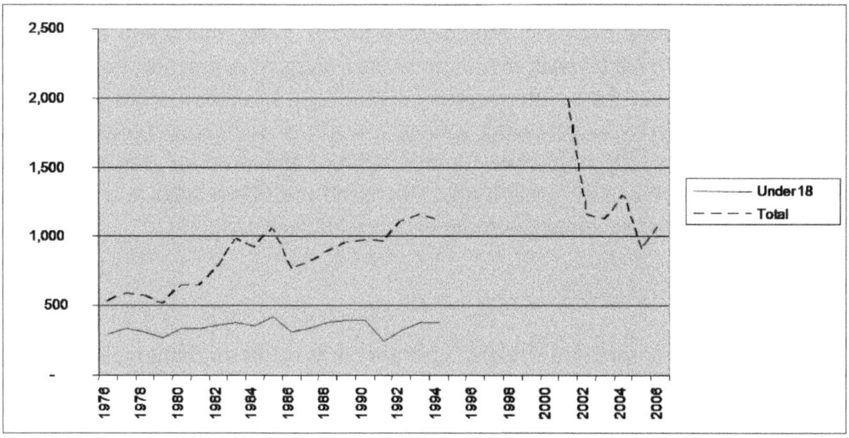

Figure 3.6 Number of offenders committed to St. Patrick's Institution

Source: Annual Reports on Prisons, various years; Irish Prison Service, Annual Reports 2001–2006.

Further support for the idea of a steady or falling rate of juvenile detention in Ireland can be derived from the numbers of those committed to special schools (institutions for offenders under 16). Walsh (2005b: 455) examined the total numbers of boys and girls committed to these schools from 1978 to 2002 inclusive and found a fairly steady downward trend from 159 in 1978 to 57 in 2002.

Before leaving the issue of juvenile detention rates, it is important to gain some sense of Ireland's standing relative to other countries. Statistics published by the Council of Europe (2003) indicate that Ireland is midrange in terms of the proportion of the prison population under 18. The Irish figure of 1.5 per cent was at the European average in 2002 and recent figures supplied to the International Centre for Prison Studies (ICPS) indicate that this rate has remained relatively unchanged (1.7 per cent in October 2007, ICPS 2007). As observed by Muncie (2008: 114), however, 'arguably the most accurate estimate of rates of *juvenile* incarceration can be derived by combining custody data collected by ICPS and population data gathered by UNICEF'. Muncie's estimates of juvenile custody rates per 1,000 under-18 population again place Ireland in the midrange. Ireland's 2006 rate of 0.05 is higher than those for the Nordic countries but also lower than the rates for the Netherlands (0.57), England and Wales (0.25) and Germany (0.23).

Overall, it is difficult to locate Ireland's juvenile justice system on the punitive 'map', so to speak. Decades of neglect and an absence of policy or legislative change may have resulted in a relatively punitive system (Kilkelly 2006), particularly in the way certain institutions such as St. Patrick's are run, bringing to mind Nelken's (2005) discussion on the subjectivity of punitiveness. In Ireland, it would seem that unintentional harshness may be equally as harmful in its effects as deliberately stigmatising policies. While the enactment of the Children Act 2001 represents progress in this area, perhaps bucking the international trend towards the responsibilisation of young offenders (Muncie, 2008), much will depend on the extent to which the legislative principles are honoured in practice. Falling rates of juvenile detention can be interpreted as signalling a less punitive era in juvenile justice but appear to be occurring less as a result of deliberate policy choices (the 2001 Act was fully implemented only in 2006) and more for reasons that are not well understood. It is possible that this trend may be related to a declining juvenile crime rate (Seymour 2006) and a more buoyant economy.

Index E: Prison Conditions

It is likely that in most regards Ireland's penal system meets minimum international standards (US Department of State, 1994–2008). There remain significant difficulties with the physical conditions in which prisoners are housed, however, not least in relation to overcrowding and 'slopping out'.

Despite an occupancy rate of 95.2 per cent (ICPS 2006) overcrowding is a severe problem in certain Irish prisons which often results in 'double-bunking'. Reports of the Visiting Committees for Cork and Castlerea prisons in 2006 (Cork Prison Visiting Committee 2007; Castlerea Prison Visiting Committee 2007) both expressed concerns about levels of overcrowding. Cork prison was originally designed for 150 prisoners yet regularly holds around 250. These problems are compounded in nineteenth century prisons such as Cork and Mountjoy by the lack of in-cell sanitation so that over 25 per cent of the prison population continue to 'slop out' night waste on a daily basis. In *Napier v Scottish Ministers*[4] the Scots

4 2005 SC 307.

courts held that the overcrowded conditions in Scottish prisons – which included 'slopping out' – were contrary to human dignity and this decision has prompted a number of Irish prisoners to institute proceedings (without success). In this regard, it is significant that a Prison Hygiene Policy Group established in September 1993 at the instigation of the Minister for Justice roundly condemned the practice as 'demeaning and degrading' for prisoners (1997: 22). Similarly, the European Committee for the Prevention of Torture (2003) has repeatedly condemned as 'degrading' and 'humiliating' the continued use of slopping out in the Irish prison system adding that it also debased the prison officers who supervised it. The government's response has been dilatory to say the least: a commitment made to provide in-cell sanitation in all places of detention by 1999 (Prison Hygiene Policy Group 1997) has still not been acted upon.

Given the poor physical conditions many Irish prisoners experience it is questionable to what extent it is even meaningful to talk about rehabilitation. While rehabilitation certainly remains an aspiration of the Irish Prison Service – according to their mission statement the Service is 'committed to managing custodial sentences in a way which encourages and supports prisoners in *their* endeavouring to live law-abiding and purposeful lives as valued members of society' (note: the responsibility clearly lies with the individual prisoner) – this is seriously compromised by overcrowding and, since 2004, cutbacks on staffing costs. These have been severely felt in the area of prisoner education; for example, both library services and evening classes for inmates in Mountjoy Prison have been curtailed over the last number of years. Moreover, the general poverty of the daily regime to which prisoners are subjected leaves many prisoners bored and frustrated and in most institutions prisoners are locked up for 18 hours per day. In Cloverhill prison and St. Patrick's Institution, for example, the lack of any meaningful activity has been recognised as one of the biggest problems (Inspector of Prisons and Places of Detention 2003, 2005).

An even more recent problem to have emerged in Irish prison life is the risk of violence. Since the tragic death of a prisoner at the hands of another mentally ill inmate in 2006, there have been a number of violent incidents in Irish prisons. It was striking that the 2007 CPT Report categorised three Irish prisons, namely, Mountjoy Prison, Limerick Prison and St. Patrick's Institution as 'unsafe' for both prisoners and prison staff due to prisoner-on-prisoner intimidation and violence (CPT 2007a). The delegation noted that stabbings and assaults with various objects were frequent and that many prisoners met by the delegation bore the marks of such incidents. The report cited the availability of drugs and the lack of purposeful activities as reasons behind the increase in violence. The use of such strong language by the CPT is exceptional and marks the gravity of the situation in the prisons. Considered together with the fact that deaths in Irish prisons reached record levels in 2006 with 12 inmates dying as a result of drug overdoses, murder and natural causes (*Irish Times* 2007), the situation warrants concern. Violence and bullying appear endemic in Irish prisons (Leddy and O'Connell (2002) found that almost two-thirds (57 per cent) of inmates questioned were involved in prison bullying in some way) and the significant increase in the number of deaths in Irish prisons since the late 1990s bears testament to the intensification of this problem (Irish Prison Service, various years).

While these and other concerns have led some to argue that Irish penal policy and practice is worryingly out of line with international human rights standards in a range of areas (see, e.g., Hamilton and Kilkelly 2008), it would be misleading not to acknowledge the positive aspects of the system. First, most institutions are small in size and relations between prisoners and staff are reasonably good and constructive (CPT 2003, 2007a). Secondly, the risk prediction tools so central to the new penological techniques adopted in other jurisdictions are not in evidence here. Indeed, the release of a significant number of prisoners every Christmas testifies to what Kilcommins et al. (2004: 265) describe as 'the humanity that continues to characterise the Irish system, for all its flaws'. Finally, shaming schemes for prisoners do not exist in Ireland and prisoners are not required to wear a uniform.

In addition, some recent developments can justifiably be claimed as significant improvements in the system. New prisons such as the Dóchas centre for female prisoners have been built providing better facilities and there have been improvements in psychiatric care and in the condition of strip cells (CPT 2003). A significant change also occurred in 2006 when, following a decision of the European Court of Human Rights, prisoners were given the right to a postal vote. Hitherto, they had been denied the practical means to exercise the franchise despite there being no formal prohibition on prisoners voting (Hamilton and Lines 2009; Behan and O'Donnell 2008). Further, an important source of accountability has been opened up with the establishment of the Office of the Inspector of Prisons and Places of Detention in 2002.

Index F: Post Release Controls

One of the features of the new penological age discussed in Chapter 2 is a desire to control certain risk groups and behaviour (Feeley and Simon 1992, 1994). According to Garland (2001), in this new climate of control, public safety is accorded absolute priority and the citizenship rights of the offender, such as his/her right to privacy, tend towards zero. In contrast to the welfarist era, the prevailing assumption is that 'there is no such thing as an "ex-offender", only offenders who have been caught before and may strike again' (Garland 2001: 180–1) and this is well evidenced by the spread of community notification schemes and paedophile registers across the US and in some Western jurisdictions. The extent to which ex-offenders are accorded rights in a country's criminal justice system therefore serves as a useful index of the 'new' penality.

In Ireland, actuarial risk assessment is not employed in most areas of the criminal justice system although there is ample evidence of what O'Malley (1992) terms the 'new prudentialism'. Civil orders and reporting requirements have proliferated in recent years increasing levels of control over certain categories of offender but perhaps most clearly in relation to sex offenders. These offenders have long been the subject of tighter controls by the state as evidenced by the fact that historically they were not considered eligible for early release, only statutory remission (O'Mahony 1996). Since the introduction of the Sex Offender Act 2001, they are also obligated upon release to provide details of their name, date of birth, address and travel plans to the Gardaí and may be made the subject of a civil sex offender order where it is deemed necessary to protect the public from serious harm. Failure to provide the requisite details or breach of a sex offender order constitutes a criminal offence. Finally, the 2001 Act imposes a legal obligation on the judge to consider whether a post release supervision order should be imposed on a sex offender, a development which O'Malley (2006) has criticised as being possibly unconstitutional on proportionality grounds. Interestingly, these provisions have now been extended to other categories of offender with the Criminal Justice Act 2006 requiring drug trafficking offenders sentenced to over one year's imprisonment to 'register' with the Gardaí.

While there would appear to be a raft of exclusionary policies directed at former sex offenders in this jurisdiction, there may be an important gap between the law in books and in practice in this area given that the degree to which these offenders are actively monitored by the Gardaí has been called into serious question (*TV3 Nightly News with Vincent Brown* 2008). The failure of the Gardaí to fully implement such laws and others relating to, for example, antisocial behaviour is evidence of what Kilcommins et al. (2004: 199) have termed a 'politics of neglect' or sense of apathy in Ireland. Further evidence of this approach is provided by the long delay in introducing expungement laws which prohibit disclosure of an offender's criminal record after a certain period of time has passed. While many Western jurisdictions introduced expungement laws in the 1960s and 1970s, Ireland has only recently addressed the issue[5] and remains the only country in the European Union which lacks an adult scheme (Kilcommins and O'Donnell 2003). (Juvenile convictions can be expunged in certain circumstances under the Children Act 2001). Finally, as with rehabilitation in the prisons, there remains a residual commitment to reintegration in the community, albeit sometimes purely at a rhetorical level (National Economic and Social Forum 2002). Community notification schemes do not exist in Ireland and ex-offenders enjoy full voting rights.

Index G: Death Penalty

The Criminal Justice Act 1964 abolished the death penalty in Ireland for murder and reserved it for: treason; certain offences under the Defence Act 1954 and Offences Against the State Act 1939; and the new offence of capital murder. This latter offence involved the murder of a member of the Gardaí or a prison officer or certain other persons. As it transpired, no person was put to death under this Act (the last execution was carried out in 1954), although husband and wife, Noel and Marie Murray, were both sentenced to death for capital murder in 1974

5 The Spent Convictions Bill 2012 was at the time of writing at Committee stage in the Seanad.

(the conviction was reduced to murder *simpliciter* on appeal). The death penalty was abolished in Ireland in 1990 and this abolition received constitutional status in 2002 after a referendum on the issue.

Conclusion

In light of the above discussion, is it correct to talk about an increased level of punitiveness in crime control in Ireland? An accurate depiction of punitiveness in Ireland over the period of the study must attempt to capture both the changes which have occurred in this area but also the stagnation which appears endemic to Irish criminal justice (O'Donnell 2008). Looking first at the changes, a low imprisonment rate in international terms belies significant increases in the prison population since 1996 and an over reliance on short sentences of imprisonment. These increases do not appear to relate to an increase in the number of offenders sentenced to imprisonment, however, rather an increase in the number of longer sentences imposed (and served) and an increase in the number of those remanded in custody. While there is little evidence of overly punitive policing practices in the public or private sectors, legislative changes augmenting police powers and eroding defendants' rights in the 1990s and 2000s are very much in line with Hinds's (2005) argument that change is occurring at the front end of the system. Further, in the last number of years, legislation reflecting crime risk thinking has emerged, often employing civil remedies at the expense of procedural protections and concerned with the control of certain offender populations such as sex offenders. There has also been some evidence of a shift away from the principle of individualised sentencing. By 2007 there were three major Acts on the statute book making provision for mandatory or presumptive sentencing, in addition to the mandatory life term for murder, thus marking a significant departure for a country where proportionate sentencing has been elevated to near-constitutional status. Other new departures concern a bold new blueprint for change in the juvenile justice area (Children Act 2001) which, if properly implemented and resourced, will insulate young offenders from increases in punishment severity.

Despite these changes one could be forgiven for indulging in deep cynicism about Irish criminal justice. The disjuncture which often occurs between policy and practice speaks to the apathy which characterises this area and the tendency for change to 'come dropping slow'. For example, the controversial 7-day detention provision enacted in the wake of the Guerin and McCabe murders has never been invoked. Bold measures introduced as a response to a crisis are often not fully effectuated and occasionally completely abandoned such as the €10 million unit for young offenders constructed in 2002. Kilcommins et al. (2004: 291) may well be correct in surmising that this inertia has paradoxically acted a bulwark against a punitive shift in Ireland. Certainly, if leniency is to be interpreted as something more than a deliberate choice to reduce punitiveness (Nelken 2005), it is clear that a more favourable verdict may be returned on the indifference which has characterised the

Irish criminal justice system over the period. Yet, the failure to act has had pernicious consequences in certain areas too. Issues relating to youth justice, prison conditions and expungement laws are only now being addressed, and it is well to remember the highly punitive consequences which may flow from such neglect.

Chapter 4
Scotland 1976–2006: From Divergence to Convergence

Introduction

Scotland has gained a reputation internationally for both 'penal harshness and innovation' (Young 1997: 116). This paradoxical situation stems from its historically high rates of imprisonment but also the stronger commitment to rehabilitation which has traditionally permeated the criminal justice system. For a large part of the period under examination Scotland has preserved this commitment aided in no small way by the 1707 constitutional agreement between Scotland and England which guarantees its separate legal identity. Since the mid 1990s, however, commentators have argued that criminal justice policy has taken a more punitive turn leading to core aspects of penal welfarism being abandoned (McAra 2006). This process appears to have gained momentum with the advent of devolved government in 1999, resulting in yet another paradox: self-government leading to increasing policy convergence with England and Wales or what McAra (2006) has called the 'de-tartanisation' of Scottish criminal justice. These arguments are explored in the first section below before proceeding to an assessment of punitiveness in Scotland on the seven chosen indices.

Criminal Justice in Scotland 1976–2006

Clearly, Scotland differs from the other two countries under examination in that it is not a sovereign nation. This has clear implications for criminal justice policy, even in a post-devolution age where justice has been devolved to the Scottish Parliament. The first is that many critical areas of policy, such as anti-terrorism legislation and legislation on firearms and misuse of drugs continue to be reserved to Westminster and as such lie largely outside the Scottish Executive's control. It goes without saying that these are areas which have in recent years witnessed a great deal of legislative activity, much of it punitive in its effect. Another consideration is that, owing to the closeness of media and political networks between the two countries, English criminal justice policy is sometimes regarded as the 'off the shelf' solution whenever a new problem arises or a fresh initiative is required. It is for this reason that the section below on the evolution of criminal justice policy over the period is framed largely in terms of Scotland's ability to distance itself from the criminal justice policies of its more powerful neighbour.

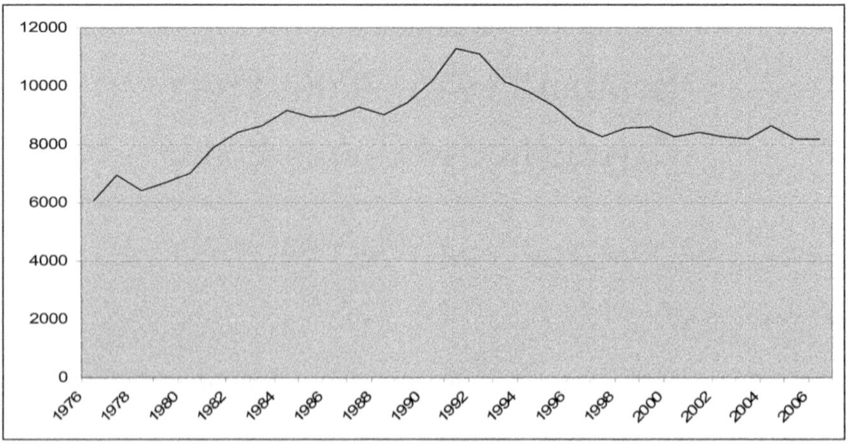

Figure 4.1 Crimes in Scotland per 100,000 population

Source: Statistical Bulletin, Recorded Crime in Scotland 1983–2006.

1976–95: Divergence and Diversion

Scottish crime trends follow those for most developed jurisdictions in that they rose sharply in the post-war period, although the rate of increase was lower than in England and Wales (Smith and Young 1999). There was a significant increase in the rate of crime[1] between the mid 1950s and the mid 1960s after which it fell off for a brief period. Thereafter, crime rates continued an upward spiral until 1991 when they fell slightly and then stabilised. Figure 4.1 shows the broad trajectory of crime rates in Scotland for the period under examination.

One aspect of the crime problem which merits separate attention is the prevalence of violent crime given Scotland's reputation as a violent country. In 2005 a World Health Organisation report found that Scotland had the second highest murder rate in Europe (although this was not a like with like comparison) and this followed a UN report published earlier that year which described Scotland as 'the most violent country in the developed world' (*Guardian* 2005). Certainly, the country's homicide rate (at 2.26 victims per 100,000) is significantly higher than England and Wales (1.59) and many other European countries (Scottish Executive 2007c) and this has been attributed largely to the exceptionally high rate of violence, particularly gang violence, in Glasgow (6.17 victims per 100,000). This picture is further confirmed by victimisation data from the 2004/5 sweep of the International Crime Victimisation Survey (ICVS) which show that Scotland

1 In Scotland, statistics are published on both crimes and offences. Crimes are generally regarded as the more serious of the two for working purposes, roughly equivalent to indictable/headline offences in Ireland.

had a higher than average rate of both assaults and threats. A more complex story, however, is revealed by lower than average rates for burglary, robbery and several other index crimes (Van Dijk et al. 2007). Particularly relevant to the instant inquiry are victimisation data showing lower prevalence rates for burglary, robbery, personal theft, sexual assault and physical assaults and threats in Scotland than in Ireland and New Zealand (Van Dijk et al. 2007).

The shift towards a highly partisan politics of crime detected by Downes and Morgan (1994, 2002) south of the border was little in evidence in Scotland which showed few obvious signs of a more populist approach until Michael Forsyth assumed control of St Andrew's House in mid-1995 (Duff and Hutton 1999).[2] A good illustration is provided by the rather considered way in which the Scottish Office handled the 'moral panic' surrounding the 'not proven' verdict which erupted in 1992/1993.[3] The same fairly measured approach was in evidence in other areas. The 1993 parole reforms introduced by Secretary of State Ian Lang followed five years of careful and detailed study by the Kincraig Committee appointed in the aftermath of the prison riots of the late 1980s (Scraton et al. 1988). Even the controversial Criminal Justice (Scotland) Act 1995 – which tightened up bail laws and eroded the right to silence – was the product of seven consultation papers, five research studies, a White Paper and a report from the Scottish Law Commission (*Herald* 1997). It was as if in Scotland the privileged position held by Loader's (2006) 'platonic guardians' together with their 'culture of deliberation' had been preserved. Indeed, McAra (2008) has identified the role of the Scottish 'quasi-state' (comprised of 'essentially progressive' civil servants in the Scottish Office and elite policy networks such as directors of social work and the judiciary) as being of key significance in the pre-devolutionary period, particularly their ability to forge a connection between welfarism and Scottishness.

It must also have been of some moment that the Scottish Secretaries who headed up the Scottish Office during the period (1976–95) for the most part held political views which could be described as 'ambiguously centrist' and 'inclining towards consensus'(Torrance 2006: 317). Malcolm Rifkind (1986–90), for one, was known to be sympathetic to penal reform and in 1988 gave an address to the Howard League which was decidedly anti-custodial in tone (Rifkind 1989). The

2 Unfortunately, it is not possible to consult Scottish party manifestos for this period as the main Scottish political parties did not normally publish separate manifestos for Scotland.

3 A three-verdict system operates in Scotland whereby judges and juries may not only acquit or convict but may also return a verdict of 'not proven'. The controversy over the verdict began in November 1992 when a verdict of 'not proven' was returned after the trial of a young man for brutally killing a fellow student. With mounting political pressure to abolish the verdict, the Scottish Office announced that it would incorporate the three-verdict system into its ongoing review of the criminal justice system. Following a consultation paper on juries, however, (Scottish Office 1994b) it concluded that the verdict should be retained (Scottish Office 1994a: para.3.19).

Secretaries for the most part enjoyed a good deal of autonomy from Westminster (Torrance 2006), aided in part by geographical distance, thereby affording elite policy networks a space within which they could operate. Moreover, given that the 'constitutional question' of devolution of power to Scotland dominated politics during this period it may also have been the case that the penal matters didn't receive the same attention they were attracting south of the border. Whyte (2007) observes that 'in contrast to the flood of papers and reports from London in the 1990s, with the exception of Rifkind's paper, much of the philosophical and policy debate in Scotland at the time was muted'. Indeed, with the notable exceptions of the Stewart and Kincraig reports (see below), few consultation papers or reports on criminal matters were published by the Scottish Office until the major review preceding the Criminal Justice Act 1995.

The view that Scottish criminal justice remained relatively sheltered during this period is held by many commentators. Smith and Young (1999: 27), for example, writing about the 1980s, observe that 'at a time when US policy was moving decisively and fast towards greater punitiveness and much higher imprisonment rates, Scottish policy was moving firmly in the opposite direction'. In support of this contention they cite the dramatic increase in offenders diverted from the criminal justice system (from 8 per cent in 1981 to 47 per cent in 1991, Moody and Tombs 1993: 367) as a result of the introduction of the 'fiscal fine' in 1988 and the creation of other alternatives to prosecution. These developments were encouraged by the recommendations of the Stewart Committee (1980, 1983) established by the government in 1977 to study alternatives to prosecution for minor offences. Similarly, Duff and Hutton (1999: 7), writing in the late 1990s, were able to state that 'there is little evidence of populist punitiveness in Scotland ... although the prison population has continued to rise'. McAra (2008: 489) too is unequivocal in her view that 'between the late 1960s and early 1990s, Scottish criminal justice and penal policy resisted the punitive and/or more actuarial turn evidenced in a range of other jurisdictions (including England/Wales) and fully embraced penal welfare values'. While managerialism was introduced to the various criminal justice institutions in the 1980s and early 1990s, it did not supplant welfarism. For example, a major review of the prison system which was undertaken during the late 1980s produced a policy document *Opportunity and Responsibility* (Scottish Prison Service 1990) which shifted the emphasis away from treatment towards managerialism and the exercise of individual responsibility. However, as McAra (1999, 2005) notes it did so 'within the context of prison regimes aimed at assisting prisoners to change their behaviour and lifestyles, and to reintegrate into mainstream society' (2005: 291). Similarly, National Standards for criminal justice social work introduced in 1991 retained a greater commitment to non-custodialism than their English counterparts and community sentences were not reinvented as 'punishment in the community' (McIvor and Williams 1999).

1995–97: The Forsyth Years

The appointment of Michael Forsyth as Scottish Secretary in July 1995 marked a watershed in the criminal justice arena. Torrance (2006: 326) describes Forsyth as 'the first, and only, genuinely Thatcherite Scottish secretary' who was, further, 'unashamedly populist and unmistakably right-wing'. This was a man who had little time for the lofty musings of the Scottish platonic guardians discussed above. As Torrance writes, Forsyth's attitudes to law and order were guided by those of the ordinary man or woman and he entered St. Andrew's House determined to 'inject ... some energy and populism into a political world obsessed by the constitutional question' (ibid.: 329). Extra urgency was added by the need to revive flagging Tory fortunes in the upcoming general election.

Given these conditions it is little wonder that the Forsyth administration was marked by frenetic activity on crime. At his inaugural media conference in July, Forsyth provided strong indications that he would adopt a tough line on crime, noting the feeling around the country that the criminal justice system was imbalanced in favour of the perpetrators of crime (*Scotsman* 1995). Some of his first acts were to introduce mandatory drug testing in prisons, propose uniforms for offenders carrying out community service and announce plans for Scotland's first private prison. In January 1996, the Scottish Office published a consultation paper, *Making the Punishment Fit the Crime* (1996a), in which Mr Forsyth made clear that prisoners should serve 'real time' to restore 'meaning and force' to sentences and to promote public confidence in the criminal justice system. These proposals attracted a barrage of criticism from some of Scotland's most senior judges, who expressed concern at the government's 'superficial' approach to law reform (*Herald* 1996a). The Secretary remained unmoved, however. At the Scottish Police Conference in April Forsyth declared a 'war on crime' and attacked 'do-gooders' and certain members of the judiciary who had accused him of being politically motivated. More prisons were promised using private money if necessary as well as 200 extra police officers (*Scotsman* 1996a).

A short few months later, the Scottish Office published a White Paper entitled *Crime and Punishment* (1996b) which contained proposals on a wide range of issues such as mandatory sentencing, crime prevention, criminal legal aid, sex offenders, the victims of crime and parole. Again, his proposals on sentencing reform drew criticism from the judiciary. Lord Hope, outgoing Lord Chief Justice, attacked Mr Forsyth's 'error of judgment' in allowing English proposals for mandatory life sentences for repeat sex and violent offenders to be 'dragged' across the border (*Herald* 1996b). Other stakeholders expressed serious concern about the short consultation period of only six weeks, fears which appeared confirmed when, on 30 September after the consultation period had ended, Mr Forsyth announced a fresh plan for minimum sentences for drugs offenders (*Scotsman* 1996b). As one commentator wrote at the time, 'Michael Forsyth is a man in a hurry. Blink and you run the risk of missing another major law and order announcement' (*Herald* 1996c). This pace continued throughout most of his administration. The following year witnessed the introduction of legislation to give effect to the controversial parole and sentencing reforms. The flagship Crime and Punishment (Scotland) Act 1997 effected reform in five main areas: minimum sentences for serious offences; increased powers for the sheriff courts; the abolition of parole and automatic early release; stricter controls on teenage drinking; and action to control the cost of criminal legal aid. This was accompanied by legislation creating a new national sex offenders register, an Act providing for non-harassment orders and a police Act making provision for wiretapping.

The legacy of the Forsyth years is mixed. Certainly, his administration marked the end of the divergence which had characterised the Scottish system for some time and saw the synchronisation of criminal justice policies north and south of the border (Duff and Hutton 1999; McAra 2008). Perhaps harking back to his previous role as Prisons Minister in the Home Office, Forsyth's policies during the period bore more than a passing resemblance to policies announced by the English Home Secretary, Michael Howard. His actions on parole, mandatory drug testing, private prisons, mandatory sentencing, stalking, a sex offenders register and knives all neatly coincided with Howardite law and order offensives and led to accusations that the 'English agenda [was] being unquestioningly aped' (*Scotsman* 1996c). This approach made for a dramatic increase in the number of criminal justice Acts passed in this period: 16 for the three years from 1995–97 as opposed to 4 in the previous three years and 7 for the period 1998–2000. It is also notable that the Scottish Crime Surveys conducted in 1993 and 1996 both register a significant increase in public concern about crime (Anderson and Leitch 1996: 36). While the spike in concern in the 1993 sweep of the survey may have been the result of the widespread media coverage of the James Bulger murder[4] in England (or indeed the home-grown 'moral panic' over the not proven verdict), the fact that similar levels were registered in 1996 does suggest some change in public perceptions.

Despite these developments, sight should not be lost of the influence which continued to be wielded by Scottish elites. Amendments tabled during the passage of the Crime and Punishment Bill through parliament scuppered Forsyth's parole plans and also seriously diluted his mandatory sentencing proposals. In the event, the only 'mandatory' sentences which were introduced into Scottish law were those relating to repeat offenders convicted of drug trafficking and even these provisions were subject to an 'interests of justice' exception (*Scotsman* 1997). Proposals that offenders wear uniforms on community service were also eventually withdrawn (McIvor and Williams 1999). Further, while it is tempting to highlight the discontinuities between Forsyth's administration and previous Secretaries, a tendency towards increased crime control values and managerialism was already in evidence by the early 1990s. The Criminal Justice (Scotland) Act 1995 severely limited the right to silence in the courtroom by allowing the prosecutor to comment on an accused's failure to give evidence at trial, a reform which generated much

4 Two-year-old James Bulger was abducted and murdered by two 10-year-old boys in Liverpool in February 1993.

adverse comment at the time. Managerialist strategies such as the introduction of performance indicators, the responsibilisation of offenders (Scottish Prison Service 1990) as well as the growth of victim-focused initiatives were already present in Scotland in the late 1980s and 1990s. Moreover, one of the Acts which is often identified by commentators (McAra 2006, 2008; Mooney and Poole 2004) as signalling a shift away from welfarism in Scottish youth justice – the Children (Scotland) Act 1995 – was introduced by Ian Lang, not Forsyth. In line with an increased focus on risk, this Act created a 'public protection' exception to the principle that consideration is to be given to the best interests of the child at all times.

1998–2006: A Distinction without a Difference? The 'Detartanisation' of Scottish Criminal Justice

The advent of devolution in 1999 following a referendum on the issue two years earlier, 'promised an era characterised by a "new politics", with greater participation and involvement of more Scots, and a policy-making agenda that was more closely in tune with "Scottish needs"' (Mooney and Scott 2005: 2). While certain aspects of criminal justice policy such as drugs, firearms and terrorism laws continued to be controlled by Westminster, the prospect of devolution held much promise given the severe criticism made of past attempts by the Conservatives to impose punitive measures north of the border (Duff and Hutton 1999: 8). Unfortunately, the promise was not fully realised in the seven years immediately following devolved government; indeed, the paradoxical effect of devolution may have been to bring the criminal justice system closer in some respects to the English model.

Policy convergence between the two jurisdictions during this period can be seen in several areas. The publication in 1998 of *The Tough Option* (Scottish Office 1998) restated the aims of the criminal justice social work services (CJSW) as being primarily concerned with public safety and this was reiterated in the 2001 *National Priorities* (Croall 2005, 2006). While Robinson and McNeill (2004) correctly point out that the document retained as its secondary and tertiary goals the reduction of unnecessary custody and promotion of the social inclusion of offenders, there were signs that the goal posts may be shifting. For example, proposals for the establishment of a single 'corrections' agency combining prisons and social work services were mooted in 2004, signalling convergence with England and Wales where the single agency approach has been associated with offender management and punishment (Scottish Executive 2004). Faced with staunch opposition the Executive did not proceed with this idea establishing instead the National Advisory Board on Offender Management in 2006 to provide expert advice on policy and practice. What appears as a victory for welfarism may ring somewhat hollow, however, for as McNeill (2005) has written, the 'shift towards the language of offender management may be more significant than any change in organisational arrangements'.

A similar shift away from welfarism towards public protection and risk management was in evidence in the youth justice system, reflecting what Piacentini and Walters (2006: 55) have termed 'the crisis of civil society's relationship to young people in Scotland'. Following media and public disquiet around the functioning of the Children's Hearing System[5] and the publication in 2000 of a report by the Advisory Group on Youth Crime (Scottish Executive 2000), persistent young offenders were identified as a particularly problematic group. The problem was addressed with a pilot system of 'fast track' hearings for those young offenders referred frequently to the Children's Hearing court and the establishment of youth courts as a tough option to tackle serious and persistent offenders aged between 16 and 18. While the first reform drew criticism from commentators for shifting the emphasis of the hearings from *needs* to *deeds* (McAra 2004), it was the second proposal which sparked most controversy. Although this latter group were effectively being diverted from the adult sheriff court (the hearing system only deals with children aged 8–16), Piacentini and Walters (2006) observe that youth courts do not necessarily adopt a more lenient approach. Drawing on work that was conducted for an evaluation of the youth courts, the authors argue first, that those offenders under the supervision of the Children's Hearing court would normally have had their case remitted back to the CHS and, second, that the youth court functions in the same manner as an adult court. In fact, it results in more guilty pleas and higher rates of detention.

The more punitive mood in relation to young offenders was encouraged by New Labour's 'respect' agenda and recent campaigns against antisocial behaviour. Indeed, Croall (2006: 599) argues that 'some of the clearest examples of penal populism can be found in the consultations leading up to the 2004 Antisocial Behaviour (Scotland) Act and in its subsequent implementation'. The Act introduced a number of measures, among them ASBOs and electronic monitoring for under 16s, parenting orders and police powers to designate 'dispersal zones' and disperse groups. Despite the concerns expressed by several key groups about the draconian nature of such measures, among them the Children's Commissioner, the Executive pressed ahead, determined to minister to the needs of 'ordinary Scots'. Its desire to appeal to popular opinion on this issue indicates further convergence between New Labour policies north and south of the border. Indeed, this was most evident during the 2003 election campaign when the First Minister, Jack McConnell, vigorously attacked 'ned culture' and 'antisocial behaviour' (Croall 2006).

The above measures would appear to signal a clear bias towards risk management in post-devolutionary crime control policy, a reading which is further confirmed by the introduction of extended sentences for sex and violent offenders in 1998 and orders facilitating the lifelong restriction of high-risk sexual and violent offenders in 2003 (see below). As with Ireland, however, 'volatile and contradictory' currents in criminal justice policy are also evident. Drug

---

5 The Children's Hearings System replaced the juvenile court structure in Scotland from 1968 onwards. It operates entirely within the civil jurisdiction and deals with both children who offend and children who are in need of care and protection.

courts were piloted in Glasgow and Fife in 2001 and 2002 and announcements made at the time signalled a longer term commitment to these initiatives (*BBC News* 2006). Moreover, the Executive has called for restorative justice approaches to be extended across Scotland (Scottish Executive 2002) and has introduced pilot schemes offering restorative conferencing and mediation (McAra 2008). While the incorporation of restorative principles to date has been fairly shallow in that they are mostly restricted to minor offences committed by young offenders (Dignan 2007), there appears to be a willingness to expand initiatives in this area.

Overall, it is clear that during this period criminal justice underwent a process of 'detartanisation' and that 'the grip of [elite] networks over the strategic direction of policy has been loosened' (McAra 2008: 494). Whether this can be better understood as a function of the 'ideological congruence' between the Labour/Liberal Democrat coalition in Scotland and New Labour in England or the populism which may accompany increased democracy and accountability (Ryan 2003; Canovan 1999) is difficult to say.

Punitiveness in Scotland 1976–2006 by Index

As with Ireland, situating Scotland on a punitiveness 'scale' is fraught with difficulty owing to the different, even contradictory, conclusions which may be returned depending on the signifier used. As will be seen below, Scotland's continuing heavy use of imprisonment and recent moves towards actuarialism (particularly with regard to sexual and violent offenders) do not sit easily with the welfarist ethos of the prison service and Children's Hearings System. Scottish punitiveness therefore varies considerably, not only over time but also within the criminal justice system itself.

Index A: Policing

In Scotland, as elsewhere, the 'diverse totality' of current policing is 'complex and ambiguous' (Fyfe 2005: 127). However, there are some indicators of a more punitive approach to law enforcement over the last number of decades. Prime among these, at least at a symbolic level, is the introduction of a more intensive, so-called zero-tolerance policing (ZTP) campaign by Strathclyde police in 1996 to tackle minor crime and late night disorder. 'Operation Spotlight' was associated in the media with zero-tolerance and shares some broad similarities with the New York initiative, despite the protestations of the then Chief Constable, John Orr, that it was misleading to label the campaign in this way (Orr 1997). The focus on combating 'quality of life' crimes such as drunkenness, public drinking, begging and truancy through a maximum street presence in parks, transport networks, licensed premises and sporting events mirrors the strategies employed by the NYPD. Indeed, Orr himself paid homage to the 'broken windows' thesis which underlies ZTP: 'I hold the firm belief that minor and serious crime are not poles apart. Indeed, I believe that minor crime is often simply the breeding ground and nursery that spawns and nurtures more serious and violent crime' (Orr 1997: 113).

As Jones and Newburn (2007: 132) point out, however, there were important differences between the New York and Scottish operation, most notably the scale of resources employed and the absence of a management-information process such as Compstat. It is also significant that ZTP has since been abandoned by Strathclyde police as 'an inappropriately short-term approach to crime prevention' (MacLeod 2002: 616) and replaced with Street Liaison Teams which aim to improve communication between the police, the public and those on the margins of society (Fyfe 2005). This is perhaps unsurprising given that research at the time indicated that such a heavy handed approach to policing was actually out of step with mainstream public opinion in Glasgow (MacLeod 2002).

Thus, while it is important not to overstate the significance of the Strathclyde experiment, viewed in conjunction with other developments the episode can be construed as part of a drift towards more intensive modes of policing or a 'sovereign state' strategy of crime control (Garland 1996). Fyfe (2005) observes a trend in recent years towards legislative changes which enhance the range of police powers, citing the new statutory powers to seize the proceeds of crime by means of a civil procedure (Proceeds of Crime Act 2002); to take DNA samples without authorisation from a senior officer (and retain samples given voluntarily) (Criminal Justice (Scotland) Act 2003); and, most controversially, to disperse groups in certain designated areas where a view is formed that any members of the public have been alarmed or distressed (Antisocial Behaviour (Scotland) Act 2004). These Acts were followed in 2006 by the landmark Police, Public Order and Criminal Justice (Scotland) Act which is the first comprehensive statute on policing since 1967 (Donnelly and Scott 2005: 188). The Act introduced football banning orders and increased powers in relation to suspects. For example, police officers are now empowered to require a suspect to give certain information in addition to their name and address and have been given a mandatory power of drug testing in certain circumstances. While this can be viewed as part of a longer term trend towards incrementally increasing police powers dating from the Criminal Justice Act 1980 (which provided for a six-hour period of detention), it is clear that the legislative pace quickened in the post-devolutionary era. Indeed, Donnelly and Scott (2005: 189) argue that the result of devolution has been a 'much closer set of linkages between policing and politicians', resulting in an increased volume of legislation and a more 'hands on' approach to policing matters.

In this new institutional context, the issue of police numbers has been hotly debated. The organisation and resourcing of the police has been a key issue in all Holyrood elections since devolution and pledges by political parties to significantly increase police strength are contained in most election manifestos from 1999 onwards. In 2003, for example, both the Conservatives and the Scottish National Party promised 1,000 more police while the Liberal Democrats pledged a whopping 3,500 extra officers. Against this background, it is likely that the upward trends in police rates and expenditure observable in Figures 4.2 and 4.3 below will continue for some time.

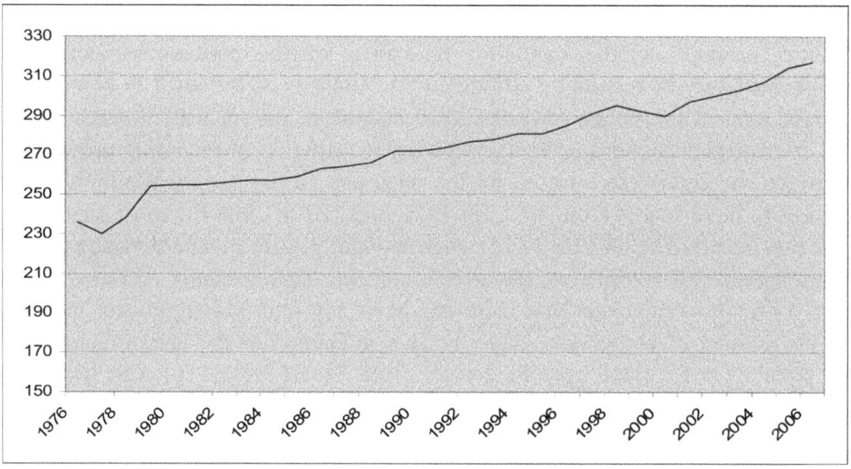

Figure 4.2 Police numbers per 100,000 population in Scotland

Source: Scottish Executive: Police Powers, Performance and Resources Division (data request).

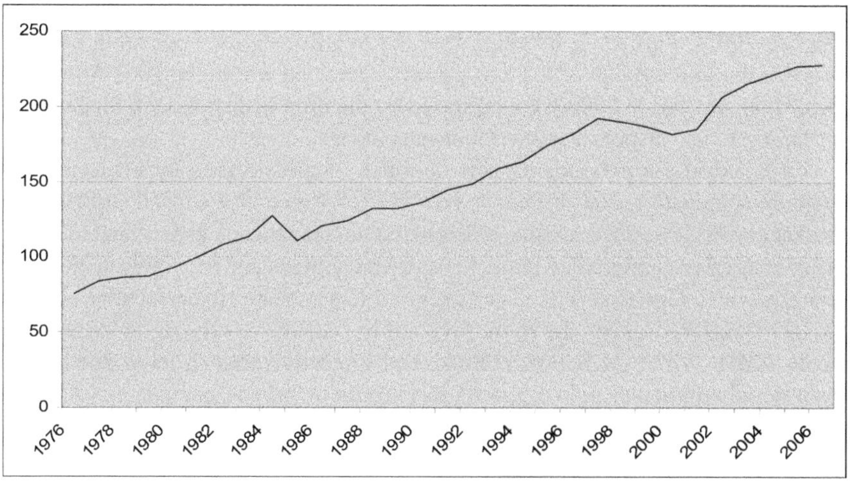

Figure 4.3 Net police expenditure (£s) per capita in Scotland

Source: Scottish Executive Police Powers Performance and Resources Division (data request); Her Majesty's Chief Inspector of Constabulary Annual Reports 1995-2004.

Note: Nominal figures have been adjusted to take account of inflation and are expressed in 2008 prices.

While increases in police resources may signify a drift towards 'law and order' politics, on their own they can tell us little about whether policing is experienced as exclusionary or restrictive (Hinds 2005). Analysis of the level of complaints lodged against the police provides some insight in this regard, although this is far from straightforward in Scotland owing to variation in recording procedures between the eight police forces for the most part of the period. While numbers appear to have soared from 1,125 in 1976 to 3,122 in 2006 the most significant increase occurred in 2001 (to 2,913) when nationally uniform recording procedures were agreed (all complaints, however minor, are now formally recorded). It is thus difficult to conclude that there has been any real and significant increase in the number of complaints made. Further indication of the predominant style of policing in Scotland may be derived from Fyfe (2005: 116) who considers community crime prevention rather than a 'sovereign state' strategy to have been the pre-eminent trend in Scottish policing over the last 20 years. Since the 1980s the government has been keen to diffuse responsibility for crime control to individuals and communities through initiatives such as the Neighbourhood Watch scheme in 1986 and the Safer Cities crime prevention programme launched three years later (Fyfe and Bannister 1999). This has been enhanced in recent years with the rapid spread of CCTV cameras throughout Scottish cities and the introduction of pilot community warden schemes and antisocial behaviour teams (McAra 2008). Further, it is telling that the Scottish Police Federation actually opposed the introduction of the new powers contained within the 2004 Antisocial Behaviour Act and in 2006 were criticised by the First Minister, Jack McConnell, for failing to use dispersal orders (*Scotsman* 2006).

As noted in the previous chapter, the idea of private security being used to spatially segregate social difference has less relevance in a smaller jurisdiction. Walker (1999: 103), for example, refers to the 'lesser salience in Scotland of a new urban underclass marginalized from mainstream political and economic institutions and practices'. However, this is certainly not to say that private security activity has not flourished under the more favourable neo-liberal climate (Mooney and Poole 2004). While the Scottish Office, and Executive after it, have shied away from devolving actual police powers to citizens or private companies (with the long standing exception of Special volunteer constables, see further Donnelly and Scott 2005: 189–91), the private security industry itself has undergone significant growth. As in other jurisdictions, it is very difficult to gauge the size of the industry although a 2001 Consultation Paper on *Regulation of the Private Security Industry in Scotland* (Scottish Executive 2001) placed the number of employees at 12,000.[6] In any event, the increase in the strength of the sector is likely to have

6 If accurate, this would suggest public police still outnumber those in the private security sector by a narrow margin of 1.25:1. This figure should perhaps be revised upwards, given that the UK-wide regulatory body, the Security Industry Authority, considers that the number employed by the private security industry is roughly 2–3 times greater than the size of the police force (Security Industry Authority 2006: 7).

been significant. Fyfe and Bannister (1999) have attempted to quantify this growth by measuring the number of entries in the Yellow Pages for 'security services and equipment' in Glasgow and found that they have increased from less than 10 in number in the mid 1960s to over 80 in the late 1990s.

Index B: Procedural Protections for Defendants

In approaching the issue of 'due process' rights in Scotland an immediate difficulty concerns the relevance of the very concept to a 'mixed' legal system such as Scotland's.[7] Young (1996/7: 22) issues a stern warning to those who would attempt to unthinkingly apply concepts such as due process and adversarialism to certain features of the Scottish criminal justice system: 'an analysis of … [certain] procedures couched in terms of concepts such as "due process" and "crime control" would miss their point and style altogether and could lead to a serious misunderstanding of procedures which are a characteristics of the Scottish system'. Bearing this caveat in mind, it is still possible to consider 'fair trial' rights as they apply to criminal justice in Scotland, in a manner akin to assessing compliance with Article 6 of the European Convention on Human Rights. Moreover, it is clear that Young's admonitions apply only to certain aspects of criminal justice in Scotland: the right to jury trial, for example, is necessarily weaker owing to the wide discretionary powers of the Fiscal. In other regards protections afforded the accused in Scotland bear close similarities to the English system (Duff 2007).

Historically, Scotland presents as a country where the procedural rights of the suspect and the accused have been accorded considerable respect. This is reflected in the short period of detention of six hours and the continued existence of the right to silence in the police station. If detained for questioning, the accused is under no obligation to answer any question other than to give his/her name and address (Donnelly and Scott 2005) although more information may be required in certain circumstances under the Police, Public Order and Criminal Justice Act. The accused also has the right to remain silent at a trial without any assumption of guilt being drawn from that silence, although importantly since 1995 the prosecutor may comment upon the accused's failure to testify. The presumption of innocence is further safeguarded in Scotland by the corroboration rule, i.e. the need to show evidence from at least two sources that the alleged offence has been committed, and that it was the accused who committed the offence (Duff and Gibb 2002). Indeed, such was the respect afforded the presumption in Scotland that until recently, sentencing discounts were not permitted for a guilty plea on the grounds

7 The system differs from England and Wales in that it displays elements of both the Anglo American and European systems (Young 1997). While the Scottish trial is adversarial in nature, other stages of the criminal process more closely resemble inquisitorial systems. Most notably, the public prosecutor or Procurator Fiscal as s/he is known makes key decisions whether to prosecute, in what court the prosecution will be brought and what type of procedure (summary or solemn) will be used.

that this represented an effective penalty on those who decided to contest their case (Ashworth 1998). It is noteworthy that these principles were often the envy of commentators abroad who called for such policies to be emulated in their own jurisdiction (see, for example, O'Mahony 2002; Ashworth 1998; Hamilton 2007).

From the mid-1990s onwards, however, an increased hostility to the rights of accused persons is detectable in Scotland. This mirrors developments south of the border at a time when, as Lea (2004: 81) has written, 'the yardstick of an effective criminal justice system [became] simply the control of crime'. Policy documents emanating from the Scottish Office during this period described the need for greater efficiency in the criminal justice process and for a balance to be struck between the rights of the accused and the need to convict the guilty (Scottish Office 1994a; 1996b). The Criminal Justice (Scotland) Act 1995 introduced a raft of reforms in order to redress this balance, namely, restrictions on bail for repeat serious offenders; prosecution appeals against sentence; compulsory hearings to agree evidence prior to trial; a sentencing discount for a guilty plea; provisions allowing the prosecutor to comment on an accused's silence; prosecution appeals against acquittals in summary cases and provisions permitting the introduction of previous bad character evidence where the character of a prosecution witness is attacked *outside* the witness box. While these reforms were widely construed at the time as much milder than expected and in stark contrast to Michael Howard's proposals for England and Wales (*Scotsman* 1994), they nevertheless represent incremental moves towards a crime control model of criminal justice (Packer 1968).

More recent reforms have continued this trend but with an increased focus on risk management and concomitant resort to hybrid criminal/civil provisions. Civil orders have been introduced which aim to control those who engage in antisocial behaviour and those who have been previously convicted of sex offences (Crime and Disorder Act 1998, Criminal Justice and Courts Services Act 2000). Breach of such orders constitutes a criminal offence punishable by imprisonment. Civil powers of recovery were also introduced in the UK-wide Proceeds of Crime Act 2002, permitting confiscation of assets irrespective of a criminal conviction. As discussed in the previous chapter, these new civil techniques arguably constitute frontal assaults on due process principles as they deny defendants on a (*de facto*) criminal charge proper protection (Hamilton 2007). Finally, the right to bail, a practical manifestation of the presumption of innocence, has also come under much greater scrutiny. The Criminal Procedure (Amendment) (Scotland) Act 2004, for example, now provides for tagging as a condition of bail.

Despite these – far from inconsequential – inroads into the procedural rights of Scottish accused persons, reforms have been more measured than in England and Wales. For example, the Criminal Justice Act 2003 which increased detention periods, removed the double jeopardy rule and allowed evidence of previous convictions to be admitted at trial was not introduced in Scotland. Reports at the time suggested that First Minister, Jack McConnell, was reluctant to announce similar measures for Scotland prior to the 2003 general election owing to their 'perceived unpopularity'(*Evening News* 2002). Given that tough measures to tackle antisocial behaviour were part of the same New Labour anti-crime package, however – and Scottish Labour ultimately decided to enthusiastically embrace these – it is unclear why procedural reforms were sidelined. One possible explanation may have been fear of a backlash from elites similar to that witnessed during the Forsyth years (see the first part of this chapter above).

Index C: The Use of Imprisonment

Scotland has historically imprisoned proportionately more of its population than many other European countries and it is only in the mid to late 1990s that its imprisonment rate has been exceeded by that of England and Wales (ICPS 2008). It has recently found itself near the top of Western European imprisonment rates with a rate of 148 (ICPS cited in Scottish Consortium on Crime and Criminal Justice 2008) and the picture appears even more gloomy if one considers the flow of entries into Scottish prisons rather than the stock figure. Recent statistics published by the Council of Europe (2009) rank Scotland as the country with *the highest* rate of entries to penal institutions in the Council of Europe. The reasons underlying such a heavy use of imprisonment are unclear but an overuse of short sentences and the high proportion of fine defaulters who are imprisoned have certainly been significant contributory factors. Since the late 1960s fine defaulters have consistently comprised over 40 per cent of all receptions under sentence and as Young (1997: 128–9) notes 'by international standards, these are very high figures'.

Table 4.1 Indices of change in Scotland's use of imprisonment (per 100,000 population)

	Imprisonment rate	% change on previous decade	Convicted prisoner rate	% change on previous decade	Reception rate	% change on previous decade	Receptionrate under sentence	% change on previous decade
1976	93.3	–	79	–	656	–	346	–
1986	109.3	17	89	13	808	23	454	31
1996	117.7	8	98	10	767	-5	460	1
2006	140.4	19	110	12	857	12	399	-13
% change 1976–2006	50		39		31		15	

Source: Statistical Bulletins: Prison Statistics Scotland, Scottish Prison Service Annual Reports, Scottish Home and Health Department Annual Reports on Prisons, various years.

In terms of overall trends, the prison population experienced rapid growth during the 1960s and then hovered around the 5,000 mark before entering a second period of growth in the early 1990s (McManus 1999). This growth has continued apace since, going from an average prison population of 4,738 in 1990 to over 7,000 in 2006. Table 4.1shows the changes which have occurred in the use of imprisonment over the study period examining: (i) imprisonment rates, (ii) convicted prisoner rates, (iii) reception rates and (iv) reception rates under sentence. It is notable that, while the average daily population has continued to rise decade-on-decade, the outline of the reception figures is more uneven: the rate actually fell by 5 per cent between 1986 and 1996 before increasing again in the following decade. Particularly noteworthy are developments between 1996 and 2006: while the reception rate under sentence dropped by 13 per cent, the total number of receptions rose. This is strongly suggestive of an increased use of custodial remand. Indeed, as McAra (2008: 488) notes, there has been a 40 per cent increase in the number of remand receptions since 2000 and many of these offenders do not end up with a custodial sentence. Analysis of the data in the table also points to another critical driver of the recent prison population increase, namely, sentence length. Increases in the committal rate under sentence over the 30-year period (15 per cent) have fallen far behind increases in the convicted prisoner rate (39 per cent), indicating that sentence lengths have increased. Indeed, these two indices appear to be going in opposite directions for the most recent period: while the rate of committals under sentence fell by 13 per cent between 1996 and 2006, the convicted prisoner rate rose by 12 per cent in the same period. This is most likely explained by an increase in both sentence lengths imposed and the actual time served.

This argument is borne out by examination of the data on the proportion of prisoners receiving sentences of imprisonment of two years or more. Seven per cent of offenders (including young offenders) fell into this category in 1988 and this rose to 11 per cent in 2006. Figure 4.4 shows the numbers of adult[8] offenders entering prison who received sentences of (i) under two years, (ii) two years or more and (iii) life sentences using 1976 as a base figure. It is clear the biggest increases have been among those receiving determinate sentences of two years or more, although there have also been increases in the other two categories. This is supported by data from Tombs's study on sentencing (2004: 25) which found that between 1993 and 2002 there was a steep rise in the numbers of adult prison receptions for longer sentences: 'Those sentenced to four years or more increased by 51 per cent, from 428 in 1993 to 645 in 2002 and those sentenced to life imprisonment increased by 115 per cent, from 33 in 1993 to 71 in 2002'. While precise causal factors for increasing sentence lengths are difficult to determine, Tombs (2004) argues that it may be due to changes in patterns of offending (i.e. more serious offences such as serious assault/attempted murder and drug crimes coming before the courts), a more punitive climate and legislative

8 Data dating from 1976 were only available in respect of adult offenders. Statistics relating to young offenders (under 21s) are therefore excluded.

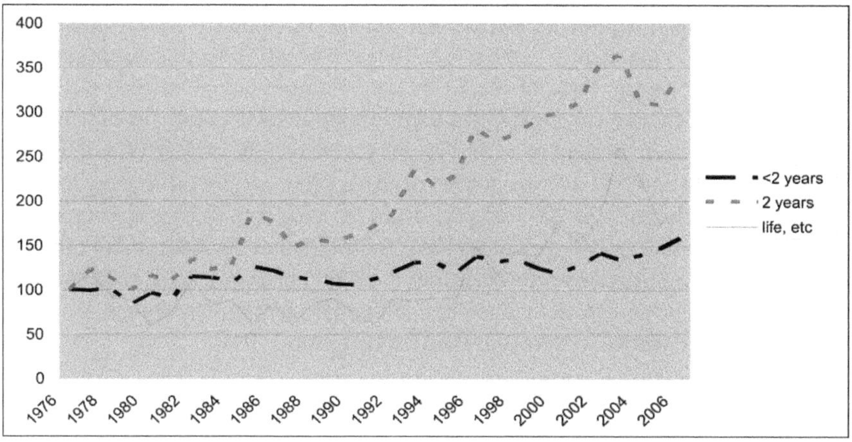

Figure 4.4 Number of adult offenders in Scotland receiving life sentences, determinate sentences of two years imprisonment or more and determinate sentences of less than two years, using 1976 as an index year

Source: Scottish Executive: Statistical Bulletin: Prison Statistics Scotland 2005/06 and 2006/07; Scottish Prison Service, Annual Reports 1992/3-1995/6; Scottish Home and Health Department, Prisons in Scotland: Reports 1986–1990/1991.

and policy changes which have encouraged an inflationary drift in sentencing. Another factor which must be considered is changes in release policy and practice. Reforms made to the system of parole in 1993 are on the whole likely to have increased the lengths served by longer term prisoners and this, combined with increasing terms served for life sentences, have probably contributed to a rising prison population (ibid.).

On the other hand, it may be said that certain measures of the use of imprisonment in Scotland militate against any increase in punitiveness. The number of prisoners per 1,000 crimes remains at a similar level to that in 1976 (15 in 1976 compared to 17 in 2006) and the juvenile detention rate (per 100,000 population) has dramatically declined from 23.7 in 1978 to 11 in 2006. As in Ireland, the ratio of custody to community orders has steadily declined over time and it now appears that an equal number of people are received into prison as begin probation or community service (compared to four times as many in 1976). Caution should be exercised in interpreting these figures, however. As has occurred in other jurisdictions (Ashworth, 2003), Scottish sentencers appear to be using community disposals not as alternatives to custody but as alternatives to financial penalties such as fines. In her study Tombs (2004: 28) observed that a 14 per cent increase in the prison population between 1993 and 2002 occurred alongside a 41 per cent increase in the use of community penalties.

Another important point is that Scotland has also remained relatively immune to the trend towards mandatory sentencing. Two presumptive sentencing provisions were introduced in the form of the Crime and Punishment (Scotland) Act 1997 but only one of them (which provides a minimum of seven years for repeat drug traffickers) has been implemented and it looks increasingly unlikely that the other legislative provision will ever be commenced. Another presumptive sentence was introduced for firearms in 2003 as part of a UK-wide Act. While of course it is possible that these legislative changes have contributed to the inflationary effect in sentencing referred to above, the fact that the 1997 measures were both strongly resisted at the time and are not currently operational speaks to the weight accorded to individualised justice in Scotland (Duff and Hutton 1999).

Index D: Juvenile Justice

Muncie's (2008) bipartite framework for assessing punitiveness in youth justice will be recalled from the previous chapter. He identified two key measures of punitiveness, namely (a) the degree of compliance with international rights conventions and (b) comparative rates of juvenile custody. It is proposed to examine below these two indices in a Scottish context.

Turning first to Scotland's compliance with human rights treaties, Scotland has long had a youth justice system in place which chimes strongly with many of the principles espoused in the UNCRC and other treaties. The Children's Hearings System – a radical system of juvenile and welfare justice which has been in operation since 1971 – in many respects represents a 'triumph of welfarism' (McAra 2002: 446). Indeed, it may be described as:

> a paradigm example of a welfare based system: the prominence accorded to social work and other expert opinion; the emphasis placed on participatory and consensual decision making and the informal character of the hearings themselves; the degree of indeterminacy with respect to disposals; and the focus on needs rather than deeds, with efforts made to secure behavioural change by viewing offending in its wider social context. (McAra 2004: 29)

Despite its strong welfarist orientation, the system has not fallen prey to one of its main dangers – an excessively interventionist approach – owing to the 'minimum interventionist' ethos adopted by the panels (Cavadino and Dignan 2006). This principle is protected in law through the rule that no order or requirement of any kind should be made unless it would benefit the child (Children (Scotland) Act 1995) and is given practical effect by the gatekeeping role performed by the Reporter to the Children's Hearing. The Reporter must be satisfied that there is a *prima facie* case against the offender and also that the child is in need of compulsory measures of care. Further, in keeping with the diversionary and anti-custodial ethos of many international juvenile justice conventions (such as the UN Standard Minimum Rules for the Administration of Juvenile Justice – the

'Beijing Rules' 1985 and the UNCRC 1990), the system has consistently strived towards maximum diversion and minimum use of custody. Cavadino and Dignan (2006) note that the proportion of offences in which no action is taken in the hearings has risen from 39 per cent in 1980 to 71 per cent in 1999 and there has also been a fall in the proportion of cases referred to a Hearing from 48 per cent to 20 per cent (most referrals come from the police). Moreover, both the number of placements made by the panels and the proportion of those placements which involve residential care has steadily declined over this period (ibid.).

While the political achievement in establishing and sustaining such a radical system over the last 40 years cannot be minimised, there remain difficulties with the system in terms of rights compliance (Edwards 2001; UK Children's Rights Commissioners 2008; Law Society of Scotland 2009). In a recent submission to the Joint Committee on Human Rights on the criminalisation of children, the Law Society (2009) identified a number of areas where Scottish child law may be vulnerable. The first point concerns the transition point between the adult and juvenile justice systems which, at 16, is out of kilter with many European countries (McAra 2002). Indeed, it should be noted that, while the vast majority of children who infringe the criminal law in Scotland are dealt with through the Children's Hearings System, it remains possible for a child in the 8–15 age group to be prosecuted in the ordinary criminal courts and offending young people aged 16 and over are usually dealt with in that forum. It is arguable that adult courts tend to fail to recognise the particular needs of young people and there are questions about the discriminatory nature of this practice (as between 16/17year olds and those under 16) (UN Committee 2007). As noted in the first part of this chapter, the Scottish Executive has recently moved to establish specialist youth courts for persistent young offenders yet far from offering a more individualised approach it would appear that there are real concerns about their operation, mainly, that they are simply adult courts designed to process offenders at a quicker pace and in a manner which encourages guilty pleas (Piacentini and Walters 2006). A further concern must be that if a young person is referred to the court on the basis that s/he is a 'persistent offender', then the sheriff knows *a priori* that the accused has a criminal record – something that is in breach of the usual rules of criminal evidence.

Second, Scotland's low age of criminal responsibility (it is currently fixed at eight) has been the focus of much adverse comment from the UN Committee (2002, 2008). The dilatory attitude of the Executive in taking forward proposals to increase it is telling (McAra 2004) as was the eventual compromise struck (the age at which children could be prosecuted was raised to 12 in the Criminal Justice and Licensing Act 2010). This leads on to broader questions about the more punitive edge to juvenile justice policy and rhetoric since devolution. It is a matter of some concern that the welfare principle has come under attack during this period and may actually be compromised by new initiatives to deal with bad behaviour by young people, such as the antisocial behaviour orders and tagging of young people under 16. McAra (2004: 39) goes so far to assert that since devolution welfarism

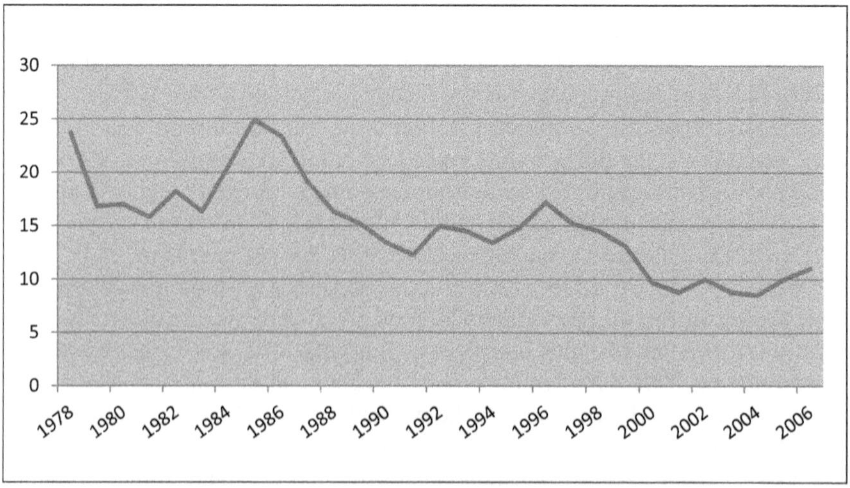

Figure 4.5 Number of juveniles committed to prison per 100,000 population in Scotland

Source: Scottish Executive: Statistical Bulletin: Prison Statistics Scotland 2005/06 and 2006/07; Scottish Prison Service, Annual Reports 1992/3-1995/6; Scottish Home and Health Department, Prisons in Scotland: Reports 1986-1990/1991.

has 'been supplanted by an eclectic and somewhat contradictory set of penal rationales (punitive, preventive, restorative, actuarial)'.

A mixed verdict can also be returned on the other aspects of the youth justice system. Diversion would appear to be operating effectively. Court proceedings statistics from the mid 1990s show a downward trend in convictions of young offenders, most likely indicating the successful implementation of diversion from prosecution schemes targeting young offenders (Hogg 1999; McAra 2002). Conditions in young offender institutions are generally good although children's care homes which house young offenders under 16 have also come in for considerable criticism in recent years, most notably in relation to the calibre of staff caring for these young people. In 1992, a report by Angus Skinner, Scotland's former chief inspector of social work, recommended radical reforms to ensure that staff were adequately trained though unfortunately the situation does not appear to have improved dramatically (*Scotsman* 2007).

The fact that young offenders aged 16–17 are not subject to the hearings system has implications beyond compliance with international human rights standards in that these offenders form part of the adult prison estate. Scotland is one of a number of European countries (alongside England and Wales) with the highest proportion of offenders under 21 (Cavadino and Dignan 2006: 223). The most recent Council of Europe data indicate that the proportion of minors in the Scottish daily prison population was 6.2 per cent in 2007, well ahead of the European average of 1.2 per cent. When a more accurate measure of punitiveness is used, however – estimates of juvenile custody rates per 1000 under-18 population – Scotland's juvenile detention rate appears midrange. At 0.17, it pales in comparison to the US (1.4) and even the Netherlands (0.57) yet remains higher than corresponding rates in the Nordic countries (Muncie 2008: 166).

Moreover, Scottish Executive statistics (1999, 2007) indicate that the adult and young offender (under 21) populations are diverging sharply in the last number of decades: the average daily population of young offenders in custody has decreased substantially whereas the opposite was true for adults. The young offender population decreased from 813 in 1989 to 621 in 2006, a fall of about a quarter. Similar trends can be detected in the receptions data per 100,000 population (see Figure 4.5) which are broken down by age and therefore allow examination of the under 18 population alone.

It may therefore be the case that while the political rhetoric relating to young offenders has hardened in the decade since devolution, punishment practices have as yet been unaffected. In relation to ASBOs, research published in 2007 suggests that only six ASBOs have been made against children since their introduction in 2004 (Donoghue, 2007) and, importantly, under the Scottish legislation children under 16 cannot be detained for breaching ASBOs.

Index E: Prison Conditions

The roots of the current guiding principles of the Scottish Prison Service lie in its experience of protracted and widespread prisoner unrest in the late 1980s. Overcrowding and changes to parole system made prisoners (particularly those serving long sentences) very difficult to manage leading to an outbreak of riots and hostage takings throughout 1986 and 1987 and calls for a new initiative (Scraton et al. 1988). A series of position papers led to the publication in 1990 of *Opportunity and Responsibility* (Scottish Prison Service 1990) which replaced the treatment philosophy with facilitated change. It emphasised prisoners taking responsibility for their own actions, while the prison's role was to provide humane custody and 'positive' regimes. The Service's mission statement remains largely unchanged today, exhibiting the same 'mixture of managerialism and rehabilitation' (Croall 2005: 187).

To a considerable degree, it must be acknowledged that the Service has made good on its promise to deliver humane custody, albeit in a somewhat dilatory fashion. While overcrowding continues to blight many Scottish prisons, in particular local prisons and the sole facility for female prisoners at HMP Cornton Vale (CPT 2005; Audit Scotland 2008), real progress has been made over the last 15 years in improving the physical conditions in which prisoners are kept. New prisons have been built, old or unsuitable institutions have been closed and in cell sanitation has been fitted to cells in Barlinnie, Edinburgh, Perth and Polmont prisons, among others. Indeed, the former Chief Inspector of Prisons, Clive Fairweather, notes that 'once modernisation is complete at Perth, Peterhead and possibly Aberdeen, within the next few years, the Scottish Prison Service

(SPS) will be able to boast, rightly, that all its prison buildings will be fit for purpose' (2006: 53). The improvement has been particularly marked in the case of remand prisoners who are now kept in uniformly decent conditions for the first time in over two centuries (Fairweather 2006). The transformation has been such that the Innocent Until Proven Guilty group representing remand prisoners in the UK extols the virtues of the 'Scottish example' on its website. In a feature on the site, Fairweather (2002) describes how, one after one, prison governors moved to transfer remand prisoners into new or refurbished wings of their institutions, with a corresponding fall in the suicide rate in some cases.

This leads on to a second area of progress, which concerns the improved safety of prisoners in Scotland in recent years. In the early 1980s there had been a spate of suicides in HM Young Offender Institution Glenochil, prompting an inquiry into the matter by the Scottish Home and Health Department (1985). The subsequent report found that the methods of managing inmates thought to be at risk of suicide were 'inhumane and unacceptable'. This was followed in the mid 1990s by a significant increase in the number of unconvicted and female prisoners taking their own lives. At the time, the Chief Inspector of Prisons raised grave concerns about the remand system and a report on Cornton Vale commissioned by the SPS was published in 1997 (Loucks 1997). Fortunately, the annual number of suicides – while still a serious problem (there were 10 suicides in 2006 down from 17 in 1996) – now appears to be on the wane, despite the steadily increasing prison population (Ross 2006; Fairweather 2006). The same can be said of the level of violence in Scottish prisons. Both prisoner-on-prisoner assaults and the number of assaults on staff have fallen to their lowest levels in some years (Ross 2006) and levels of unrest and indiscipline are incomparable to those experienced in the 1980s (Fairweather 2006). On its visit to Scotland's largest prison, Barlinnie, in 2003, the CPT described prisoner-staff relations as 'relaxed' (CPT 2005: para 68).

Scottish prisons have traditionally shown a commitment to rehabilitation and are known for their pioneering efforts in this regard as exemplified by the well-known Barlinnie unit with violent prisoners (Young 1997). Opened in 1973, the unit was a 'bold penal experiment' (Scottish Prison Service 1990) created for the treatment of long-term, difficult-to-manage and disruptive prisoners. It operated on a therapeutic basis and allowed prisoners a large degree of freedom in determining their daily programme and generally deciding how the unit should be run. Another distinguishing feature was that visits and personal possessions were allowed on a more generous scale than normal, and inmates were encouraged to develop links outside the prison. Despite achieving international acclaim and some considerable success in reducing levels of violence (not least the reform of Glasgow gangster Jimmy Boyle), it attracted criticism locally and nationally for its 'lax' procedures and in 1995 the unit was closed (Cavadino and Dignan 2007). Though in a much less radical guise, there continues to be a commitment to rehabilitation today with cognitive behavioural programmes being rolled out in many prisons. Writing in the late 1990s, McAra (1999) noted that there were then more rehabilitation programmes operating in Scottish prisons than in heyday of welfarism (albeit within a 'what works' philosophy) and this has shown little sign of changing (Croall 2005). In relation to the high proportion of offenders with serious substance misuse problems, a number of initiatives have been put in place, although it has been argued that more could be done to tackle alcohol addiction (Fairweather 2006).

Even the best efforts at rehabilitation, however, are seriously hampered by overcrowding among and within prisons. As we have seen, since 2000/01 there has been a significant rise in the number of remand prisoners, short-term prisoners (sentenced to less than four years) and female prisoners. This puts pressure on local prisons which are already among the most overcrowded in Scotland, and on the limited facilities for female prisoners at HMP Cornton Vale (Audit Scotland 2008). Indeed, in many respects the smooth operation of the Scottish Prison Service is severely compromised by the need to receive all the prisoners sent to it by the courts. The prison population has continued to swell despite official policy documents recognising its ineffectiveness in reducing offending (Scottish Executive 2002). This is best illustrated in the case of female prisoners whose numbers have increased disproportionately to men in the last decade or so (Croall 2005; Tombs 2004) *despite* the publication of an influential report (Social Work Services and Prison Inspectorates for Scotland 1998) and the full agreement of the Executive and judiciary that the majority of these damaged individuals should not be in prison.

As a final point, it should also be noted that to a significant degree, the hand of the Scottish Executive has also been forced in relation to the improvements in physical conditions related above. As discussed in the previous chapter, a successful legal challenge brought by a remand prisoner under the ECHR[9] led to a flood of compensation claims and it is likely that this development rather than humanitarian considerations prompted the rapid modernisation programme. Indeed, it is worth recalling that the SPS had in previous years come in for considerable criticism from the CPT about its slow rate of progress in relation to slopping out (CPT 1996; 2005).

Index F: Post Release Controls

The greater focus on public protection in the period following devolution has led to stricter controls on certain types of offender following conviction, particularly sexual and violent offenders (McAra 2008). The government initiated a review of the sentencing and management of these offenders with the establishment of the MacLean Committee in 1999 and the recommendations which followed from this review were implemented in Part 1 of the Criminal Justice Act 2003. The Act established a new Risk Management Authority (RMA) tasked with ensuring the effective assessment and minimisation of risk and introduced a novel type of incapacitative order termed the Order for Lifelong Restriction (OLR). If an OLR is imposed by a court (following a recommendation by the RMA) an offender will

9 *Napier v. Scottish Ministers* [2005] SC 229 OH.

be released from custody only when the Parole Board considers s/he is suitable for release. For the remainder of his/her life s/he will be subject to risk assessment and must abide by conditions designed to minimise risk to the public. If the level of risk rises to an unacceptable level, or s/he breaches the conditions of his release, s/ he may be returned to custody (OLRs differ from life sentence conditions in that a life sentence offers no element of lifelong risk assessment). The new arrangements therefore show a clear desire to extend control beyond prison, using level of risk posed as a justification for intervention, not solely a criminal act. As McAra (2008: 113) has observed, the 'principal components of the Act reflect the general trend in post-devolutionary criminal justice policy in Scotland away from penal welfarism and towards more actuarial forms of justice and increased punitiveness'.

Even prior to the introduction of OLRs, the range of legislative provisions aimed at the control of sexual and violent offenders was considerable: extended sentences providing for periods of post release supervision of up to 10 years could be imposed on serious violent and sexual offenders (Crime and Disorder Act 1998) and this was extended to include the offence of abduction by the 2003 Act. Civil sex offender orders and reporting requirements can also be imposed on those convicted of sexual offences (Sex Offenders Act 1997; Criminal Justice and Courts Services Act 2000) and, unlike Ireland, it would appear that these provisions are enforced (given the significant police resources devoted to them, see Justice Committee 2008). At the other end of the spectrum there has been a tough approach taken to antisocial behaviour and outbreaks of public disorder. Since 2006 those convicted of football related offences (as well as those whose behaviour has given cause for concern) may be made the subject of a Football Banning Order (Police, Public Order and Criminal Justice (Scotland) Act) instead of, or in addition to, any sentence the court could impose for the offence. As with ASBOs and sex offender orders, these orders are civil in nature but breach constitutes a criminal offence. Banning orders imposed following conviction can last for up to 10 years.

Thus, in relation to certain (and expanding) categories of offender, it would appear that Scotland has moved closer to an actuarial model of justice where, based on risk assessments or perception of risk, government controls are imposed after conviction or release. As noted above in the section on procedural protections, many of the new initiatives to increase public protection from certain offenders operate in ways outside the context of the criminal law. In other regards the law is more inclusionary. Scotland has the same spent convictions provisions in place as in the rest of the UK so that prison sentences of up to two and a half years are deemed 'spent' after a defined 'rehabilitation period' has elapsed (Rehabilitation of Offenders Act 1974). Further, genuine attempts at reintegration have been made recently with the establishment of 'throughcare' programmes in several Scottish prisons and in the community. In Scotland local authorities have a statutory responsibility to provide throughcare services to offenders sentenced to prison terms of over four years and aftercare to other prisoners in the first 12 months of their release from prison. The programmes are distinctive as they provide assistance with employment, accommodation and other problems from the point of sentence or remand, during the period of imprisonment and following release into the community (Croall 2006).

Index G: Death Penalty

The first restriction on the death penalty in Scotland came with the Homicide Act 1957 which abolished it for certain attempts to murder and distinguished certain types of homicides as 'capital murders'. These included murder of police or prison officers and murder committed in the course of a theft or by shooting or explosion. The death penalty was also retained for repeated murders. Complete abolition (save for the offence of treason) came with the Murder (Abolition of Death Penalty) Act 1965 and this Act was made permanent four years later (Walker 2004). The death penalty was abolished for treason in 1998. The last execution in Scotland took place in 1964.

Conclusion

The Scottish criminal justice system presents as a series of paradoxes which make simple conclusions concerning punitiveness very difficult to draw. First, the same civic and political culture which has been crucial in sustaining the commitment to welfarism in prisons, probation and youth justice over the period, has also played a part in sustaining the burgeoning prison population. Second, the advent of devolution appeared to have resulted in greater policy convergence with the rest of Great Britain rather than less although serious questions must now be asked as to what degree this was simply the result of the unwillingness of the Scottish Labour Party to depart from New Labour orthodoxy on crime. Policy trends discussed in Chapter 2 are undoubtedly in evidence in the period since the mid-1990s when a rise in levels of public concern and significant increases in media attention point to the increasing politicisation of crime. These include: a rebalancing of the criminal justice system in favour of the police and prosecution; increased managerialism and actuarialism; a focus on dangerous and sexual offenders; and increasing numbers of police and prison places. Yet sight must not be lost of the commitment to individualised justice and rehabilitation which continues to permeate Scottish criminal justice institutions. Both the prison service and youth justice system remain wedded to welfarist principles and genuine efforts are made at reintegrating prisoners. Further, in so far as can be determined, both private and public policing practices do not appear to be overly punitive or exclusionary. Even in contemporary times, Young's (1996/7) view that punitiveness 'has not bitten so deep either at the level of political representation or at the level of institutions and policy' continues to have a ring of truth about it. An explanation can most probably be found in the association of certain welfarist policies and institutions with 'Scottishness', combined with strong resistance to punitive policies from the judiciary and criminal justice professionals.

Chapter 5
New Zealand 1976–2006: Perfecting the 'Perfect Society'

Introduction

New Zealand is a jurisdiction which has a historically high rate of imprisonment compared to Australia and Western Europe (Cavadino and Dignan 2006). As with Scotland, the reasons for this are difficult to identify, although Pratt (2006) has argued that cultural factors have been an important contributory factor, most notably, an excessive emphasis on conformity arising out of a desire to create a 'Better Britain'. It is also clear that race is a large part of the explanation given the alarming overrepresentation of Māori and Polynesian populations in the criminal justice and imprisonment statistics. Imprisonment rates in New Zealand have continued to rise over the period under examination, yet, as will be examined presently, this increase cannot be attributed solely to increases in crime. From the late 1990s crime has in fact been falling and increases in imprisonment are more likely the result of a coalescence of populist forces campaigning on the law and order issue (Pratt 2007). Indeed, while there have been brief pockets of populism in the past (most notably the 1987 general election), crime in recent years has been intensively politicised culminating in a 1999 referendum in which 92 per cent of the electorate endorsed, among other things, hard labour and mandatory minimum sentences.

Criminal Justice in New Zealand 1976–2006

In line with the observations made above, examination of the development of criminal justice in New Zealand over the period of analysis is divided into three sub-periods: 1976–87, 1988–99 and 1999–2006.

Consensus and Conflict: Law and Order before and during the 1987 General Election

As is evident from Figure 5.1, crime[1] increased significantly between 1976 and 1992: from 7,471 offences per 100,000 to 13,155, an increase of 76 per cent.

1 There is no distinction made in New Zealand between serious and minor crimes and the crime rate simply refers to the number of offences recorded by the police per 1,000 or 10,000 population.

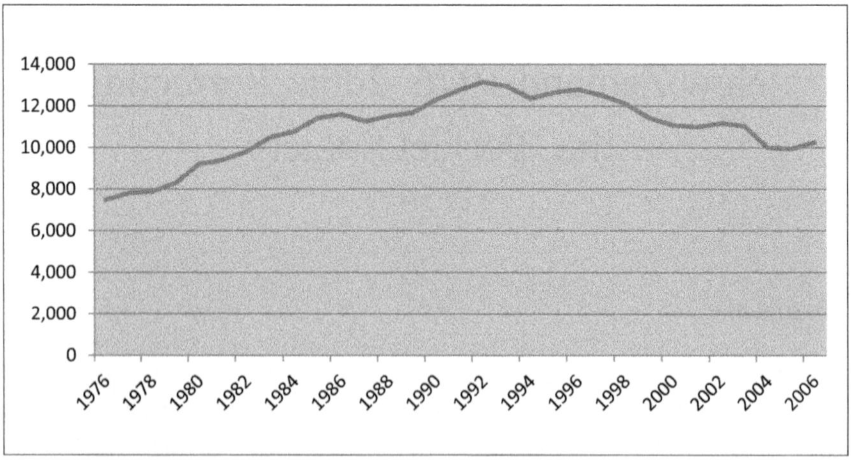

Figure 5.1 Crimes per 100,000 population in New Zealand

Source: Statistics New Zealand: Long Term Data Series. (http://www.stats.govt.nz/browse_for_stats/economic_indicators/nationalaccounts/long-term-data-series.aspx)

It should be emphasised, moreover, that increases were particularly significant in respect of violent crime and serious violence: between 1960 and 1985 recorded violent crime increased sevenfold, with an 80 per cent increase between the years 1980 and 1989 alone (Newbold 1992, 2007). After 1992, the crime rate dropped relatively sharply until 1994 after which it increased again until 1996. The overall trend is downward from 1996 to 2005. The rises in violent crime which New Zealand had been battling since the 1970s also fell off, so that the number of recorded violent crimes peaked in 1996 and the number of murders peaked in 1993 at 73 (Newbold 2007: 101).

In the public eye at least, the sharp increases in violent offending over this period were associated with the rise of organised drug trafficking and related gang activity which were both high-profile issues in the 1970s and 80s. Given that the two largest gangs in New Zealand – the Mongrel Mob and Black Power – are both overwhelmingly Māori, this affirmed the growing realisation that the country had an 'indigenous crime problem' similar to that experienced in other colonial jurisdictions. In a comparative context, New Zealand has also been found to have a relatively high rate of property crime victimisation in both the international crime surveys in which it has participated (Van Dijk and Mayhew 1992; Van Dijk et al. 2008). In the most recent sweep of the ICVS in 2004/5, it ranked third highest of 30 countries in terms of the prevalence of 10 of the most common crimes. Rates of burglary, car theft and theft from cars are consistently higher in New Zealand than in European countries although the rate for robbery is lower (Van Dijk et al. 2008).

Despite these crime problems, justice and the control of crime were not foremost in the minds of most New Zealanders for the first 10 years of the study period. Pratt (1988: 104–5) cites the following rejoinder by a Police Commissioner to press criticisms in his 1978 Annual Report as evidence of a general lack of public concern about crime at that time: '...some sections of the news media have accused me of being repetitive in my references to the development of organised crime ... *notwithstanding police efforts there is still very clear evidence of a public reluctance to accept the seriousness of the law and order issues of 1978*' (Police Department 1978: 3 cited in Pratt 1988, emphasis added). Prior to 1987, most general elections were fought on policies to manage the economic crises facing New Zealand such as unemployment, inflation and interest rates (New Zealand's economy was badly hit by the UK's entry to the EU and the oil crises of the 1970s) and the position which both parties took on the crime issue was actually strikingly similar. Indeed, in this early period Newbold (2007: 84) describes Labour and National's views on criminal justice as being 'closer than in probably any other area'. In the election manifestos of both the main parties published prior to the 1978, 1981 and 1984 general elections, tough rhetoric on crime is generally absent save perhaps for references to the need to tackle offences of serious violence and drug trafficking.

In government, both National and Labour had taken steps to increase the numbers of police, particularly community police, and had expanded the range of alternatives to custody in an effort to reduce the prison population (e.g. community service orders in 1981 and community care (probation) orders in 1985) (Pratt 1988). Indeed, despite the high imprisonment rate, official rhetoric had for a long time been anti-custodial in nature, with two major Commissions of Inquiry in 1981 and 1989 (Penal Policy Review Committee 1981; Roper 1989) recommending that imprisonment should be used sparingly and for violent offenders mostly. The 1981 inquiry largely formed the basis for the Criminal Justice Act 1985 which enshrined in statute the principle of imprisonment as a last resort as well as introducing a sweeping presumption against custody for property offences punishable by less than seven years imprisonment. Further, the Act introduced the automatic deduction of periods on remand from sentences and liberalised the rules relating to parole, moves which resulted in the immediate release of more than 1,000 inmates (Newbold 2007: 86).

All semblance of bipartisanship vanished, however, with the 1987 general election. National clearly resolved to exploit 'law and order' in a manner similar to the Conservatives in the 1979 general election in Britain (Downes and Morgan 1994). The attractiveness of crime derived from its usefulness as an issue on which a united front could be presented as Labour's decision to adopt Thatcherite economic policies had thrown the party's economic policy into disarray. It was also an issue on which the Labour government appeared unsure of itself: although Labour had in 1984 introduced radical neo-liberal reforms of the public sector, its policies on law and order appeared out of line with such 'possessive individualism' and had remained firmly wedded to its social democratic base (Pratt and Treacher 1988). As Pratt and Treacher (1988) have termed it, National felt that a form of 'provincial populism' could be reignited by appealing to its traditional agrarian base of small landowners and shopkeepers: criminals, along with bureaucrats, dole-scroungers, 'yuppies' and other 'useless' people were portrayed as receiving favour at the expense of this constituency. Consequently,

National's election platform made it clear that Māori, youth and gang crime were to be some of the main issues on which the election was to be fought. It pledged to 'return law and order to our land' and presented National as the party who were *not afraid* to do something about crime (National Party of New Zealand 1987). When a few months before the election a child murder and a violent gang rape led to marches demanding the restoration of capital punishment, National intensified its campaign by calling for harsher penalties for rape and promising a referendum on the issue of restoring the death penalty for murder. This strategy did not bring the anticipated gains in the polls, however. The opportunistic nature of National's response to these events and the incoherence which this generated in terms of their election strategy (previously emphasising Māori/youth crime), left them open to accusations of exploitation of the crime problem and this appeared to be affirmed when the murdered child's father made a public statement requesting that National should stop using his child's name to suit political ends (Pratt and Treacher 1988).

Thus, in the final result crime didn't pay for National and the Labour government was returned with a strengthened majority. Local conditions in New Zealand – most notably the fact that it was the Labour party, not the Conservatives, which had first moved the new neo-liberal economic agenda (known as 'Rogernomics' after the Labour Minister Roger Douglas) – did not allow the National Party to reproduce the success of the British Conservatives. National did succeed in one important regard, however. As both Pratt (1988: 265) and Havemann and Havemann (1995: 232) have observed, the opposition may have lost the election battle but 'they won the war to establish the parameters of crime talk and set down the terms on which Labour was forced to compete to be tough on the law and order front during 1987–1990'. This was evidenced by the manner in which the Criminal Justice Act 1985 was rebranded as a 'get tough' measure to curb violent crime (rather than divert non-violent offenders) and by an important amendment to the Act in 1987 which severely reduced parole options and remission for violent offences.

Continuity and Change: Law and Order Politics in the 'Decent Society' 1988–1998

During its three-year term in power following the 1987 election Labour vacillated on the crime issue, alternating between efforts to address demands for crime control and more liberal initiatives. Minister for Justice, Geoffrey Palmer, had established a Committee of Inquiry into the penal system in 1987 and when it reported in 1989 it argued for a 'new way' (*Te Ara Hou*) in corrections which would involve the overhaul of the prison system and its replacement with a number of small 'habilitation centres' providing specialist treatment to specific types of offenders (Roper 1989). Perhaps sensing the public mood had changed since the publication of the previous review (Penal Policy Review Committee 1981), or perhaps due to the perceived unworkability of the proposals (Newbold 2007), its recommendations were never fully implemented. Further reflecting concern about crime, increased attention was also focused on victims. The Victims of Offences

Act introduced shortly before the 1987 election increased compensation for victims and allowed the victim to make representations to the judiciary prior to sentence. The Act also provided for a Victims Task Force to be established for a five-year term to consider how the position of victims within the criminal justice system could be improved and this was actioned in 1988.

On the other hand, legislation was introduced which enhanced rights and promoted due process. The New Zealand Bill of Rights Act was passed, albeit a diluted version of the 1985 proposal, and the law relating to young offenders was radically reformed with the enactment of the Children, Young Persons and Their Families Act 1989. Considered to be groundbreaking legislation at the time, the Act introduced a regime based on diversion, family group conferences and restrictions on the use of police powers of arrest. Detention was to be used only as a last resort. Thus, as Havemann and Havemann (1995: 223) observe, '[a]mbiguity and complexity have blurred the parameters of a law and order agenda over the decade [1984–1994], especially under Labour'.

Nor did the accession of a National government to power in 1990 bring radical change. Although it has been suggested that Labour's 'soft on crime' image may have cost them the 1990 general election (Vowles and Aimer 1993; Havemann and Havemann 1995), the differences between the policies of the two parties in practice were not that great. National's slogan in the 1990 general election was a return to a 'decent society', suggesting a break with the Thatcherite policies Labour had pursued, yet the new government continued its predecessor's Rogernomic policies and even some of its more progressive ideas on the environment and the inclusion of Māori. The same continuity was also present in relation to crime policy.

The new Minister, Douglas Graham, was a lawyer by profession who, like Palmer and McLay before him, was 'a man of liberal sympathy and humanitarian principles' (Newbold 2007: 98). During his eight years in office, a new optimism about rehabilitation emerged, both in prisons and probation, as well as an increasing emphasis on diversion and restorative justice (Brown and Young 2000). Plans for a new rehabilitative system within the prisons, called *He Ara Hou* in recognition of its relationship with *Te Ara Hou*, continued apace under the watchful eye of its architect, Kim Workman, Assistant Secretary of Penal Institutions. Under *He Ara Hou*, rehabilitation was upgraded to give it equal status to security within the prisons and prison officers were encouraged to become directly involved with the inmates and their rehabilitative programmes (Newbold 2007). Even when security breaches at several prisons forced Workman to resign in 1993, the rehabilitative approach was continued with the introduction of a new system called Integrated Offender Management (IOM), albeit with a much more scientific and managerialist bent.

IOM was rolled out in 1995 by the new Department of Corrections which assumed responsibility for both prisons and community sentences. The new system essentially followed a 'what works' agenda, drawing on mostly Canadian research which advocated a psycho-therapeutic approach to reducing offending. In a manner similar to Scotland, therefore, rehabilitative efforts were updated and modernised in the mid 1990s and provided with a much sharper focus (McAra 1999;

Brown and Young 2000). The period also witnessed the expansion of specialist sex offender units and the establishment of habilitation centres (residential rehabilitative centres) for offenders who are released on parole, although the latter have now ceased to exist.

Criminal justice did not remain entirely insulated from National's neo-liberal policies, however. As per their 1993 election platform, legislation enabling the establishment of private prisons was enacted in 1994 and calls for tenders were issued in 1995 and 1998. New Zealand's first private prison – the Auckland Central Remand Prison – was opened in July 2000. New managerialist principles which had been infiltrating the public service since 1984 also eventually reached the justice system so that in 1995 (on foot of an inquiry into departmental efficiency), the government disassembled the Justice Department into discrete departments to manage the operation of the courts, prisons, etc. A Ministry of Justice was created to provide advice and policy coordination over the broad spectrum of justice issues.

A more punitive edge is also discernible in some of National's policies to control violent and sexual offenders. The bifurcatory strategy set out in the 1985 Act and the 1987 amendments was consolidated with the Criminal Justice Amendment Act 1993. The Act *inter alia* increased the maximum penalty for rape, expanded preventive detention to first time sexual offenders, extended the non-parole period which could be set by the courts beyond 10 years and provided for the right to recall prisoners on remission. It also introduced risk-based interventions to the criminal justice system, most notably electronic monitoring, which was used in combination with home detention. In a similar vein was the introduction of mandatory random drug testing via an amendment to the Penal Institutions Act in 1997 which permitted high-risk offenders to be more easily identified and singled out for restrictions on visits and other privileges.

Despite these changes it would be simply incorrect to characterise the period as one of unthinking obeisance to new penological principles of risk and incapacitation. The context for the 1993 changes had been a period of rapidly increasing violent crime (Meek 1995) and the immediate impetus was provided by a particularly horrible child rape/murder, similar to the James Bulger case in England. The murder led to a petition being drawn up to increase sentences which attracted 300,000 signatures. Given the strength of public feeling on the crime issue and climbing rates of violent crime, the extent of the reforms introduced in 1993 and the years that followed appears modest, certainly in light of later moves. Significantly, as Cavadino and Dignan (2006) note, there was no attempt to legislate for mandatory sentences or 'truth in sentencing', despite the fact that minimum sentences were promised in National's 1990 election manifesto. Indeed, it is difficult to disagree with Cavadino and Dignan's (2006: 88) overall assessment of the period: 'The National Party government of 1990–9 toned down its penal stridency on coming to power, preferring to stress managerialism and limited privatization rather than ever-increasing harshness'.

Penal Populism Unleashed: 1999–2006

During its period in opposition, it would appear that the New Zealand Labour Party adjusted its views on crime and refashioned itself as a party of law and order. Havemann and Havemann (1995) discern a change in attitude as far back as the 1993 general election, observing that Labour were now taking seriously the crime control agenda and matching National 'item for item' in their manifesto. Indeed, Labour's 1993 manifesto is particularly noteworthy for its early use of the Blairite soundbite: 'tough on crime, tough on the causes of crime'.

In New Zealand, as in England, the New Labour mantra was translated as being, first and foremost, tough on criminals (Tonry 2004; Workman 2008). It was operationalised by Phil Goff who held the justice portfolio from 1999 to 2005, a man described by Kim Workman (the former Assistant Secretary of Justice mentioned above) as the 'architect of the tough on crime stance' (Rethinking Crime and Punishment 2009). His statements on criminal justice certainly bear this moniker out. For example, in 2000 when three prisoners brought successful actions claiming compensation for beatings and other ill treatment that they had received in Hawkes Bay Prison, the Minister referred to the case as an 'alleged' assault and publicly labelled the victims a 'bunch of scum bags' (Workman 2008: 9). Similarly, when four years later the High Court and then the Court of Appeal found that the confinement of six complainant prisoners in a 'Behaviour Management Regime' similar to an American Supermax prison was in breach of the New Zealand Bill of Rights Act, the Minister rejected the notion that time served in prison atoned for the prisoner's crimes (Pratt 2007). In response, he rushed through Parliament the Prisoners and Victims Claims Act 2005 which allowed victims of crime and their families to sue ex-prisoners for financial compensation up to six years after their release, thus permitting the damages awarded in court actions, as well as the fruits of a lottery win or even simply a successful career to be claimed by the victim. As Pratt (2006: 557) has said of this development, '[c]learly, New Zealand's punitiveness has moved to a new level. Going to prison is no longer enough punishment; nor, of course, will punishment cease on release from prison'.

The significance of the Labour's party repositioning on crime is that law and order auctioneering has become a regular feature of election campaigns, which are held quite frequently in New Zealand, namely every three years. The punitive ante has been further upped by the formation in the 1990s of a number of fringe parties such as New Zealand First and ACT (Association of Consumers and Taxpayers) which have taken a hard-line on crime and its control. An excerpt from ACT's 2002 election manifesto gives a flavour of the rhetoric employed: 'No one is safe from callous violence. We are suffering from a failed 30-year experiment of being nice to criminals, hoping they will be nice back to us…' (ACT 2002). The party goes on to promote zero-tolerance policing, 'truth in sentencing' (so that early release and parole are abolished and life means life), mandatory minimum sentences and the end of family conferencing. These parties can now wield considerable influence since the move in 1996 from the 'first past the post' (FPP) electoral system to 'mixed member proportional' (MMP)[2] and have frequently formed part of governing coalitions. The 1996 referendum which authorised the introduction of the MMP system, also paved the way for the introduction of non-binding Citizen Initiated Referendums (CIRs), a development which, as will be discussed presently, is not without some significance.

One might well wonder how the situation changed so dramatically in New Zealand, given the relative stability of criminal justice policy in the 1990s. A national debate on crime was sparked in January 1998 when Norm Withers, a Christchurch shopkeeper, organised a petition seeking the necessary 252,336 signatures (10 per cent of registered voters) for a citizen's-initiated referendum on violent crime. Withers's 71-year-old mother had been beaten with an iron bar in July 1997 during the course of a robbery in his menswear shop and he was angered to discover her assailant had a long list of convictions and was on parole at the time (he was sentenced to 10 years imprisonment for the crime). The petition was successful, having obtained 285,000 signatures, and the referendum question was put to the electorate as part of the 1999 election. It read: 'Should there be a reform of our justice system placing greater emphasis on the needs of victims, providing restitution and compensation for them and imposing minimum sentences and hard labour for all violent offences?' As observed by several commentators (Pratt 2007; Workman 2008), the message contained in the referendum question was internally contradictory and incoherent, presenting the needs of victims and offenders as diametrically opposed. Whatever its intentions, it was approved by 92 per cent of the electorate and its dramatic success drew expressions of support from politicians of all political hues.

The high-profile achieved by Withers prompted the formation of several other victims' advocacy groups, most notably, the Sensible Sentencing Trust (SST), led by Napier farmer Garth McVicar. The SST has campaigned for longer sentences for violent offenders and the immediate enactment of legislation giving effect to the 1999 referendum. The government responded with the Sentencing, Parole and Victims Rights Acts 2002 which repealed much of the Criminal Justice Act 1985 and overhauled the way in which sentences were administered. These pieces of legislation were not as draconian as might have been expected, however. Rather they were very much a mixed package such that one might even describe them as 'Blairite' (Cavadino and Dignan 2006). On the one hand, the Acts significantly expanded preventive detention (so that it was made available for all offenders aged 18 and over who commit a serious sexual or violent offence); provided for a 17 year minimum non-parole period for several forms of aggravated murder and restricted the early release of serious and 'high-risk' offenders. On the other, the Acts promoted the use of fines and restorative justice, provided for automatic release at half sentence for those offenders serving two years or less and abolished

2 The MMP system is one in which roughly half of the seats are elected by FPP; and the remainder are filled from party lists to top-up the local seats so as to ensure a proportional overall result.

the mandatory life sentence for murder. Thus, the need to increase sentences for some offenders was married with both the administrative necessity of easing pressure on the prison population and meeting the demands of Labour's junior partner in government (the Alliance Party) to incorporate restorative justice principles (Pratt and Clark 2005: 318). Indeed, the provisions contained in the Act have been so carefully calibrated that Roberts (2003) actually describes it as holding the line against populist punitiveness in an era of punitive sentencing legislation. While it may therefore have been somewhat disingenuous for the Minister of Justice to have telephoned Norm Withers prior to the passing of the bills to congratulate him on the referendum's success (Pratt and Clark 2005: 314), the legislation is nevertheless testament to the considerable degree of influence which such victims' groups wield in New Zealand.

A similar level of deference was shown to victims' groups during the 2002 election campaign in which law and order featured prominently. Indeed, Pratt (2007: 27) writes that 'these groups led the campaign, with politicians running to catch up with their demands'. For example, the SST enjoyed substantial coverage in the press and on primetime TV and in the weeks running up to the election held two rallies in Auckland and Wellington in order to remember the victims of violent crime. These were addressed by MPs from the main political parties and government ministers who told the crowd that 'life should mean life' and 'there's no need for parole' (Pratt and Clark 2005). Those who expressed more moderate views were fiercely criticised: even Governor General and former High Court judge, Dame Silvia Cartwright, was the subject of attacks from opposition MPs for observing that 'prisons don't work' when opening a new centre of crime and justice research at Victoria University (ibid.).

Pratt and Clark (2005) have analysed the origins of this particularly busy period of New Zealand criminal justice history and have identified several factors which began to coalesce in the late 1990s. In their view the radical changes in economic policy introduced by the Labour government in 1984 – without a mandate from the electorate – created a distrust of politicians and a sense of disillusionment with the democratic process. This same sense of disillusionment, combined with growing feelings of insecurity engendered by the economic and social reforms of the 1980s, may perhaps be the most significant factors in explaining the formation of extra parliamentary groups such as the SST around the crime issue. While Pratt and Clark (2005) include in their analysis other characteristics usually associated with populist punitiveness, such as a decline in deference and the rise of the victims' movement, it is these local contingencies which they view as particularly important in the New Zealand context.

While the public debate about crime since the 2002 general election has not maintained the same level of intensity, criminal justice featured prominently in the 2005 general election. In the run up to the election, for example, National Party leader, Don Brash, promised to abolish parole, despite the fact it would increase prison numbers by 50 per cent (Brash 2005), andfor its part the Labour government announced plans to build four new prisons and to introduce the legislation discussed above restricting the rights of prisoners (Cavadino and Dignan 2006). The 'new axis of penal power' (Pratt 2007: 24) represented by organisations such as the SST appears set to continue to dictate the terms of the debate on criminal justice.

Punitiveness in New Zealand 1976–2006 by Index

Given New Zealand's high rate of imprisonment and the increasingly punitive public mood described above, it is tempting to conclude that the new punitiveness has bitten quite deep in this jurisdiction. This has been the verdict returned by several commentators. Cavadino and Dignan (2006), for example, discuss it as a particularly good example of 'neo-liberal punitveness down under'. As with Ireland and Scotland, however, there are key aspects of its criminal justice system which strongly resist such conclusions, not least the limits which are placed on police powers and the procedural protections afforded defendants.

Index A: Policing

Over the last 40 years or so policing in New Zealand has evolved from a militaristic, post-colonial model into a 'softer', more 'community-based' policing style, with crime prevention at its core (Stenning 2006).When considering the non-/punitive nature of policing in New Zealand, however, it is important to be aware of both the historical and contemporary context of Māori-police relations. There is some evidence to suggest that ethnic minorities in New Zealand may experience differential treatment at the hands of the police and that police discretion may be exercised in discriminatory ways. There is a history of animosity between the police and Māori in New Zealand dating from their heavy-handed treatment of young Māori activists in the 1970s and 1980s and this has left a legacy of distrust (Quince 2007). Research conducted in 1998 found that New Zealand police enforced alcohol prohibitions and liquor laws in selective and discriminatory ways against Māori and stopped and questioned young Māori frequently on the pretext of criminal offending (TeWhaiti and Roguski 1998). Further, following the Taser stun guns trials in 2006 there have been suggestions that Māori and Pacific Islanders were unfairly targeted (Human Rights Commission 2009).

The above may provide some explanation, perhaps, for the rise in the number of complaints against the police which have grown by 344 per cent between 1989 (795) (when the Police Complaints Authority was first established) and 2006 (3,526).[3] Looking to other indicators of punitive policing, however, as in Ireland

3 It is important to note that the newly established Independent Police Conduct Authority (ICPA) and its predecessor the Police Complaints Authority (PCA) argue that the number of *complainants* rather than number of *complaints* is a more reliable indicator of dissatisfaction with police performance (ICPA 2008).

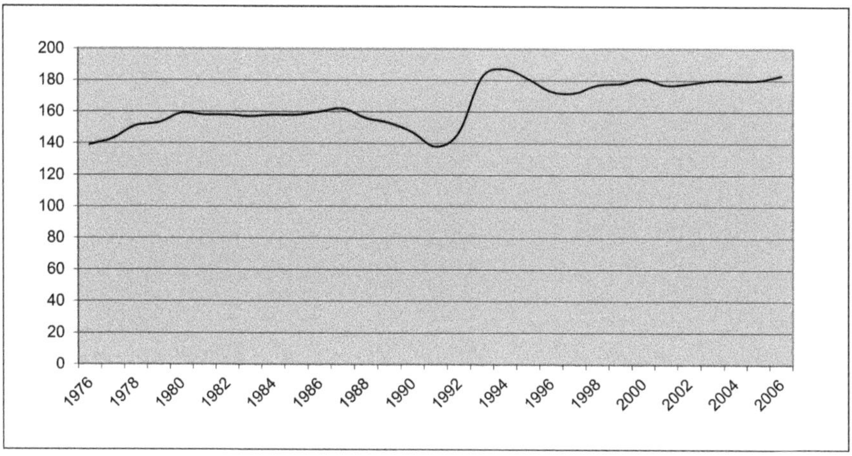

Figure 5.2 Police numbers per 100,000 population in New Zealand

Source: Statistics New Zealand: Long Term Data Series. (http://www.stats.govt.nz/browse_for_stats/economic_indicators/nationalaccounts/long-term-data-series.aspx).

zero-tolerance has been in evidence more at the level of political rhetoric than as an actual policing strategy. While far-right parties such as ACT have promised to introduce a zero-tolerance policing strategy this has not found in its way into government policy documents. Moreover, in New Zealand police powers remain limited compared to other Western democracies. The rights afforded the citizen under the New Zealand Bill of Rights have meant that to date the police do not have any powers of detention for the purpose of questioning so that a person who has been arrested has the right to be brought before a judge as soon as possible (Newbold 2000; Optican 2007). What is perhaps even more surprising is that a major project commenced in March 2006 to review and rewrite the legislative framework for policing in New Zealand and proposals emanating from that review do not contain any radical reforms (New Zealand Police 2006).

A more long-standing concern has been with police numbers, leading to accusations that there is a 'policing gap' in some of the main urban centres such as South Auckland and Hamilton (*New Zealand Herald* 2005). The statistics appear to bear this out given that the number of police per 100,000 population in New Zealand (177 in 2001) falls below that in England (241) and Australia (212) and indeed, Ireland (306) and Scotland (292) (Barclay and Tavares, 2003). However, as can be seen from Figure 5.2, numbers have, for the most part, slowly but steadily increased in line with the population (the sharp rise in 1993 is due to the merger of the Traffic Safety Service with the Police in July 1992). Police expenditure has also more than doubled over the period, even in real terms, rising from NZ$126 per head of population in 1976 to NZ$263 in 2006 (see Figure 5.3).

Of the three policies identified by Hinds (2005), namely zero-tolerance policing, calls for more police/police powers, and the exclusion of certain 'undesirable' groups

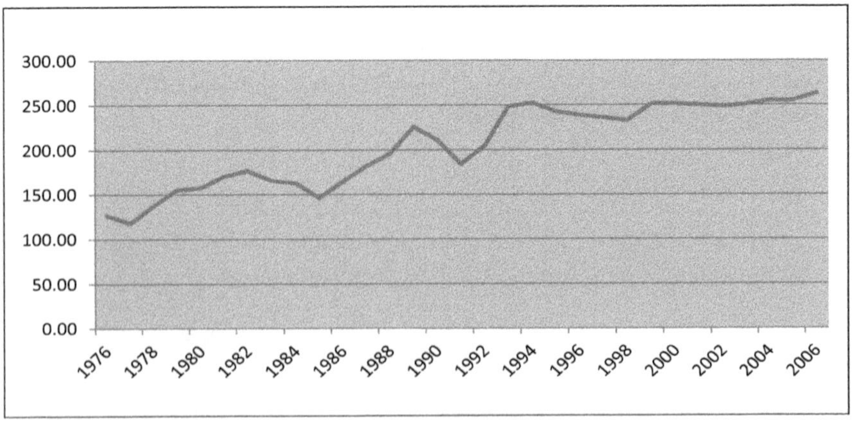

Figure 5.3 Net police expenditure per capita in New Zealand

Source: New Zealand Police (data request), New Zealand Police, Annual Reports to Parliament 1976–1989.

from public or quasi-public spaces through the increased use of private security, it is arguable that it is the third which has the most purchase in New Zealand. Increasing frustration at the policing shortfall referred to above has led many local authorities to hire private companies to perform policing services. Organisations such as Wellington's Walk Wise have been contracted to walk the beat in Wellington Central Business District and satisfy the demand for safety that is not able to be met by the public police and this situation is replicated throughout New Zealand (O'Connor 2006). Although these safety officers do not possess legal powers of arrest, with their bright yellow jackets they provide a visible safety intervention for the public and work closely with the police and council in reporting crime. Similarly, private firms can be found patrolling the wealthier suburbs of Auckland and several other New Zealand cities, reflecting the low priority which police now accord to residential burglaries and other more minor crimes (*New Zealand Herald on Sunday* 2006). Unsurprisingly, such developments have resulted in an increase in the number of private security guards and it was noted at a symposium on policing in 2006 that 'a conservative estimate of the size of the private security industry in New Zealand suggests there are already more private security guards than Police employees' (Hawke 2006; Carter 2006). Another important element in the diversification of policing in New Zealand is the activism of community groups and volunteer groups from local communities. Groups such as the 'Guardian Angels' in Auckland patrol suburban streets and shopping districts at night as a deterrent to trouble-makers (*New Zealand Herald* 2006a).

All of these developments increase the likelihood that certain undesirable 'others' may be demonised and increasingly excluded from private property and semi-public spaces such as malls. Consider the following comment from a resident describing the activities of one of these community groups: 'They're immediately suspicious of anyone who comes into their area. One guy was going door-to-door offering tree-cutting services and because he was an Islander from out of the area, emails started flying around about a dodgy character who must be up to no good, when in fact he was an honest guy just trying to make a buck' (cited in *Sunday Star Times* 2009). In this regard, it is significant that Pratt (2008c) argues that punitiveness is more *visible* in New Zealand, citing the manner in which shopkeepers display images of local offenders in their windows.

Index B: Procedural Protections for Defendants

To date the debate concerning crime control in New Zealand has centred on the *punishment* of offenders rather than their treatment during the investigative stages of the process or at trial. Thus, despite some adverse comment (New Zealand Herald 2006b), defendants continue to benefit from the right to silence in the police station and at trial; detention purely for the purpose of interrogation remains illegal (s.23 Bill of Rights Act 1990) and there is little evidence of hybrid provisions such as ASBOs (with the attendant negative consequences for procedural protections). Affirming the relative inactivity in this area – at least compared to other common law jurisdictions such as England and Wales and Ireland – Sankoff (2007: 225) writes 'without question, the criminal justice system remains one of the most conservative institutions in New Zealand'. There are signs that this is changing in some areas, however, such as the law relating to bail.

A more restrictive approach taken by the judiciary to bail has been in evidence since the early 1980s: the number of remands as a percentage of all inmates went from 6 per cent in 1980, to 10 in 1990 to 13 in 2000 and this jumped further to 20 per cent in 2006.[4] Newbold (2007) notes that there was some publicity in the late 1980s and 1990s about bail remands offending before trial and this, coupled with some studies showing that offending on bail increased during the 1990s (Lash and Luketina 1990; Howard League 2000), may explain the harsher approach taken by the courts. This trend was exacerbated with the enactment of the Bail Act 2000 which expanded the grounds for denying bail and introduced reverse onus provisions for 'repeat' sexual or violent offenders. Tolmie (2007) observes a 135 per cent increase in the male remand population between 1996 and 2005 and a staggering 274 per cent increase in the female remand population.

Other areas which have witnessed incremental, if not radical, changes concern the rights of victims within the criminal process which have resulted in many of the trial's most adversarial features being blunted. Further proposals contained in a Criminal Procedure Bill introduced in 2005 will introduce majority verdicts for juries, limit the right to jury trial in complex cases/cases of juror intimidation and create exceptions to the rule on double jeopardy. Observing these developments Sankoff (2007: 225) predicts more reforms may follow: 'While many claims of the victims' movement have been just … there is cause to worry that politicians

4 Source: Department of Corrections data warehouse.

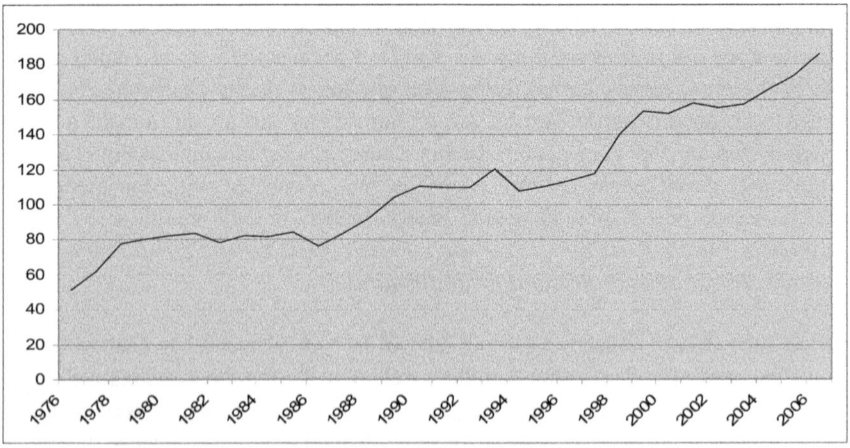

Figure 5.4 Imprisonment rates in New Zealand

Source: New Zealand Department of Corrections data warehouse (data request).

will increasingly bend to the will of a "law and order" climate at the expense of defendants'. One is struck, however, by the limited amount of change in this area compared to, say, sentencing and parole during the crisis years 1999–2002.

Index C: Use of Imprisonment

New Zealand's historically high rate of imprisonment has been noted above. Indeed, as far back as 1954 New Zealand had 50 per cent more people in prison than England, relative to its population. It is only in more recent times, however, that New Zealand's rapid penal expansion has meant that it has outstripped comparable countries (in 2006 it had a rate of 185 per 100,000 population). It has now one of the highest rates of imprisonment in the OECD and is frequently described as being the second most punitive country in the developed world (second only to the US) (Tolmie 2007).

Turning the focus to the period under analysis, as Figure 5.4 demonstrates, New Zealand has experienced several periods of growth in terms of its prison population. There has been a sharp rise in imprisonment rates after 1986 and again after 1997. The imprisonment rate appears to be increasing at a faster rate from 2003 onward.

Taking these periods of growth in turn, Cavadino and Dignan (2006) observe that, while rates increased steadily from the 1970s onwards, the prison population jumped by 58 per cent in the period between 1986 and 1996. The causes of this sharp upward turn can be attributed in part to an increase in the number of serious offences coming before the courts (Ministry of Justice 1998). However, Brown and Young (2000: 7–8) argue that this also reflects key changes in policing, sentencing and parole practices. First, the semi-mandatory arrest policy adopted in relation to domestic violence cases after 1992 drove up the numbers of assaults recorded by the police (from 741 in 1987 to 3,128 in 1996). Secondly, the average sentence length

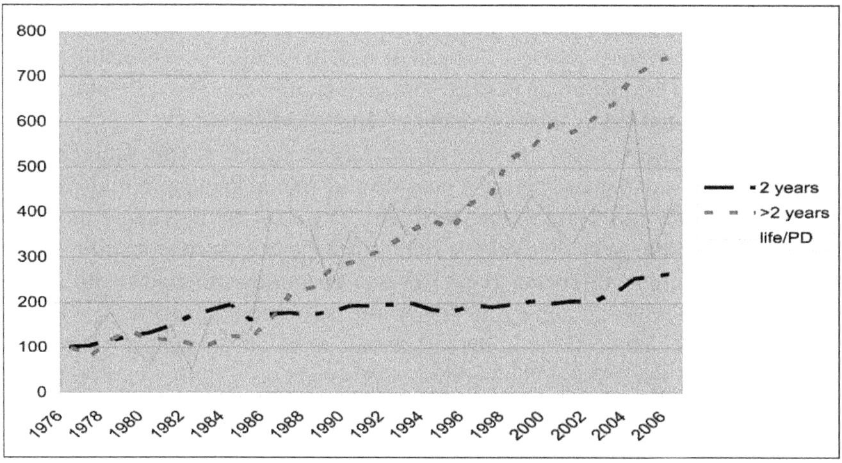

Figure 5.5 Number of offenders in New Zealand receiving determinate sentences of two years or less; over two years and life sentences/sentences of preventive detention 1976–2006, using 1976 as an index year

Source: New Zealand Department of Corrections data warehouse (data request).

handed down for all types of offences also increased during this period, although the proportionate use of custody remained the same. Finally, reforms made to the parole laws in 1987 and 1993 meant that the effective sentence served by violent offenders significantly increased. As averred to above, the 1987 Criminal Justice (Amendment) Act effectively abolished parole for serious violent offenders so that they were required to serve out at least two-thirds of their sentence and in 1993 judges were empowered to impose non-parole periods that exceeded the statutory maximum of 10 years. Thus, as Brown and Young (2000: 7) remark 'the serious violent offender group … produce[d] a multiplier effect in the prison population data, raising overall population by a factor far beyond what their numbers would suggest'.

Brown and Young's (2000) conclusions would also appear to hold good for the following 10-year period. The rate of committals under sentence over the period increased slightly between 1986 and 2006 (from 171 per 100,000 population to 186, an increase of 9 per cent) but this falls far behind the huge increases in the convicted prisoner population (from 71 to 146 per 100,000 population, an increase of 106 per cent).[5] There is also clear evidence that sentence lengths have increased: the average custodial sentence imposed by the courts went from 9.5 months in 1987 to 14.2 months in 2001 (Spier 1997, 2002). Indeed, as Figure 5.5 illustrates, while sentences handed down in all categories have increased, it is the number of offenders receiving determinate sentences of over two years and those receiving indeterminate sentences which have witnessed the biggest increases.

5 Source: Department of Corrections data warehouse.

Tolmie (2007: 64) explains this 'punitive sentencing creep' by reference to a rise in 'popular punitiveness' in New Zealand as well as changes in sentencing policy which increased the maximum penalties for certain offences. She maintains that it is largely unrelated to any increase in the severity of offending.

As observed above there has been an increase in the use of custodial remands over the period and this has played a considerable role in the upturn in the prison population which took place in the late 1990s. The most obvious cause of this is the reforms introduced by the Bail Act 2000 which made it much more difficult for repeat serious violent offenders to get bail as well as those offenders with a long history of more minor offending. It should also be observed that the increases in imprisonment which occurred in the last decade or so did so against a backdrop of falling crime rates. While the number of prisoners per 1,000 crimes remained steady for much of the period under examination, only increasing from seven in 1976 to nine in 1996, this figure more than doubled between 1996 and 2006 (18 prisoners per crime). This latter decade would therefore appear to be the most punitive, judged according to this criterion.

In addition to the Bail Act, the most recent (post-2003) increases in the prison population are at least partly a result of the Sentencing and Parole Acts which were implemented in July 2002. As discussed in the first part of the chapter, these Acts increased penalties for some types of offences (such as aggravated forms of murder) and replaced automatic release on remission for all prisoners with selective release contingent on their level of risk. These new rules combined with a new conservatism on the part of the parole board (Newbold 2007) have most likely exacerbated the penal crisis by driving effective sentence lengths upwards.

New Zealand appears less punitive when the use made of alternatives to custody and mandatory sentences are considered. Newbold (2007: 257) describes the country as 'something of a leader in community corrections' on account of the proportion of offenders receiving community sentences relative to those receiving prison sentences. This has grown steadily in favour of the former for most of the period: for every prison sentence handed down in 1980, 1.9 community sentences were imposed and this rose to 3.8 in 1990 and 2000. (Since 2001, numbers have fallen somewhat with the ratio of prison to probation declining to 2.8 in 2006.) As in Scotland and some other Western jurisdictions, however, the rising number of offenders in community corrections as well as the increasing diversity of community sentences (e.g. home detention since 1999), has failed to stem the seemingly inexorable rise of the prison population. Somewhat remarkably, given the level of public agitation on the matter, by 2006 there were no mandatory sentences on the statute book in New Zealand, a fact which may perhaps be attributable to the prohibition on 'disproportionately severe punishment' in the New Zealand Bill of Rights Act. Control over the judiciary has tightened over the period, however. Writing before the 1999 referendum, Brown and Young (2000: 25) were able to conclude, 'most of the responses in New Zealand have been driven by and are under the control of the judiciary themselves'. Merely one year later Justice Minister, Phil Goff, sent a clear message to the judiciary that they risked losing their discretionary powers if public concerns were not taken seriously (*The Press* 2000, cited in Pratt 2007: 15). The proposal to establish a Sentencing Council with a remit to draft sentencing and parole guidelines appears to be a further move in this direction.

It is also arguable that for the majority of the non-Māori population in New Zealand the country may be a very *un*punitive place. Rates of imprisonment fall dramatically when the Māori and Pacific Island populations are removed: from 196 for all ethnic groups to approximately 100 per 100,000 for the non-Māori population (Department of Corrections 2007). Indeed, as in the US, there is a 'new ethnic toxicity' (Pratt 2006) about the rises in the imprisonment rate in New Zealand discussed above. Data provided by the Department of Corrections data warehouse show that Māoris comprised 17 per cent of sentenced receptions in 1976, 32 per cent in 1986, 45 per cent in 1996 and 53 per cent in 2006. Although this increase must be considered in light of the fact that these groups comprise an increasing proportion of the population, they represent worrying increases particularly when there has been no significant shift in racial patterns of apprehensions over the last decade or so (Department of Corrections 2007).

Index D: Juvenile Justice

In stark contrast to the punitive adult criminal justice system, New Zealand's youth justice system is internationally renowned for its diversionary and restorative approach. Reforms were first introduced to the system in 1989 with the unique provisions contained in the Children, Young Persons and Their Families Act. Under this Act a new philosophy was introduced in relation to youth offending which was closer to the justice model than the welfare model previously in place, but which still incorporated welfarist principles. Thus, young offenders are expected to be accountable for what they have done and to take responsibility for their behaviour while at the same time offering rehabilitative options and support for families. The aim was also to 'culturally sensitise' the youth justice system: the empowerment of *whanau*, *hapu* and *iwi* (family, clan and tribe) through the processes adopted in the Act were intended to respond to Māori criticisms of the criminal justice system which left them feeling locked out from the care of their children.

Thus, at the heart of the system is the Family Group Conference (FGC) which is a diversionary mechanism introduced to deal with offenders under the age of 17. Attended by the child, his/her family group, the police and possibly the victim of the offence, the aim of the conference is to confront the child and their families with the consequences of their actions and decide on responses to the child's offending. While at the time that the Act was implemented, the philosophy of restorative justice had not yet been clearly articulated, the practices have developed in a distinctively restorative direction (Maxwell 2007). Thus, young offenders are expected to have regard to the victims of their offending, make amends for their actions and are dealt with in a manner that facilitates their reintegration back into their community. While FGCs are generally convened for more serious young offenders under the Act; diversionary mechanisms for more minor offences include police warnings and youth diversion and these currently deal with an impressive 70–80 per cent of offenders aged 14–17 (Chong 2007).

To date, evaluations of the youth justice system have been positive (Morris and Maxwell 1993; Maxwell et al. 2004), with the scheme generally achieving its aims of accountability, family empowerment and cultural responsiveness, in addition to significant advances in the field of diversion and decarceration. A smaller proportion of young offenders now appear in court in New Zealand than in any other country and the number of custodial outcomes resulting from court appearances has fallen dramatically (from approximately 300 in 1987 to just under 70 in 2001) (Maxwell 2007). While more critical accounts of the system have recently appeared, attempting to 'demythologise' youth justice in New Zealand (Bradley et al. 2006), these have mainly centred around the claims of the system to be both culturally responsive and restorative in nature. It is contended that in reality elements of cultural practice are incorporated into the system in a largely tokenistic manner while denying Māori any real control over the way youth offending is dealt with. Bradley et al. (2006) further argue that the empirical evidence shows that many victims are neither 'restored' nor 'empowered' by the Act, given the high rates of non-attendance and lack of participation.

On the basis of the above, it would appear that New Zealand presents as a paragon of lenient and balanced youth justice policy (if yet with some way to go in achieving *all* of its goals). Employing once again Muncie's (2008) measures of punitiveness in youth justice as a guide, namely, (a) the degree of compliance with international rights conventions and (b) comparative rates of juvenile custody, a number of positive aspects of the system emerge. First, New Zealand has implemented many of the principles laid down in the UNCRC and Beijing Rules in the 1989 Act, namely, a preference for diversion from courts and custody over other outcomes; application of the least restrictive sanction (ss.208(a) and (f)(ii) and 209); separation of welfare and justice matters (s.208(b)); and age-appropriate time frames for resolving matters (s.5(f)). Moreover, the emphasis on participation and empowerment of children (and families) also contained within the Act provides the child with a voice in the proceedings in line with Article 12 of the UNCRC. Secondly, and importantly in light of the significant gatekeeping role played by the police, Lynch (2008) has observed that the police service has been provided with appropriate training to deal with young offenders, as required by international standards. Finally, while New Zealand has come in for some criticism from the Committee on the Rights of the Child (2003) for its low age of criminal responsibility (of 10), it should be noted that young children aged 10–13 may only be prosecuted in homicide cases and then only when it can be proven that the child knew what he/she was doing was wrong. These children may be dealt with informally and if necessary a FGC will be convened and an application made to the Family Court. If it is found that a child is in need of care and protection, a wide range of orders, including counselling and support orders, can be made. Again, therefore, 'although there is a low age of criminal responsibility, younger children are generally dealt with in a manner which promotes reintegration and recognizes the child's needs in line with international standards (Article 40.1, CRC)' (Lynch 2008: 219).

On a less positive note, there are some features of the system which give cause for concern. In her human rights audit of the youth justice system in New Zealand, Lynch (2008) has identified a number of areas where it can be seen to be falling short of international norms. These include: the mixing of child prisoners with adults in adult correctional facilities; the exclusion of 17-year-olds from the youth justice system; the lack of oversight of police diversion/warnings given the large amount of discretion they wield; the absence of free legal advice for children participating in FGCs and, the fact that children are frequently remanded to police cells owing to a shortage of places in residential units (Becroft 2002). Certain of these points merit further development. First, the protections afforded by the youth justice system only extend to children and young people under the age of 17 in New Zealand so that once the offender turns 17 s/he is dealt with in the adult system. This has attracted criticism from the UN Committee on the Rights of the Child (2003) who have argued that the age jurisdiction of the Youth Court should be extended to include everyone under the age of 18. A second important issue concerns the mixing of children and adults in the penal system, in clear breach of Article 37(c) of the UNCRC. The shortage of residential youth facilities has created problems for young offenders in both pre and post-trial detention. On conviction, male young offenders are placed in one of four youth units attached to prisons which are intended to house 17–20-year-old males and females are always placed in adult women's prisons. In addition, children who are remanded in custody are remanded to police cells in the absence of places in youth residential units. In some cases, remands in police cells have stretched to 14 days or even longer and children are left in situations that are inhumane and degrading (Becroft 2002). Strong concerns about this situation have been expressed by the UN Committee on the Rights of the Child (2003), as well as various NGOs and the Human Rights Commission (ACYA 2003; Human Rights Commission 2004). Indeed, the Principal Youth Court judge has described the situation as 'intolerable in a civilised society' (Bell 2004: 4).

While there are clearly some difficulties with the youth justice system in New Zealand, the high rate of diversion and declining number of custodial sentences imposed on the under 16s by the courts between 1987 and 2001 (Maxwell et al. 2004) speak to its success. Further, more recent data published by the Ministry of Justice (Chong 2007) show that the number of proved cases that resulted in any type of custodial sentence has remained steady (at around 60 cases) since 2001. These data do not include the sentencing of 17-year-old offenders, however. This cohort of offenders should not be forgotten, particularly given that, as we saw in relation to Scotland, it is possible for a jurisdiction to have both a lenient youth justice system and a high proportion of young offenders in the prison population. Figure 5.6 shows the number of 'new starts' (receptions to prison) in New Zealand for offenders aged under 18 for the period 1976 to 2006. The sharp rise in receptions in 1982 is due to the abolition in 1981 of borstals for young offenders in favour of ordinary imprisonment. As was to be expected, the Children, Young

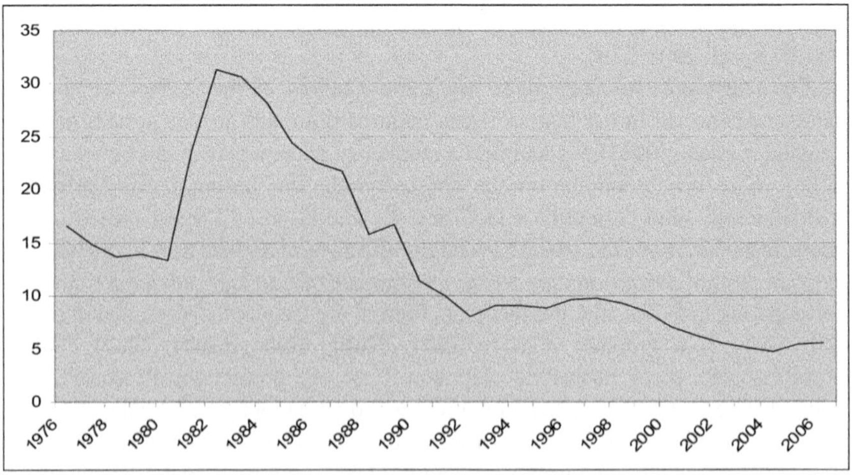

Figure 5.6 Receptions of offenders aged under 18 per 100,000 population in New Zealand

Source: New Zealand Department of Corrections data warehouse (data request).

Persons and Their Families Act 1989 had a depressive effect on the number of juveniles committed to prison but to a large extent it merely consolidated a pre-existing downward trend in the numbers since 1982.

The continuing decline in the juvenile reception rate in recent years is particularly interesting given that the youth justice system as a whole has increasingly come under attack. Indeed, Bradley et al. (2006: 81) write that the system now faces 'a growing political challenge to its previously dominant liberalism' such that 'the liberal coalition has been forced to issue a constant stream of denials and defences'. In the 2005 general election, both National and the far right-wing party ACT proposed tough reforms of the juvenile justice system to tackle the supposed 'spiralling problem of youth crime' (ACT 2005 cited in Bradley et al. 2006). National argued that the age of criminal responsibility should be lowered to 10, that there should be less use of diversion and that children who offend on two or more occasions should be automatically referred to the Youth Court (Brash 2005 cited in Bradley et al. 2006). ACT for its part pledged to introduce non-association orders for young offenders and to incorporate shaming techniques into the system. Echoing policy developments in the UK, both parties wanted parents held to account for their children's actions. In this environment, criminal justice actors may feel under pressure to take a tougher line. Research by Maxwell and Popplewell (2003), for example, indicates that the police are making increased use of referrals to the Youth Court and there is also some evidence that it has affected sentencing practice in the courts. Data published by the Ministry of Justice (Spier and Lash 2004) show that the youth courts are making increased use of supervision orders since the late 1990s, including supervision orders with residence requirements. Despite these developments, however, juvenile reception rates remain at their lowest levels since 1976.

New Zealand's youth detention rates also fare reasonably well in comparative terms. According to the World Prison Brief (ICPS 2009), minors make up only 1 per cent of the prison population and juvenile custody rates per 1,000 under 18 population are midrange at 0.09 (ICPS 2009; UNICEF 2009). To conclude, therefore, it is clear that the principles on which the system is based generally comply with international standards, despite some difficulties with implementation (Lynch 2008). Over the course of the study period, the juvenile area would also appear to have remained relatively untouched by the populist forces sweeping the adult system.

Index E: Prison Conditions

Despite a hardening of public attitudes, the corresponding surge in the prison population and the overrepresentation of Māori and Pacific Islanders in the prison estate, there is no sense of penal crisis in New Zealand (Cavadino and Dignan 2006). Indeed, it has been described as a country with 'a history of liberalism in its prison system' (Newbold and Ekridge 2005: 437) given that nearly half of all inmates are housed in small, modern prisons with open, minimum security conditions and the possibility of 72 hours home leave every two months (Newbold 2007). Additionally, nearly all inmates can apply for leave as they approach the end of their sentence. While conditions are less pleasant for those classified as medium-high security, usually accommodated in the older nineteenth century prison buildings, security classification is reviewed every six months and most inmates gradually move to less secure units over time (Newbold and Eskridge 2005). Historically, overcrowding has been less of a problem in New Zealand than in other jurisdictions so that nearly all inmates continue to have their own cells. Significantly, despite the dramatic increases in prison population, the government remains committed to the construction of small, 60-bed units enabling closer staff–inmate relationships (ibid.). Low security prisons offer a good range of programmes, which include activities such as farming, gardening or forestry work (ibid.). There are comparatively few escapes from prison in New Zealand and suicide rates have been low and stable since 1996, trends which Newbold (2007: 162) attributes to better management practices since 1995 (when Integrated Offender Management was introduced).

With the swelling numbers of prisoners, however, some of the more positive features of the prison system have been undermined. Double bunking has been used in some prisons as inmate numbers exploded over the last number of years. Moreover, the proportion of inmates in education or on work programmes has gradually declined with closures in prison education courses, library hours, horticulture, nurseries and other employment programmes (Newbold 2007). Access to families and release to work schemes has also been restricted in more recent years, as prisons become more security-minded. Workman (2008: 10) refers to the increasing tendency of prison officials to 'objectify' offenders: 'prisoners became less eligible for such privileges as release to work and family visits, and more likely to be described in official reports as culpable, deserving of punishment and sometimes dangerous. They were no longer clients in need of support, but risks to be carefully managed'.

Moreover, even prior to the current concerns with overcrowding and security, New Zealand's prisons were not without their problems. Along-standing difficulty for the past quarter of a decade or so has been increasing levels of violence as reflected in the increase in the proportion of inmates requiring protective custody since the 1980s (from 4 per cent of the population in 1983 to between 16 and 20 per cent of inmates in 2006) (Newbold 2007: 159). This is most probably the result of the emergence of internecine gang warfare, an increasing proportion of offenders committed for violent and sexual offences and the influx of psychiatric inmates who previously had been treated in hospital. Unlike Ireland, however, increasing gang tensions and overcrowding do not appear to have resulted in an increased number of prison deaths. Unnatural deaths (suicides, homicides, etc., have remained fairly constant over the last decade, with six recorded in 1997 and the same number in 2006 (Department of Corrections, various years).

Violence perpetrated by staff on inmates has also been a problem. In the space of a number of years, the country has witnessed *two* major inquiries into prison brutality at Paparua prison in Christchurch and in Paremoremo, the country's only maximum security prison (Workman 2008). The first of these concerned the militaristic approach taken by the Canterbury Emergency Response Unit (or 'Goon Squad' as they became known) which was formed in 1999 to deal with the drug problem and any other crises which may occur. Allegations of night time raids on cells, attempts to provoke inmates, and the death of one inmate when he was being moved by officers led to several internal inquiries and the publication in 2004 of a devastating report by Ailsa Duffy QC. The report found that the Unit developed an 'inappropriate militaristic culture' and had routinely acted outside the law (*New Zealand Herald* 2004). Similarly, in 2004 the High Court found that the Behaviour Management Regime in operation at Paremoremo prison was unlawful and in some cases in breach of the Bill of Rights. Prisoners alleged that under the regime they were stripped naked and photographed, underwent ritual humiliation and mental abuse as well as unlawfully long periods spent in solitary confinement. The High Court described the treatment as inhumane and awarded four of the applicants a total of NZ$325,000 in compensation. In the wake of these scandals the Ombudsmen's Office, took the unusual step of conducting an 'own motion' to investigate the treatment of prisoners within the Department of Corrections (Office of the Ombudsman 2005). While the report found little evidence of systemic ill treatment of inmates across the prison estate or of a culture of abuse among staff, it was nevertheless very critical of a number of aspects of prison governance, including the lack of meaningful activity for prisoners, the shortage of drug and alcohol programmes and the restrictive rules concerning access to rehabilitative programmes.

Index F: Post-Release Controls

Garland's (2001: 180–1) observation that in contemporary penal politics 'there is no such thing as an ex-offender' has a particular resonance in New Zealand, given the jurisdiction's increasing preoccupation with risk and dangerousness. A good illustration is provided by the history of the sentence of preventive detention (PD), an indeterminate sentence which was originally envisaged to deal with repeat sexual offenders (Criminal Justice Act 1954) and which was limited in 1967 to repeat child sex offenders. Offenders subject to PD are only released from prison when they are considered to no longer pose a risk to the community and those who are released can be recalled at any point for the rest of their lives. Its indeterminate nature and stated aim of 'protecting the community' have led some commentators to compare it to civil commitment statutes in the US (Vess 2005). Preventive detention went from a marginal measure which had practically fallen into desuetude at the time the 1985 Act was passed (indeed the Penal Policy Review Committee (1981) recommended its abolition) to a key weapon in the government's 'law and order' arsenal at the start of the new millennium. As already noted, it underwent a major revival in the 1987 and 1993 Criminal Justice Amendment Acts when the age limit for the sentences was lowered and it was made available to sex offenders on a first offence and violent offenders on a second offence (Meek 1995). Further, the recent Sentencing Act 2002 significantly extended the scope of preventive detention to include a wider range of qualifying sexual and violent offending, such as conspiracy to murder, aggravated robbery, and kidnapping. Importantly, a record of previous serious violent offending is no longer required. The 2002 changes have resulted in a significant increase in the number of sentences of preventive detention imposed and in the five and a half years following the Sentencing Act coming into force, preventive detention was imposed in 30 more cases than the preceding five and a half years (Hurd 2008). While the actual numbers involved are relatively small, it arguably illustrates the increasingly forward-looking orientation of New Zealand criminal justice interventions. As Pratt (1995: 30–31) has written dangerousness as a concept is not that new; what changed has been the emergence of a 'growing interest in the kind of crime one might commit in the future, rather than the quantity of crimes one had committed in the past'.

Further control over serious offenders was brought about in 2004 with the introduction of extended supervision orders (ESOs) in the Parole (Extended Supervision) Amendment Act 2004. These orders allowed the Department of Corrections to monitor medium and high-risk child sex offenders for up to 10 years following release from prison. They were intended to provide a regime for managing the release of child sex offenders who had not been sentenced to preventive detention, but were assessed as having a high risk of re-offending against children on release (Hurd 2008). The order is made on the basis of a civil standard of proof: the judge must be satisfied, having considered the matters addressed in the health assessor's report, that the offender is likely to commit further sexual offences against children. Moreover, the courts have interpreted the legislation in a manner which appears on all fours with the categorical logic of the 'new penology'. In *Belcher*,[6] the Court of Appeal approved the use of group-based re-offending data in upholding an extended supervision order imposed after Belcher had served his sentence and had been living in the community for three and a half years. Brown (2008: 259–60) has described this decision as 'distinctly unjust' and as illustrative of the 'latitude courts are prepared to grant executive power in the face of special threats'.

It appears from the above that discourses of risk and danger in New Zealand have come to place offenders' liberty rights on an increasingly unstable footing (Brown 2008). Where the risk to the community is deemed intolerable, determinate sentences are replaced with preventive detention or supplemented with ESOs. Indeed, as noted, the 'lesser eligibility' of offenders to resume a normal life upon release from prison was made explicit in 2005 by Justice Minister, Phil Goff: prisoners do *not* pay their debt to society in prison and therefore do not leave their crimes behind at the prison gates.[7] The Prisoners and Victims Claims Act 2005 makes it clear that victims will continue to lay claim to restitution for a period of six years following release.

New Zealand currently does not have a drug or sex offenders' register, although a private member's bill has been under consideration by Parliament since 2003 and unofficial versions of the latter are maintained by the SST. Reintegration into the community has been the focus of renewed efforts by the Department of Corrections in recent years but the Department has yet to develop a comprehensive strategy (Workman 2009). Further, it is somewhat challenged by punitive practices such as shopkeepers displaying pictures of local undesirables in their windows and the distribution of flyers by the police warning local residents about offenders' imminent release into the community (Pratt 2008).

Index G: Death Penalty

The death penalty was temporarily suspended in 1935 when the Labour government commuted all death sentences to life imprisonment. Legislative change followed with the Crimes Amendment Act which changed the penalty for murder from death to life imprisonment with hard labour. This provision was revoked when the National government assumed power in 1950, although pressure for abolition grew. The matter came to a conscience vote in Parliament in 1961 and the death penalty was subsequently abolished for murder, being retained only for treason and other similar acts. The penalty was finally removed for all offences, including treason and piracy, in 1989. While, as noted above, there have been occasional calls for it to be restored, it is notable that in recent years no political party, not even those belonging to the far-right such as ACT, have made capital punishment

6 *R v. Belcher* [2007] 1 NZLR 507.

7 Similarly, during the course of the Parole (Extended Supervision) Amendment Act, United Future MP Marc Alexander commented that in respect of sex offenders 'they have lost their right to humanity' (Dalziel 2008).

a part of their manifesto. Newbold (2007: 252) observes that 'it is unlikely that the idea of reinstatement would [today] get any sustained support'.

Conclusion

Of the three countries examined in this study it is clear that New Zealand is the jurisdiction most affected by populist rhetoric and demands by citizens for harsher measures on crime. In some respects the country is an exemplar of the effects of penal populism (Pratt 2008c): despite the fall in crime rates over the last 15 years and the surge in the prison population, citizen's groups continue to call for mandatory sentencing, truth in sentencing and the reform of even 'sacred cows' such as the country's renowned youth justice system. It is clear that there is a lack of correspondence between reality and perception in New Zealand such that communities feel under threat from crime even when this is not the case. Indeed, the very visibility of punitiveness in New Zealand, in the form of various measures aimed at excluding the dangerous 'other', suggests the explanation may well be found in the country's cultural heritage (Pratt 2006). Other aspects of the country's criminal justice system speak to traditions of social justice and fairness, however: faith in rehabilitation is far from dead in corrections and it is significant that over the period of the study politicians have continued to resist calls for mandatory sentencing. Further, police powers remain limited and civil orders such as ASBOs, sex offender orders, etc., are notable by their absence.

Chapter 6
The Measurement of Punitiveness

Introduction

Prior to considering the overall punitiveness scores of the three countries, it is proposed in this chapter to consider what has been learned about the definition and measurement of punitiveness from the three countries under examination. The data suggest a number of ways in which a fuller understanding of the concept can be achieved. First of all, there is a need to have regard to *qualitative* as well as *quantitative* indices; secondly, to assess punitiveness over the criminal justice system *as a whole*, not just at the point of sentencing; and thirdly, to consider the various dimensions of imprisonment and its use, including its relationship with crime rates. As illustrated below using the three case studies, the approach taken by researchers to these matters will strongly determine the conclusions they will ultimately draw on the punitiveness question.

The Need for Qualitative Data

The concept of punitiveness has eluded precise definition by many scholars (Daems 2007) and further enquiry often appears to yield more questions than answers. Nelken (2006: 270–71), for example, identifies the following knotty issues:

> Does harshness mean the same thing across cultures and societies? Is mildness the deliberate and repeated exercise of leniency? To what extent is mildness just an 'absence', a low position on the continuum of harshness, to what degree is it an approach to punishment which has its own independent roots and standing? Should we call it mildness where illegal conduct is dealt with outside the criminal law, through using regulatory regimes, welfare interventions or restitution programmes? What about low levels of incarceration which are the intended or unintended result of inefficiency and delay? ... Is harsh justice a descriptive or also an evaluative concept? Conversely, is mildness always and inevitably a good thing?

Partly perhaps because of the intractable nature of these complex questions, punitiveness is treated by many criminologists as synonymous with imprisonment rates, namely, the numbers of those detained in prisons per 100,000 population (e.g. Cavadino and Dignan 2006; Lacey 2008). As the questions posed by Nelken demonstrate, however, while criminal justice statistics shed much light on the operation of the system they are necessarily limited in the amount of information they can provide about a system's 'ethos' or ideology. Some may view this is no bad thing. Brown (2005), for example, has argued that the preoccupation with discourse analysis amongst criminological researchers has led to a neglect of the empirical dimension. Equally, however, the values which permeate a particular criminal justice system *do* have an impact on practice and indeed may play a critical role in nurturing resistance among practitioners to reforms perceived as alien or punitive in nature (Hutchinson 2006). Moreover, it is highly probable that penal culture will impact upon the experience of the offender in his/her journey through the criminal justice system. As King and McDermott (1995, after Downes 1988) have argued, the experience of imprisonment can differ widely from country to country and in this sense, the 'weight' of imprisonment in terms of the burden it imposes on offenders should be considered. Few would argue that the experience of prisoners in the southern states of the US, for example, is not qualitatively different to that of a prisoner in Western Europe (Whitman 2003). Even within Europe, the European Committee for the Prevention of Torture and Inhuman and Degrading Treatment or Punishment (the 'CPT') (a body which has privileged access to the penal institutions of all 46 member states of the Council of Europe) has noted that not only the *quantity* of punishment but also its *quality* varies widely from country to country (Daems 2007: 130).

Another danger in focusing exclusively on statistical data is that we may mistake outcomes for intentions or, worse still, project our own ethnocentric ideas of the factors which are driving these outcomes onto the social actors we are studying. Clearly, 'bad' outcomes can result from the most worthy of reasons and 'good' outcomes for less. Daems (2007) cites as an example ECHR reforms to the Belgian early release process designed to increase fairness but which will more than likely result in a longer effective sentence being served by prisoners. In a similar vein, Nelken (2008, 2009) seeks to unpack assumptions commonly made about 'punitiveness' and 'leniency' in Italian/English youth justice. Italy and England are often put at opposite ends of the punitiveness spectrum in terms of their youth justice system and are often characterised as 'lenient' and 'punitive' respectively. Yet, researchers often fail to engage with what policymakers and other actors think they are doing and why it makes sense *to them*. Nelken notes that legal actors in the English and Welsh youth justice systems simply claim to be doing their best for young people before they get into further trouble and that 'different working assumptions lie behind the levels of tolerance or leniency in dealing with young people in different places' (Nelken 2009: 307–8). In the same piece, he takes issue with Cavadino and Dignan's (2006) arguments concerning the links between neo-liberalism and punitiveness, noting, 'there does seem to be something ethnocentric about a thesis so well suited to telling policy makers in countries affected by neo-liberalism that evidence from other countries shows us that only more welfare provisions and government regulation of the economy can provide a prophylactic against punitiveness' (2009: 299). In actuality, he argues, the (highly controversial) raft of procedural guarantees which defendants enjoy in Italy, and which lead to a high rate of attrition in criminal cases, form a larger part of the explanation for its low rate of imprisonment than the government's economic policies.

The importance of distinguishing between intentions and outcomes, or what Nelken (2005) has termed 'objective' and 'subjective' punitiveness/leniency is critical to understanding a country's criminal justice system and can generally only be explored through qualitative means. Indeed, the interview material from the three countries in question served to complicate (yet also illuminate) any simple conclusions which could be drawn from the quantitative data. Scotland provides the best example, with its strong welfarist ethos yet high rate of imprisonment. Many respondents struggled to square this circle when asked whether they considered their country to be a punitive one:

> Imprisonment rates … are taken to mean punitiveness but actually in the Scottish case they have always been high, even in a period when we had a very strongly welfarist system, so what do imprisonment rates actually mean? I don't think they necessarily signify punitiveness. (Scotland Interviewee #3, p. 1)

> I think we are probably [more punitive]. There is a dilemma there because we probably like to think as a society that we are less punitive, but the statistics rather suggest that we are just as punitive. (Scotland Interviewee #4, p. 9)

> The figures would be around that it probably is [more punitive], I'm not sure it's a more punitive mentality … That's a paradox that none of us have actually … (trails off). (Scotland Interviewee #5, p. 10)

> [CH: any thoughts on why Scotland had a high imprisonment rate even back in 1976?] Not particularly, no. I suspect it is why I still like to see Scotland as having more liberal tendencies. (Scotland Interviewee #2, p. 3)

In considering this conundrum, two respondents suggested that judges were in effect sending offenders to prison as a means of rehabilitating them:

> When I have done qualitative research with and talking to sheriffs about sentencing and asking them … about their sentencing practices and why they sent people to prison and most of them would say things like 'well, actually I'm not sending someone to prison because I'm trying to punish them but I think it's the best place for a person to get help' and particularly for women that was generally the reason that was given and so there was a perception that what they were actually doing was not punitive *per se* but was actually rehabilitative … (Scotland Interviewee #3, p. 2)

> There is also a suggestion in some sheriffdoms that there were some sheriffs who took the view, and again all this is anecdotal … some sheriffs took the view that if you had someone appearing before you whose crime was largely drug related, that

> they had a better chance of getting treatment in prison than if they had to wait … some places across the country that was probably true, that the waiting time for drug treatment in civilian … was quite long. (Scotland Interviewee #5, p. 3)

Thus, in the Scottish example there is a danger in assuming that punitive intentions lie behind punitive outcomes. While any arguments remain speculative in the absence of further research, it is at least possible that a desire to assist offenders may actually form part of the explanation for Scotland's heavy use of imprisonment. The same paradoxical forces may also be at play in the case of reforms to Scottish law necessitated by the incorporation of the ECHR which are generally regarded as progressive in nature. As one Scottish interviewee observed, since 2001 Scottish judges are now required to fix a tariff period or punishment part of a sentence which a prisoner sentenced to life imprisonment must serve before becoming eligible for parole. While fairness dictates that an independent and non-political body should determine the non-parole period, it is possible that (as in the Belgian example discussed by Daems (2007)) this shift may have contributed to the rising Scottish prison population (the High Court have determined that the minimum appropriate tariff is generally 12 years whereas previously a life sentence could have been as low as 8 years).

The Scottish example also points up the complexity of punitiveness and the need to consider each country on its own terms. In Scotland there is a sense that there is something mysterious or not understood about the high imprisonment rate; it is nearly construed as operating *independently* of the views of the criminal justice actors which by and large remain wedded to welfarism. In the Netherlands, on the other hand, the tougher attitudes taken by practitioners are currently believed to be *the* critical factor in producing steep increases in imprisonment in the absence of more punitive laws or policies (Tonry 2007: 37).

As a final point on the importance of qualitative data, it should be noted that it is only through detailed discussions with policymakers and seasoned observers of the political system in individual societies than one can hope to gain a deeper appreciation of the tenor of the debate over criminal justice issues. Some of the 'soft' evidence (to borrow Nelken's (2005) term) that was gathered in the interviews, for example, was important in understanding the extent to which political parties in all three countries are exploiting crime for electoral advantage (Caplow and Simon 1999). As discussed in Chapters 3–5 there is evidence of penal populism in all three countries. Reflecting this, in all of the sample jurisdictions several interviewees acknowledged that tough policies were often proposed as a response to a high profile crime or event and were therefore ill-considered and ad hoc. Yet, as evidenced in Table 6.1 below, there are significant differences in the degree to which the crime issue has become a part of the political fabric. Politicians in Ireland and Scotland were generally more *reactive* than *proactive* in this area and concern about crime was a *transient* rather than a *permanent* phenomenon. Respondents in New Zealand, on the other hand, spoke of a constant tinkering with their criminal justice system such that it was impossible to make reasonable progress in this area which was permanent. Political parties have sought to use crime as a wedge issue during elections, particularly smaller parties since 1996 when a form of proportional representation was introduced. Criminal justice has achieved a different level of *embeddedness* in New Zealand political life than in the other two countries.

Table 6.1 Comments on populism in Ireland, Scotland and New Zealand

Ireland
We would be much less punitive than the UK … [Labour] took a much stronger line and were very *proactive*. Blair in particular was very strong in introducing things. And they tried some really extreme things that were a complete waste of time, they introduced boot camps and things like that, they were complete failures. They are continuously coming up with new ideas, you think we are bad with legislation … the amount of stuff they are churning out and trying constantly to address, it's a kind of frenzied activity, reorganisation and in the middle of it introducing extra legislation … *it's a much bigger focus there*, so there is no way Ireland is anywhere near the UK. (Ireland interviewee #3, p. 19, emphasis added)
Scotland
'I think that is one of things that has actually characterised things post devolution, is that *mostly criminal justice changes have been about reacting to specific things*, so actually although they have a national criminal justice plan … most of what they've actually done has been in response to something, a problem, and not as a kind of … I wouldn't argue that they've actually had a collective strategy. (Scotland interviewee #3, p. 5, emphasis added)
New Zealand
I would agree that 1985 and 2002 would be the two most significant changes in terms of the legislative framework *but the history would be characterised by that continual change*, probably not helped by the fact that we have a three year electoral term as well. (NZ Interviewee #7, p. 2, emphasis added)
The Prisoners and Victims Claims Act, appalling. The politics of it are just … It's Goff [former Minister of Justice] you know, *absolute political opportunist* and one of the things that has appalled me particularly is the language these so called statesmen use when they are describing offenders … (NZ Interviewee #8, p. 11, emphasis added)
(talking about law and order auctioneering) I mean they're all … it's all breast beating of a political character, entirely superficial and wrong. It will do no good. (NZ Interviewee #3, p. 5)

The Need to Assess Punitiveness Holistically

As argued in Chapter 1, punitiveness should be viewed holistically in line with the experience of the offender. Despite the (now standard) reliance on imprisonment rates *simpliciter*, for several commentators (Whitman 2003; Hinds 2005; Nelken 2006; Tonry 2007; Kutateladze 2007a, 2009) the current narrow criminological focus on this measure has the potential to oversimplify and mislead as to a state's punitiveness. As will be seen below, this conclusion finds support in the data. Countries such as New Zealand and Scotland which appear very punitive viewed through the traditional lens of imprisonment rates, take on quite a different complexion when assessed on a much broader range of criteria. Conversely, Ireland's low imprisonment rate in international terms conceals a more authoritarian trend in criminal justice legislation.

New Zealand is generally regarded as quite a punitive country using the singular index of imprisonment; it is second only to the United States in the Western World in terms of its use of custody. Yet, as discussed in Chapter 5, this occludes several factors which militate in favour of 'leniency': the limited nature of police powers (unlike many modern democratic states there is no detention for the purpose of interrogation); the extraordinary rates of diversion for young offenders (70–80 per cent) and what has been described as its relatively 'liberal' history in its prison programme (Newbold and Ekridge 2005: 437). Similarly, as noted in the section above, Scotland's high rate of imprisonment belies its continued adherence to welfarist principles and continuing commitment to the decriminalisation of children through the Children's Hearing System. The very *complexity* of the criminal justice systems within these jurisdictions (including the failure of a strongly diversionary youth justice system to reduce adult imprisonment rates) tempers any conclusions which may be drawn on the basis of one indicator alone and led many respondents to speak of paradoxes:

> That [the 1989 Act], most people in New Zealand don't associate that with the criminal justice system because it's youth and the youth system is kind of outside … These two policy streams have been rather divorced in New Zealand, it's strange really. (New Zealand interviewee #3, p. 11)

> I think it would be wrong to see us as the sort of jurisdiction in the adult area that's really pushed restorative justice more than others. That's the paradox really, we have ... restorative justice and we're known for that and we have a very punitive system actually in the adult area and that's the reason why we don't use restorative justice for these more serious cases. (New Zealand interviewee, #2, p. 11)
> [See also Scottish interviews above].

Interesting insights into the harshness of a system can also be derived from different disciplinary perspectives. While many people automatically think of imprisonment rates when questioned about punitiveness, others, particularly lawyers, consider a country's track record in criminal justice legislation. One Irish interviewee, a lawyer, opined that Ireland's tough record in terms of criminal justice legislation was sufficient to define it as a 'punitive' country, albeit honoured more often in the breach than in the observance:

> If you just looked at the black and white letters of the law and didn't know anything about Ireland you might assume it was a more punitive regime when you saw some of the provisions. In fact it's not. So *I think yes on paper, yes*

> *it is more punitive* but no ... because judges mitigate, if they think the law is unjust ... (Ireland interviewee #9, p. 4, emphasis added)

Interestingly, over the period of the study New Zealand and Ireland appear to be diametrically opposed in this regard as in the former the 'get tough' movement has concentrated on the 'back end' of the system, (i.e. on the use of imprisonment) with little attention given to 'front-end' reforms, (i.e. increases in police powers/erosions in the rights of defendants). Conversely, Ireland has maintained relatively low rates of imprisonment in international terms while the rights enjoyed by suspects have been increasingly curtailed. As suggested by some of the New Zealand interviewees, it is likely that the *direction* of crime control developments may be influenced by the presence/absence of a terrorist threat: a nation unaccustomed to wide ranging powers in an exceptional regime is much less ready to cede powers to the police in relation to ordinary crimes. It is therefore unsurprising that Ireland – a country which has faced serious threats from subversives within the state since its foundation in 1922 – continues to display a preference for a front-end strategy in its dealings with 'ordinary' criminals. Consider the following extracts from the interviews which contemplate this interesting juxtaposition in the two countries.

Table 6.2 Reflections on front-end and back-end punitiveness in Ireland and New Zealand

Ireland
It's a bit of a mixed bag ... I don't think we are more punitive in the sort of punishments that we hand down ... the broad feeling I have for it is that we don't go over the top on punishments, but on the other hand I feel we are inclined to adopt, what I would refer to as an authoritarian approach to offending, to criminal justice, unlike some of our other common law countries. (Ireland interviewee #7, p. 10)
New Zealand
I think there's been some increased attention to the right to silence and hostility to that in some quarters to some degree ... but I think that in general it's been much more muted than overseas ... One of the issues that we are having to look at with that is the extent to which we should have some of powers that exist in the UK to deal with terrorism situations and I think if we did the public would actually largely go into revolt. I mean I don't think there would be public acceptance of it because we don't have a history of it. A lot of the things in the 2002 UK Act were actually taken over from the old emergency powers and therefore people have got used to them over the last 20 years and dealing with a real threat and in New Zealand I think there's a lot less public appetite for this because the threat's more removed... [CH: It's interesting because on the one hand you've got quite a punitive public in relation to punishment practices but that hasn't necessarily translated to the defendants... That's a very good point actually. I never thought about that, that's absolutely right. (New Zealand interviewee #2, p. 5)

The Attractiveness of 'Front-End' Policies

Another factor which may have influenced the front-end bias in Irish criminal justice strategy is the central role occupied by the Garda Síochána (Irish police) in public life. One respondent commented that 'they are a much bigger, more powerful, more significant culturally ... institution in this state than police forces are in most other states ... so that crime control in Ireland was always going to be front loaded, because that's where the power of the criminal justice system in this country actually lies' (Irish interviewee #7, p. 11). Indeed, across all three jurisdictions, interviewees seemed inclined towards the view that there was a public opinion bias towards increasing police resources. The police in all three countries appeared to be held in considerable public regard, were expert lobbyists and were well connected to the media.

A further important point is that front-end measures such as CCTV and more police are more visible to communities and are more readily understood by voters. As an Irish journalist commented to me (a sentiment incidentally that was echoed by their New Zealand counterpart), 'the police don't have to be explained' whereas changes in sentencing and parole are less accessible to the public. Respondents across the three countries, including policymakers and former Ministers, were well aware of the popular appeal of front-end measures. As one former Minister of Justice remarked, 'you got far more brownie points for increasing police numbers and you publicised that...'. Indeed, in both New Zealand and Scotland, elections in 2005 and 2007 respectively have seen political parties promise 1,000 new police, targets which were difficult to meet and which in Scotland have formed the basis of a parliamentary inquiry (Justice Committee 2008).

A good example of the appeal which front-end measures hold for policy makers is provided by the slopping out debacle in Scotland. Two Scottish respondents drew attention to the fact that £13 million of the Prison Service Budget which had been originally intended to improve sanitation in Scottish prisons had been rediverted to the Drugs Enforcement Agency and the establishment of a witness support scheme, decidedly front-end measures. As discussed in Chapter 4, the failure to apply this money led to the award of damages in *Napier* for breach of a prisoner's human rights and a flood of similar claims. Responding to criticisms in the Parliament, the then Justice Minister, Jim Wallace, noted: 'Government is about making choices; those are the choices that we have made' (*Scotsman* 2004). It is noteworthy, however, that these choices were directed at the more visible front end of the system.

Figures 6.1 and 6.2 show police rates (numbers per 100,000 population) and police expenditure per head of population from 1976 to 2006 in Ireland, Scotland and New Zealand using 1976 as an index year.

As in the Hinds (2005) study (see further Chapter 1), there is a remarkable degree of convergence between the three countries in terms of police rates over the period so that homogeneity in police rates exists alongside diversity in increases

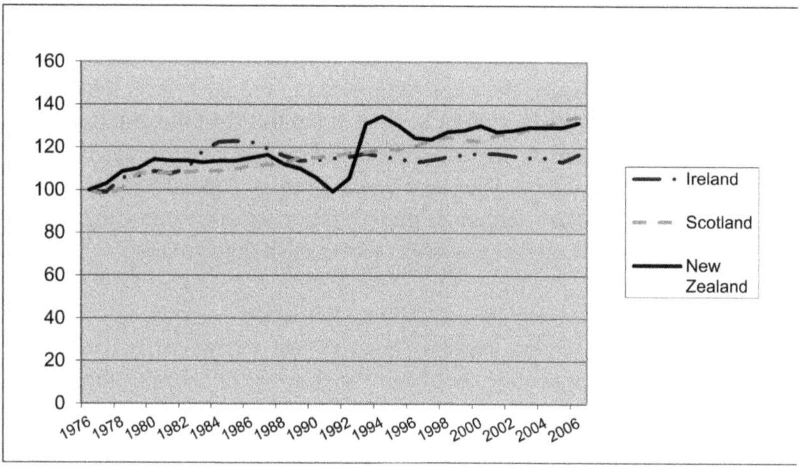

Figure 6.1 Police rates in Ireland, Scotland and New Zealand 1976–2006 using 1976 as an index year

Sources: Statistical Abstract of Ireland, An Garda Síochána Annual Reports, various years; Scottish Executive Police Powers Performance and Resources Division; Statistics New Zealand: Long Term Data Series.

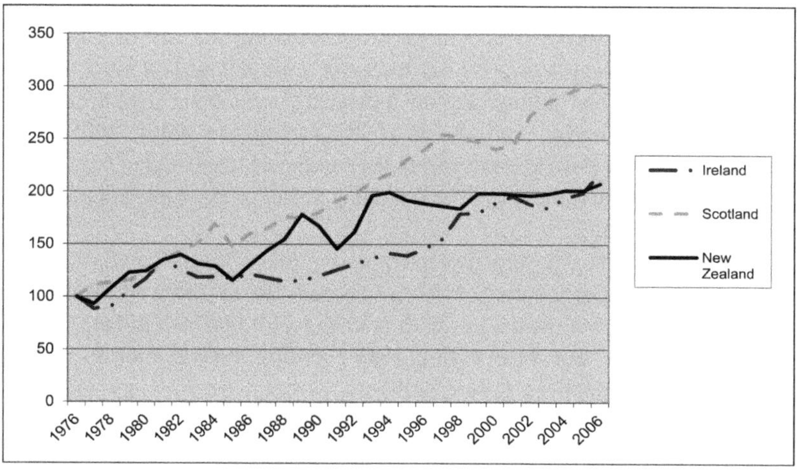

Figure 6.2 Police expenditure per capita in Ireland, Scotland and New Zealand 1976–2006 using 1976 as an index year

Sources: Irish Department of Finance (data request); Scottish Executive Police Powers Performance and Resources Division (data request); New Zealand Police (data request), New Zealand Police Annual Reports to Parliament 1976–1989.

Note: Please note nominal figures have been adjusted to take account of inflation and are expressed in 2008 prices.

in imprisonment rates.[1] Police expenditure on the other hand has doubled in both New Zealand and Ireland over the 30 years and has trebled in Scotland. This substantiates to some degree the views expressed in the interviews that front-end measures may in some circumstances be more attractive than those at the back end to politicians aiming to satisfy law and order demands, not least through their ability to provide visible reassurance. The sharp upward turn in expenditure since 2000 in Scotland (i.e. in the post devolutionary period) is particularly interesting in light of the following comments made by one former Scottish policymaker:

> Justice is one of the key responsibilities for secure societies, it's a key responsibility and therefore perhaps inevitable that a devolved government, which is getting more scrutiny than it ever did, than the old Scottish Office ever did, would work to respond by increasing police numbers as indeed you now see with the present government who announced that they would have 1,000 and are finding it rather more difficult to … implement. (Scottish interviewee #5, p. 7)

There is a strong suggestion here that in the post devolutionary period governments have sought to increase police resources as a means of bolstering their legitimacy. Indeed, it is arguable that since devolution the crime control focus of the parties holding power has been on front-end rather than back-end measures. In 2004, the Labour/Liberal Democrat coalition published *Re:duce, Re:habilitate, Re:form* (Scottish Executive 2004), which emphasised reducing the use of custody and the relative ineffectiveness of prison in reducing reoffending. Moreover, the penal policy of the current SNP administration is explicitly reductionist and decarcerative in nature (Scottish Prisons Commission 2008). Perhaps, as Hinds (2005: 58) has argued, 'as well as the *push* towards increased punitiveness and higher custody rates, it is also valid to discuss the *pull* of maintaining social order at the front end of the criminal justice system'?

It would seem that one selective index alone does not tell the whole story of punishment in a specified jurisdiction. Given both the political attractiveness of front-end strategies as a means of tackling crime and their particular salience in certain jurisdictions,[2] researchers should give serious consideration to including front-end variables such as police numbers, powers, etc., in any measure of punitiveness. As illustrated by the data from the case studies, a narrow focus on the punitiveness of the criminal justice system at the point of sentencing creates the risk of obscuring other (sometimes critical) aspects of the system.

---

1 Note: the significant increase in the number of police in New Zealand in 1993 is due to the merger of the traffic corps of the Ministry of Transport with the New Zealand Police.

2 Front-end measures will assume particular importance not only in jurisdictions with experience of a long-standing terrorist threats but also developing nations which (for financial or traditional reasons) rely on these measures as a means of social control. See further Neapolitan's (2001) work on this area.

That said, there are obvious challenges associated with such an approach (pragmatic and otherwise) and it is likely to make conclusions as to a jurisdiction's authoritarianism or harshness much more difficult to draw (Tonry 2007). To take one example: Lappi-Seppälä (2008) has conducted a quantitative analysis using data from 25 industrialised countries and found that there is a negative association between imprisonment rates and conviction data. In conviction statistics, low-imprisonment countries such as Finland and Denmark receive the highest rankings and high-imprisonment countries in Eastern Europe and the Baltic countries receive the lowest. This raises difficult (probably theoretical) questions about the extent to which punitiveness in one sector can compensate for punitiveness in another. Arguably, the increased propensity to conviction tells us something important about the perceived leniency of the Scandinavian jurisdictions, yet it is also arguable that concentration on the relatively small number of offenders which actually contest a criminal charge sidelines the experiences of the majority. In line with other fields of research within criminology, however, it is important that the model which we adopt to measure punitiveness should reflect the complexity of the concept which it is seeking to explore. Drawing on Ekblom's (2008) comments concerning crime prevention, it is useful to consider Ashby's (1957) 'law of requisite variety' which essentially says that in order for a model to be useful in capturing some aspects of the world, it must itself be sufficiently complex to handle and reflect enough of the variety in the reality it is intended to represent. Greater attention to the thorny question of how punitiveness is best operationalised at the beginning of a research study may therefore repay investment at the end.

Disaggregating Imprisonment

Turning now to imprisonment as the conventional indicator of punitiveness, it has been observed in Chapter 1 that imprisonment rates are a compound of remand prisoners, those convicted and awaiting sentence and those who are serving a sentence. In some countries, they include immigration detainees and juveniles. Without breaking imprisonment rates down further to examine the use of prison at various stages of the criminal process, they tell us little about a country's punitiveness (Kommer 1994; 2004). As the charts below illustrate, when the imprisonment rates for Ireland, Scotland and New Zealand are disaggregated in this way it dramatically changes our perception of which countries are the most punitive. With the exception of Figure 6.3, in each of the charts 1976 is used as an index year and changes are shown relative to that. It was felt that this method would have the advantage of showing most clearly in each of the countries concerned the advent of a *new* punitiveness or 'get tough' attitude which is after all the main object of the inquiry (rather than any pre-existing differences between nations).

Figure 6.3 shows imprisonment per 100,000 population in each of the three countries concerned as it would conventionally be presented. Fortunately, meaningful comparison is possible between the three countries as imprisonment

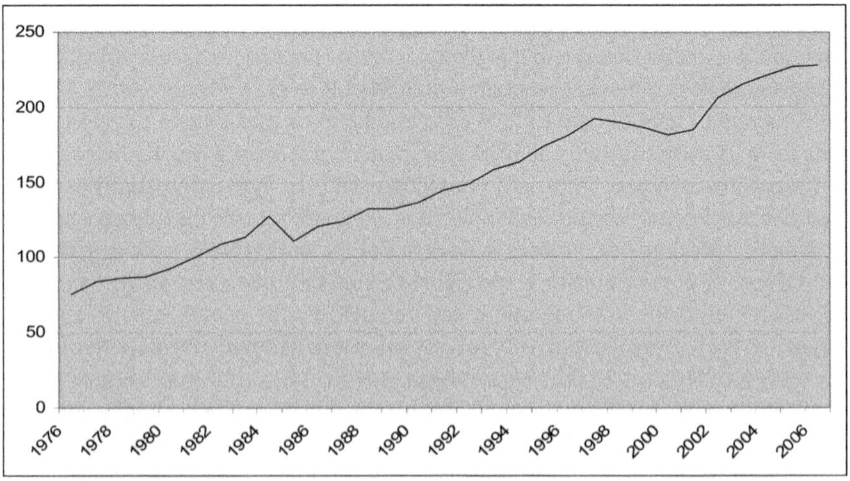

Figure 6.3 Imprisonment rates in Ireland, Scotland and New Zealand

Sources: O'Donnell et al. (2005), Irish Prison Service (2005–07); Scottish Home and Health Department, Prisons in Scotland: Reports, various years; Scottish Prison Service, Annual Reports, various years; Scottish Executive, (2006a; 2007a); New Zealand Official Yearbook, 1981; Spier (1997, 2002), Soboleva et al. (2006).

rates exclude juveniles under 16, persons in drug treatment or mental health facilities and sanctions such as electronic monitoring and house arrest. While both Ireland and New Zealand (unlike Scotland) include in their figures immigrants and foreign nationals detained on the basis of immigration laws this group form only a very small proportion of the average daily prison population in both countries (UN Committee Against Torture 2009; Irish Prison Service 2007). When the trends are examined New Zealand and Scotland both appear considerably more punitive than Ireland, although it is important to be aware that Ireland's heavy reliance on temporary release in the early to mid 1990s to ease capacity constraints means that the Irish prison population is significantly underrepresented during this period (these prisoners are not counted in the figures). While both Scotland and New Zealand follow similar trajectories, New Zealand entered a new period of growth from 1986 onward, eventually surpassing even Scotland.

Figure 6.4 now shows imprisonment rates using 1976 as an index year. Even this simple adjustment substantially changes our view of the relative punitiveness of the countries concerned. While the rates of all three countries have increased in the last 15 years or so, Ireland appears to outstrip the other two countries in terms of the *rate of growth* of its prison population. As already noted, it is arguable that historical comparison assumes particular importance in relation to the 'punitive turn' given the assertion that we have undergone a penological *transformation.* Brodeur (2007) refers to this as the 'intrinsic' meaning of punitiveness and contrasts

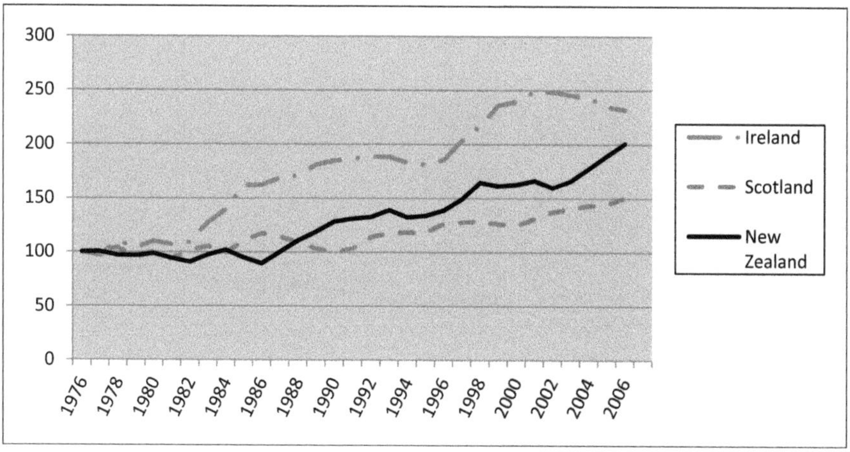

Figure 6.4 Imprisonment rates in Ireland, Scotland and New Zealand 1976–2006 using 1976 as an index year

Sources: O'Donnell et al. (2005), Irish Prison Service (2005–07); Scottish Home and Health Department, Prisons in Scotland: Reports, various years; Scottish Prison Service, Annual Reports, various years; Scottish Executive, (2006a; 2007a); New Zealand Official Yearbook, 1981; Spier (1997, 2002), Soboleva et al. (2006).

it with its 'comparative' meaning. Canada, for example, looks considerably better in comparison with its close neighbour, the US, in its use of imprisonment yet a historical view suggests less room for complacency. Conversely, Scotland and New Zealand, both countries which have historically used imprisonment heavily, benefit from a historical rather than a comparative appraisal.

Adjusting the data further to remove remand prisoners and show only the convicted prisoner rate as in Figure 6.5 again changes our perspective. This time Ireland appears to have surpassed Scotland and New Zealand by an even greater margin as while convicted prisoner rates in Scotland and New Zealand have remained quite stable, they have quadrupled in Ireland. While it is possible that this dramatic increase may in part be a function of counting practices and the poor quality of the data available,[3] it nevertheless serves to place a question mark over the extent to which Scotland and New Zealand have witnessed a transformation in

3 No data are available for the period 1995–2000. On 1 January every year many prisoners are on home leave for Christmas and thus the figures may be artificially low. The (more accurate) average daily figure of convicted prisoners was used for Scotland and New Zealand. Another factor is the reduction in the number of prisoners on temporary release in the late 1990s which meant that more prisoners were actually behind bars to be counted. The example serves to illustrate the difficulties of accurate cross-national comparison and the importance of taking into account counting practices and seasonal fluctuations when calculating the prison population and its constituent elements (Young and Brown 1993).

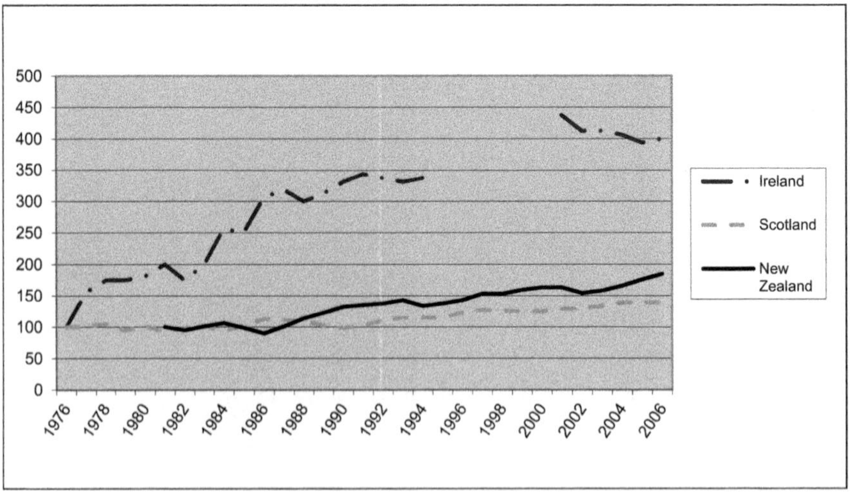

Figure 6.5 Convicted prisoner rates in Ireland, Scotland and New Zealand 1976–2006 using 1976 as an index year

Sources: O'Donnell et al. (2005), Irish Prison Service (2005–07); Scottish Home and Health Department, Prisons in Scotland: Reports, various years; Scottish Prison Service, Annual Reports, various years; Scottish Executive, (2006a; 2007a); New Zealand Official Yearbook, 1981; Spier (1997, 2002), Soboleva et al. (2006).

penal policy or 'punitive turn' over the last 30 years. This index appears to stress *relative* continuity rather than change.

To date we have only examined the prison population or 'stock' figure in the three jurisdictions. Another way in which a country's use of imprisonment can be viewed is of course by examining admissions to prison, or the 'flow' of prisoners through the prison system. This can reveal much about the way in which imprisonment is used in a particular country for, as noted by Lynch (1995), static or stock statistics tend to overrepresent more serious offenders with longer sentences. Countries with a serious crime problem may therefore appear very punitive by this measure. Figure 6.6 shows the number of prison admissions or entries per 100,000 population in two of the three countries, using 1976 as an index year. Examining the use of imprisonment in this way again suggests relative stability in the rates for Scotland, with increases of approximately 30 per cent. While Ireland experienced a sharp increase in its rate of prison receptions in the early 1990s, recent decreases have resulted in an overall increase over the period of 50 per cent.[4] Complete

4 Please note that prison entry data from Ireland are only shown from 1980 onwards as prior to 1980 data were not available for the number of entries on remand to St. Patrick's Institution. As these are significant in number (635 in 1980) it was felt that 1980 is a better starting point for comparison with later years.

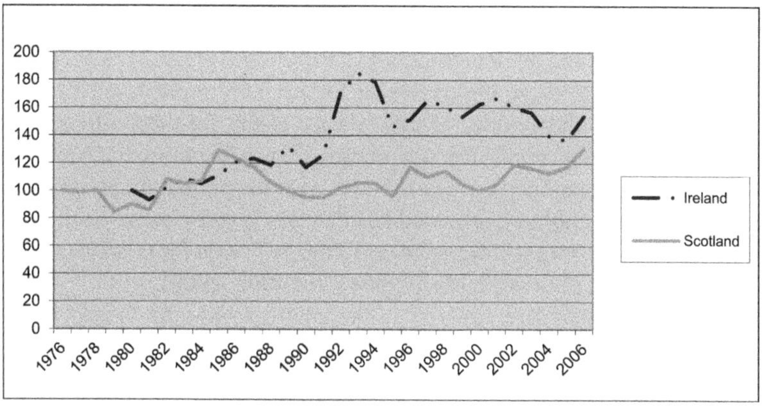

Figure 6.6 Prison entry rates in Ireland and Scotland 1976/1980–2006 using 1976/1980 as an index year

Sources: Department of Justice, Annual Reports on Prisons and Places of Detention, various years, Irish Prisons Service, Annual Reports, various years (as presented on National Crime Council website http://www.crimecouncil.gov.ie/statistics_cri_prison_table2.html); Scottish Executive (2006a; 2007a); Scottish Prison Service, Annual Reports 1992/3–1995/6; Scottish Home and Health Department, Prisons in Scotland: Reports 1986–1990/1991.

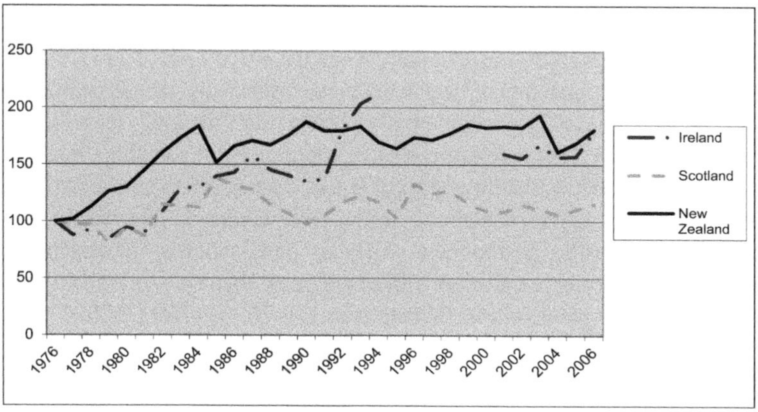

Figure 6.7 Prison entry rates of offenders under sentence in Ireland, Scotland and New Zealand 1976–2006 using 1976 as an index year

Sources: Department of Justice, Annual Reports on Prisons and Places of Detention, various years, Irish Prisons Service, Annual Reports, various years (as presented on National Crime Council website http://www.crimecouncil.gov.ie/statistics_cri_prison_table2.html); Scottish Executive (2006a; 2007a), Scottish Prison Service, Annual Reports 1992/3–1995/6; Scottish Home and Health Department, Prisons in Scotland: Reports 1986–1990/1991; Department of Corrections data warehouse (data request).

prison entry data for New Zealand (i.e. including remand prisoners) are only available from 1999 and are therefore not shown.

Similar patterns to those observable in Figure 6.6 are displayed for Scotland in Figure 6.7 which shows rates of prison entry solely for those offenders under sentence, i.e. excluding remand prison entries. The trajectories for New Zealand and Ireland suggest significant rates of growth over the period of approximately 80 per cent, although it may be questioned whether this is sufficient to justify talk of a penal *transformation.* (As will be noted, unfortunately, data for prison entries under sentence in Ireland are not available for the period 1995–2000).

To summarise, therefore, thus far in the analysis only the 'stock' figures on the use of imprisonment in Ireland have provided convincing evidence of a 'new punitiveness', although these increases are not reflected in the data on prison entries. For the most part, the empirical evidence relating to Scotland and New Zealand, both countries which were already using imprisonment heavily prior to the advent of 'get tough' period, does not bear out claims of a *profound transformation* of the sort to be found in the literature.

Two other ways of conceptualising punishment severity (relating to imprisonment) are through examining the risk of a sentence of imprisonment being imposed and the length of the custodial sentence served in a given jurisdiction. Frost (2008) has argued that these dual determinants of the imprisonment rate, which she terms 'propensity to imprison' and 'penal intensity', provide a more accurate measure of punitiveness.[5] In her empirical work into the use of imprisonment in the US, she found that state punitiveness rankings shifted substantially when these two dependent variables were used instead of the imprisonment rate. In her view, 'propensity' should be measured in terms of the likelihood of imprisonment of over one year following arrest for an index offence (Frost 2005). There are difficulties in adopting Frost's method, however, not least among them the availability of reliable and current arrest and sentencing data and this did in fact prove problematic in the three countries selected for analysis. For this reason it was decided to focus solely on 'penal intensity' or sentence length which – given its strong association with tough penal rhetoric – is arguably the best measure of the 'new punitiveness' (Kutateladze 2007b). As Frost (2008: 279) herself observes 'when those in academia speak of increasing punitiveness, they frequently refer to the influx of particularly punitive legislative initiatives that focus more on sending people to prison for longer periods of time, than on sending more and more people to prison'. Measures such as 'three strikes', mandatory minimum sentencing laws and 'truth in sentencing' have, in some parts of the United States at least, resulted in the regular imposition of disproportionate penalties (see Tonry 1996).

While ideally both the average term of imprisonment *imposed* and *served* should be used, information concerning time served simply did not exist in some of the

5 It should be noted that she defines punitiveness narrowly, and, it is submitted, mistakenly, as the use of imprisonment; see further Daems (2007).

jurisdictions.[6] In light of the data available across the three jurisdictions it was decided that counting the number of offenders committed to prison in receipt of sentences of imprisonment of two years or above would be the best proxy for increasing harshness in sentence length. This figure includes those serving determinate sentences of two years or above as well as those serving life sentences and other forms of indeterminate sentence.[7] It was adjusted for population changes over the period. As with the other data, the number of those committed in 1976 was used as an index year.

The results are shown in Figure 6.8 and, as can be seen, seem to provide the best evidence of a 'new punitiveness' in all three jurisdictions, albeit to varying degrees. In both Ireland and New Zealand the number of offenders receiving longer-term sentences has increased by approximately 500 per cent between 1976 and 2006. This trend is less marked in Scotland but the numbers of longer-term prisoners committed to prison still appear to have increased by 233 per cent over the period.

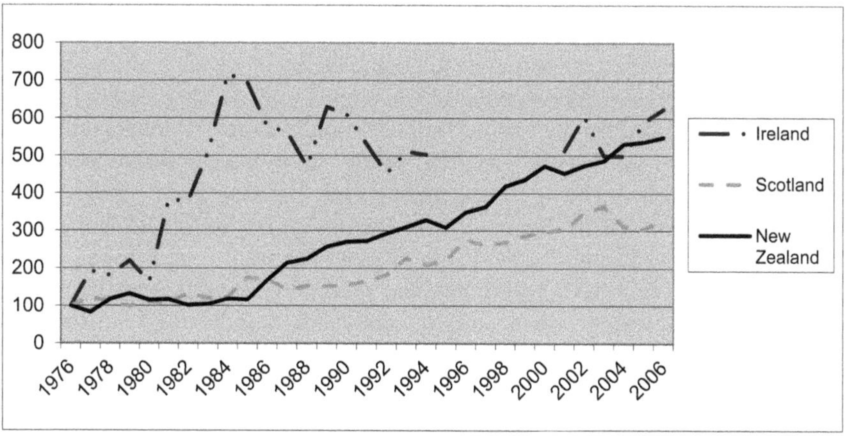

Figure 6.8 Number of offenders committed to prison receiving sentences of two years or more in Ireland, Scotland and New Zealand 1976–2006 using 1976 as an index year

Sources: O'Donnell et al. (2005), Irish Prison Service, Annual Reports, various years; Scottish Executive: Statistical Bulletin: Prison Statistics Scotland, various years; New Zealand Department of Corrections data warehouse (data request).

6 For example, in Ireland the average time served is greatly influenced not only by legal rules concerning remission and parole, but also by temporary release practices which are at the discretion of the Minister of Justice and which have varied widely over the past two decades. Data on the average time imposed or served is not collected by the government.

7 Unfortunately, due to the way the data are recorded information on the number of young offenders (under 21) sentenced to terms of imprisonment of two years or over in Scotland was not available for the period 1976–1988. In order to be able to present a data series covering the whole period, the Scottish data refer to sentences of imprisonment imposed on adult offenders only. Additionally, owing to the particular data collection methods in New Zealand, the New Zealand data do not include the numbers of offenders sentenced to terms of exactly two years.

Given the data already presented in Figures 6.3 to 6.7, what does this tell us about punitiveness in the three states in question? First of all, it appears to affirm research conducted by scholars in the US (Gordon 1989; Kutateladze 2007a, 2009) and elsewhere (Farrington et al. 2004) that there are various ways in which states can be punitive. Kutateladze (2007a, 2009) for example used 44 variables across 50 states in the US and found that Maine, the least punitive state across the majority of the indices (such as prison conditions, youth justice, absence of the death penalty), was nevertheless the one where average prison sentences – both imposed and served – significantly surpassed the national averages. This result was replicated in Frost's study (2008). She also found Maine had the second lowest imprisonment rate in the country, yet was ranked second in terms of average time served. In a similar vein, Farrington et al. (2004) in their research into crime and punishment in Switzerland found that while changes in the propensity to imprison indicated less rather than more punitiveness, the data for sentence lengths indicated the reverse.

Secondly, it is notable that this measure as a particularly important indicator of change and driver of the prison population increases found support in the case studies and interviews. As discussed in Chapters 3 to 5, in New Zealand and to some degree also in the other two jurisdictions, public discourse around crime has hardened in more recent years and judges have come under pressure to impose longer sentences. It should be reiterated, however, that sentence length is *not* the same as time served. The amount of time spent in prison in Ireland in the early to mid 1990s, for example, when early release was used frequently to relieve overcrowding, would have been much less than the sentence imposed. At that period of time, therefore, the country's punitiveness (relative to 1976 sentence lengths) would have been significantly mitigated in practice.

The Need to Relate Imprisonment Rates to Crime Rates

As discussed in Chapter 1, imprisonment rates alone tell us little about a state's reaction to crime: countries with radically different crime problems would naturally have quite different imprisonment rates even if they were similarly punitive. The importance of factoring back in what Lynch (1988) has termed the 'provocation' to which the state is exposed was stressed by some of the interviewees, namely, representatives of victims' groups and commentators to the 'right' of the political spectrum. As can be seen below, it is clear that these groups possess a sophisticated understanding of the concept of punitiveness and its dimensions, including the argument that imprisonment does not occur in a vacuum:

> You say it's higher, it certainly is higher in the number that are physically behind bars but it is interesting when you carry out the contrast with, in fact, your own jurisdiction, where in Ireland you actually per 1,000 offences jail more people than what we do in Scotland and it seems to work for you. (Scotland interviewee #6, p. 2)

> [talking about New Zealand] If you compare the imprisonment rate to the population, we're about second [in the OECD]. If you bring our crime rate into that, we're about in the middle. So where I think criminologists are failing to take into account is what is the crime rate of a particular population or country [*sic*]. (New Zealand interviewee #6, p. 21)

The views held by these groups underline the importance for criminologists to depict state punitiveness as accurately as possible, including relating this to crime (Daems 2008). In this relation, many commentators (Lynch 1988, 1995; Young and Brown 1993; Pease 1994) have argued that punitiveness is best illustrated by using admissions under sentence as a numerator and conviction rates as a denominator. As Pease (1994: 120) writes 'restricting oneself to admissions under sentence as the numerator and convictions as the denominator and analysing separately by offence type is arguably the closest one can get in a non-experimental situation to assessing national differences in "punitiveness" of sentencing as defined by the imposition of custody'. In the instant case, a lack of reliable data on convictions in the three jurisdictions meant that the ratio of prisoners to crimes was examined instead.

While this reconfiguration may provide greater conceptual clarity it does introduce a host of further methodological challenges relating to the comparison of crime rates. There are considerable difficulties with presenting imprisonment rates in this way given the differences in the way in which crimes are defined, recorded and counted in different countries (Neapolitan 1997; Kutateladze 2007b). With regard to the three jurisdictions under consideration, the most significant obstacle to comparison in absolute terms was the differences in the way crimes were counted (Brottsförebyggande rådet 1999). For example, in Ireland a hierarchical system of recording offences applies. Under the 'primary offence rule' where two or more criminal offences are disclosed in a single episode it is the 'primary' criminal offence which is counted, i.e. the offence to which the greater penalty may apply (Garda Síochána 2005). This is not the case in both Scotland and New Zealand where all offences arising from a single incident are normally counted (Ministry of Justice 2002: 2; Scottish Executive 2006b: 23). Clearly, this would tend to significantly underrepresent the number of crimes committed in Ireland in the statistics.[8]

One way of overcoming these difficulties is by abandoning absolute comparison in favour of comparing changes over time (Barclay and Tavares 2003). As noted, this has the added advantage of detecting the onset of a *new* rather than pre-existing punitiveness in the three jurisdictions. Using 1976 as an index year (1978 in the case of New Zealand as prior to that data were not collected in sufficient detail)

8 This difficulty is compounded by over-inclusive recording procedures in New Zealand. As observed by Young and Brown (1993: 27, own emphasis) '[New Zealand] unlike most other jurisdictions ... has a national computerized system on which all incidents initially classified as offenses are recorded, *no matter how trivial they are or what the subsequent outcome is ...*'.

changes in imprisonment rates per 1,000 violent crimes and per 1,000 thefts and burglaries were recorded over the 30-year period. Unfortunately, it was not possible to compare the total number of recorded crimes with imprisonment rates owing to the differences in the way these are compiled and the exclusion of certain categories such as traffic offences in New Zealand.[9] In any event, as argued by Lynch (1995) and Kutateladze (2007b, 2009), crime specific comparisons are preferable when relating imprisonment rates to crime given that countries may have a very different mix of crime. The violent crime/prison entry ratio was selected for comparison given the strong association of violent crimes with the punitiveness debate. In the absence of reliable data on sentencing for drugs offences,[10] it was also considered important to gauge how a government punishes less serious (and more prolific) offences such as theft and burglary and this forms the reason for their inclusion.

Figure 6.9 shows the growth in the use of imprisonment in all three countries relative to the number of violent crimes. This is defined to include murder, manslaughter, attempts to murder, death by dangerous driving, serious assaults, rape, sexual assault and robbery.[11] Contrary to what one might expect, the ratio of imprisonment to the number of violent crimes has actually been declining rather than increasing for Scotland and New Zealand. Indeed, from the early 1980s onward, the three countries take quite divergent paths. For the first 20 years of the study period Ireland used imprisonment to a much greater degree relative to its violent crime problem whereas Scotland and New Zealand used it less. In the last five years of the study period, however, the Irish ratio of admissions to violent crimes has dramatically fallen so that *all three* countries appear less punitive in 2006 than they were in 1976. While it is important to understand the decrease in Ireland against a background of significant changes in crime recording practices,[12] this is nevertheless a significant finding given that violent crimes are

9 Ireland records headline (serious) offences as well as the number of proceedings instituted in more minor matters; Scotland records crimes (more serious) and offences (less serious) and New Zealand records total offence numbers, excluding traffic offences. Even if serious and less serious offences were combined in Ireland and Scotland it is doubtful whether they could be compared with New Zealand's total offences category with a large degree of confidence.

10 As argued by Kutateladze (2007b, 2009) data on sentencing for drugs offences can reveal much about a state's punitiveness. For these offences it unfortunately did not prove possible to overcome definitional differences between the three states to any reasonable degree of satisfaction.

11 In all three jurisdictions, the offence of rape is gender specific and thus refers only rape of females. Attempts to rape and, where appropriate, assaults with intent to rape are included. With regard to the offence of sexual/indecent assault (and in New Zealand, unlawful sexual connection), however, the definition is gender-neutral. New Zealand data do not contain traffic offences as it was not possible to obtain information on the offence of death by dangerous driving.

12 It is important to understand the decrease in the number of prison entries per 1,000 violent crimes since 2001 in Ireland against the background of a change in the way in

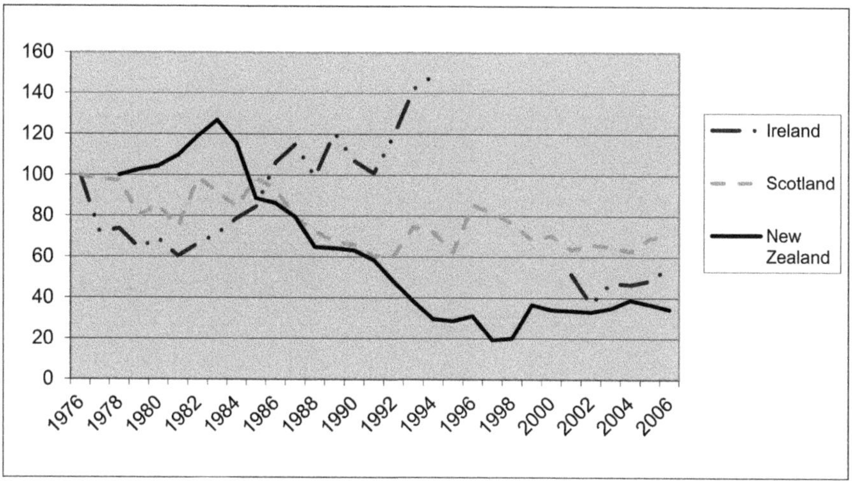

Figure 6.9 Number of prison entries under sentence per 1,000 violent crimes in Ireland, Scotland and New Zealand 1976–2006 using 1976 as an index year

Source: Department of Justice, Annual Reports on Prisons and Places of Detention, various years, Irish Prisons Service, Annual Reports, various years (as presented on National Crime Council website http://www.crimecouncil.gov.ie/statistics_cri_prison_table2.html); Scottish Executive (2006a; 2007a), Scottish Prison Service, Annual Reports 1992/3–1995/6; Scottish Home and Health Department, Prisons in Scotland: Reports 1986–1990/1991; Department of Corrections data warehouse (data request); Annual Reports of An Garda Siochana 1976–2005; Statistical Bulletin, Recorded Crime in Scotland 1983–2006; Statistics New Zealand: Long Term Data Series. (http://www.stats.govt.nz/browse_for_stats/economic_indicators/nationalaccounts/long-term-data-series.aspx), New Zealand Police (data request).

much more likely than non-violent crimes to lead to imprisonment and have the greatest potential for evoking affective resonance (Brodeur 2007).

Examination of prison admissions relative to property crimes as shown in Figures 6.10 and 6.11 also reveals a relative degree of stability for most of the study period: significant increases are not discernible in all three jurisdictions from 1976–96 but sharp increases in the use of imprisonment for both theft and burglary can be observed in Scotland and New Zealand over the last decade. This is particularly striking in the case of sentenced prison admissions relative to burglaries in Scotland which have trebled in the period from 1996 to 2006. This can be explained by reference to the fall in recorded burglaries in that jurisdiction

which crimes were recorded in 1999. The introduction of the PULSE electronic system of recording offences in that year resulted in significant increases in recorded crime since 2000 as a result of a more comprehensive recording system (see further Kilcommins et al. 2004).

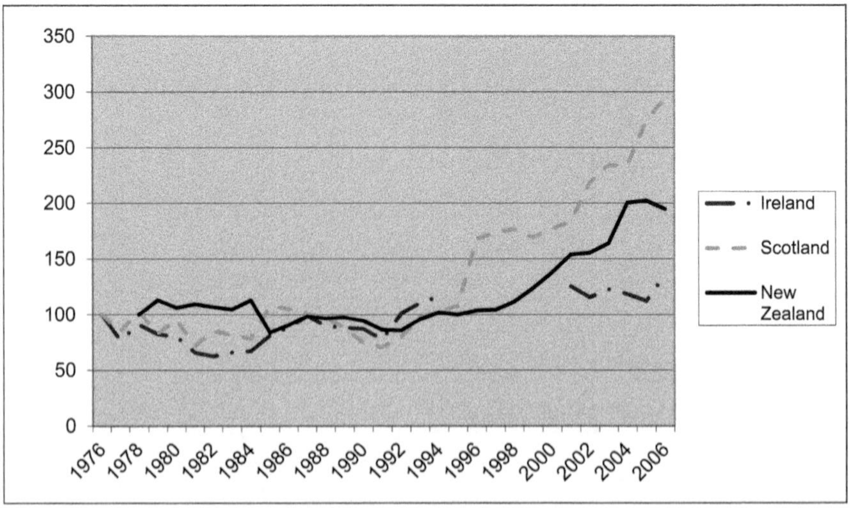

Figure 6.10 Number of prison entries under sentence per 1,000 burglaries in Ireland, Scotland and New Zealand 1976–2006 using 1976 as an index year

Source: Ibid.

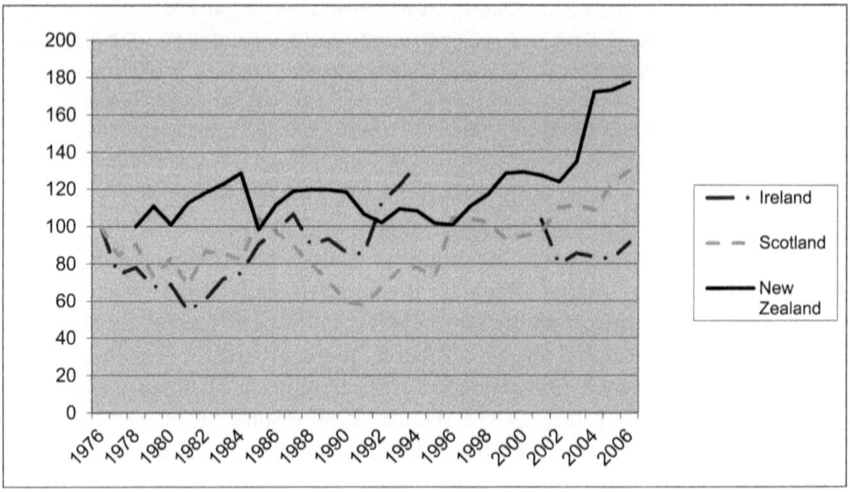

Figure 6.11 Number of prison entries under sentence per 1,000 thefts in Ireland, Scotland and New Zealand 1976–2006 using 1976 as an index year

Source: Ibid.

from the mid 1990s while the prison entry rate, as we have seen, has remained relatively stable.

Conclusion

Examining the criminal justice systems of the three jurisdictions in the above ways allows us both to draw some interesting conclusions about the punitiveness of the three states in issue and to make some important methodological points about the measurement of punitiveness more generally. Multidimensional and multi-method scrutiny has, as anticipated, served to complicate the picture of punitiveness traditionally advanced for these jurisdictions. Qualitative data speaking to the strong welfarist bent of Scottish penal culture shed important light on cross-sectoral tensions (between, for example, its high imprisonment rates and the Children's Hearing System) as well as problematising the equation of punitive outcomes (*qua* imprisonment rates) with punitive intentions. This type of data additionally differentiates the embeddedness of penal populism in the three jurisdictions. Surface similarities in tough penal rhetoric, e.g. 'zero-tolerance', often belie a singularly different approach to the politicisation of crime in Ireland and Scotland as compared with New Zealand (Jones and Newburn 2007). Punitiveness should not simply be 'read off' from rhetoric or penal statistics without (cautiously) engaging with the views of local actors and what they believe is happening (Nelken 2006).

Casting the net beyond the usual focus on imprisonment is also highly useful for gaining a better sense of how criminal justice is done in a given jurisdiction. As will be explored further in the next chapter, few states show consistency in their punitiveness levels across *all* dimensions of punitiveness. Ireland's authoritarian streak with regard to criminal justice legislation may be considered against its low imprisonment rates in international terms. Conversely, New Zealand's limited police powers and strong procedural protections force us to reflect on the punitiveness of that jurisdiction. Even the United States, considered by many to be the very acme of the 'new punitiveness' over the last number of decades, appears less punitive when prison conditions and procedural protections for defendants are placed in the balance. In this regard, it is particularly important for criminologists not to lose sight of the political attractiveness of strategies aimed at the more visible (and perhaps 'marketable') 'front end' of the system.

Returning to the more conventional indicator of imprisonment use, the utility of separately examining the many different ways in which imprisonment can be used is revealed in the marked variation which these different measures produce. With the (significant) exception of sentence length, there was no one measure which provided convincing evidence of a 'punitive turn' across all three jurisdictions. Ireland appears most punitive in regard to increases in prisoner rates and convicted prisoner rates over the period, less so when prison entries are examined. Examination of stock and flow data relating to Scotland and New Zealand, both countries which were already using imprisonment heavily prior to the advent of 'get tough' period, failed to substantiate claims of a *profound transformation* of the sort to be found in the literature. Indeed, measures such as number of prison entries per 1,000 violent crimes suggest a decline rather than increase in punitiveness levels in all countries over the 30-year period. This is of course not to ignore the substantial increases in these countries with regard to penal intensity (sentence length) nor to minimise the importance of this measure as a dimension of punitiveness. Rather it serves to point to the importance of examining *all* of these aspects in cross-national comparisons. Examining these aspects separately provides greater conceptual clarity on the precise nature a 'punitive turn' (if any) may have taken in a given jurisdiction, as well as providing a more useful guide for policy. In considering sentence length, as the Irish case illustrates, it is also critical to take into account the determinacy of the sentencing process and role played by parole boards or ministerial decisions.

Chapter 7
The 'New Punitiveness' in Ireland, Scotland and New Zealand

Introduction

In line with the arguments advanced in the previous chapter about the desirability of employing a wide range of variables when measuring punitiveness the empirical basis for the punitive turn will now be addressed below using the multidimensional (34-variable) scale of punitiveness outlined in Chapter 1. This measure will hopefully be sensitive enough to capture the (sometimes conflicting) aspects of punitiveness across the various sectors of the criminal justice system and thus better help us examine variations in punitiveness between (and within) the three jurisdictions.

Prior to embarking on a more systematic assessment of punitiveness, however, it is useful to reflect briefly on what has been learned about changes in the nature of criminal justice in three jurisdictions from the case studies in Chapters 3 to 5. There is a sense in which the punitive turn thesis does find a resonance in that in all of the countries criminal justice policy has become more severe. While considerable variation remains in relation to implementation, the historical accounts illustrate that the mid 1990s in all three countries witnessed a quickening pace of legislative activity on criminal justice issues and hardening political and public sensibilities towards offenders and their rights. As discussed in the previous chapter, a more punitive edge is also revealed in significantly increased sentence lengths.

Punitiveness Scores

Drawing on the qualitative and quantitative data gathered on the three countries in question, scores were attributed to variables and indices in an attempt to bring some degree of finality to the questions posed in earlier chapters. Each of the 34 variables identified in the tables below generated a score of 10, 20 or 30 denoting low or less than moderate; moderate punitiveness; and more than moderate or high punitiveness respectively. A score was awarded based on the punitiveness of the states at the end of 2006 but in determining the score consideration was also given to how policies and practices had evolved over the 30-year time period of the study. The year 1976 is therefore used as a basis for comparison in relation to all of the variables where possible. This was considered important given that the research was investigating the existence of a *new* punitiveness rather than pre-existing differences between the jurisdictions. The scores for all of the variables in each index were totalled and divided by the sum of the variables in that index to get overall punitiveness scores (OPSs) (Kutateladze 2009). OPSs are therefore the mean scores for each category A–G running to a maximum of 30. Finally, a mean OPS score for all the indices (the sum of the OPSs for each index divided by seven) was calculated for each of the countries. The scores for all three jurisdictions can be seen in Tables 7.1 to 7.3 together with country narratives expanding on the results.

Ireland

In Ireland over the 30-year period police powers have been significantly expanded, defendants' rights eroded and the country has become significantly more punitive in many of the ways in which imprisonment can be used. In response to various crime crises over the last number of decades, legislators have tended to focus on measures which enhance police powers and numbers and there has been some erosion of procedural protections for defendants based on the idea that the balance of the criminal justice system had swung too far in favour of the accused (O'Mahony 1996; Hamilton 2007). In this connection Walsh (2005a) has counted 27 major criminal justice enactments since the passage of the Criminal Justice Act 1984 increasing the powers of the police and the prosecution. The 2006 Criminal Justice Act was particularly significant in this respect, more than doubling the maximum period of detention and providing for the Gardaí (Irish police) to issue search warrants to themselves in certain circumstances without the traditional safeguard of judicial supervision. Policymakers have also briefly flirted with the concept of zero-tolerance policing in the period following two high-profile murders in 1996 but there has been little evidence of this in practice (Kilcommins et al. 2004). This period also provided the context for many significant reforms such as a constitutional amendment relating to the law on bail (allowing it to be denied where there is a reasonable apprehension that the accused will reoffend), civil forfeiture under the Proceeds of Crime Act and the erosion of the rights to silence for those charged with serious drugs offences (Hamilton 2007).

Despite the significance of these changes, Ireland's punitiveness appears the most severe in relation to Indices C and E. Imprisonment rates have increased by 132 per cent and convicted prisoner rates by 300 per cent, albeit from a much lower base than the other two jurisdictions. These increases, considered together with increases in nominal sentence length (the number of offenders receiving sentences of two years imprisonment or more 2006 figure is eight times the number for 1976) and imprisonment rates correlated with violent crime (an increase of 59 per cent between 1976 and 1994) do appear to substantiate suggestions that the country is experiencing a 'punitive turn'. Repeated attempts have also been made by the legislature to curtail judicial discretion. By the end of the period there were two major acts on the statute book making provision for presumptive and mandatory sentencing (in addition to the mandatory life term for murder) and this marks a significant departure for a country where proportionate sentencing has been elevated to near-constitutional status (O'Malley 2006). Turning to Index E, conditions in Irish prisons raise serious concerns about compliance with human rights standards (Hamilton and Kilkelly 2008). Increasing levels of prisoner-on-prisoner violence in recent years combined with degrading practices such as 'slopping out' and poor physical conditions in some older prisons mean that the experience of prison life may be very harsh. Indeed, it was highly significant that a contemporary Report by the European Committee for the Prevention of Torture (CPT) (2007a) categorised three Irish prisons as 'unsafe' for both prisoners and prison staff due to prisoner-on-prisoner intimidation and violence.

Measures across other indices present the Irish criminal justice system in a more positive light. Fundamental reforms relating to juvenile justice have seen the age of criminal responsibility increase to 12; statutory provision made for diversion and a greater range of community sentences and (most) juveniles separated from adults within the penal system in line with international standards. All references to the death penalty have also been removed from the Constitution following a referendum in 2001. In concluding, what should not be forgotten is that an important aspect of Irish criminal justice is the failure to translate policy into practice. The punitiveness of the system on paper is thus offset to some degree by the inherent conservatism of the system, the slow pace of change and by a certain failure of implementation. For example, there remains significant doubt about the extent to which sex offenders on the Garda 'register' are actively policed. Moreover, provisions limiting the right to silence were introduced in 1984 and 1996 but these have not been relied on by prosecutors during the study period. It is this same inertia, however, which has also meant that we are only now seeing matters such as youth justice reform and spent conviction laws being properly addressed.

Table 7.1 Summary of punitiveness in Ireland 1976–2006

#	Variable name	Source	Result	Score
			Index A: Policing	
1	Zero-tolerance policing	Literature	Strongly advocated by Fianna Fáil (then in opposition) in the 1997 general election which resulted in some increase in arrests in the period immediately following the election. For the most part, however, this policy has not been implemented (See Chapter 3, Kilcommins et al. 2004).	10
2	Law and order rhetoric which emphasises more police, more police powers	Literature/ interviews/ legislation	A significant increase in the numbers of Gardaí formed part of the government's 'anti-crime package' in 1996 but there have been no dramatic increases over the period. Police powers on the other hand have been considerably expanded. Walsh (2005a) notes there have been 27 major criminal justice enactments since the Criminal Justice Act 1984 expanding police/prosecution powers. Detention powers have recently been doubled in the Criminal Justice Act 2006 and senior Gardaí have been given the power to issue warrants. Some legislative provisions have not been implemented, however, e.g. seven day detention for drug trafficking under the 1996 Act.	30
3	Private security leading to the exclusion of marginalised groups	Literature/ interviews	The numbers of people working in this sector have dramatically increased over the period but there is little evidence of the use of private security as a means of excluding certain groups from public or quasi-public places such as shopping malls, etc. This may be due to the fact that there is a less readily identifiable 'underclass' in Ireland (O'Donnell and O'Sullivan 2003: 42).	10
4	Strength of police	Statistical abstract; Garda Síochána annual reports	Police strength has increased considerably over the period but police *rates* have remained constant.	10
5	Expenditure on police	Dept of finance/ interviews	Expenditure per head of population has doubled over the 30 year period, even when expressed in real terms. However, some of this may be due to the cost of professionalising of the force over the period rather than operations.	20

6	Complaints about police	Reports of GSCB/ Garda ombudsman	2006 figures (1,350) show only a 33% increase since 1987 although complaint rates remain low relative to other comparable jurisdictions.	10
			OPS= 15 Policing practices, both public and private, cannot be described as overly punitive in Ireland although powers have been significantly expanded.	
			Index B: Procedural protections for defendants	
7	Right to silence	Literature/ interviews/ legislation	This principle has been curtailed in 1984 and 1996 but in practice the new provisions are not invoked against defendants.	10
8	Double jeopardy rule	Literature/ legislation	Rule remains intact within the study period (amending legislation was introduced in 2009). Without prejudice prosecution appeal provided for in the Criminal Justice Act 2006.	10
9	Evidential exclusionary rules	Literature/ legislation	Reform of these rules was recommended by the Balance in the Criminal Law Review Group (2007) but there are no plans to legislate for this.	10
10	Use of civil law to control criminal behaviour	Literature/ legislation	The civil forfeiture procedure introduced in 1996 has been frequently utilised. Sex offender orders were introduced in 2001 and ASBOs (called 'behaviour orders') legislated for in 2006. Very few ASBOs have been issued by the courts, however.	20
11	Right to bail	Literature/ legislation	Bail laws were substantially reformed in 1997 following a constitutional amendment permitting bail to be denied where there was a reasonable suspicion that the offender would commit an offence while on bail. These reforms may go some of the way towards explaining the rapid expansion of the proportion of the prison population on remand over the last decade or so (from 6% in 1994 to 16%in 2006).	20
			OPS= 14 Changes in the main relate to concerns about evidential standards being eroded through recourse to the civil law as well as increased use of remands in custody.	

Table 7.1 ***Continued***

#	Variable name	Source	Result	Score
			Index C: Use of imprisonment	
12	Use of mandatory/ presumptive sentences	Literature/ interviews/ legislation	Presumptive sentences of 10 years were introduced for drugs trafficking offences over a certain value in 1999 and these have since been expanded and consolidated in the Criminal Justice Act 2006. While few 10 year sentences have actually been handed down by the judiciary, the legislation has had a considerable inflationary effect on the length of sentences handed down for drugs offences.	20
13	Use of alternatives to custody	Literature/ interviews/ legislation	There are relatively few alternatives to custody in Ireland and this is an area which has suffered from legislative neglect. The ratio of custody to community sentences would appear to have improved over the period, however, suggesting there is now a lesser risk of custody.	10
14	Imprisonment rates and convicted prisoner rates	Annual reports on prisons	These have soared over the period as the figures in the previous chapter demonstrate. Imprisonment rates have increased by nearly 150% and convicted prisoner rates by 300%. Imprisonment rates remain comparatively low but such increases, even from a low base, do appear to testify to a 'new punitiveness' in the country.	30
15	Prison admission rates and convicted prisoners admission rates	Annual reports on prisons	Data as presented in Chapter 6 show increases which are significant over the period (approximately 80%) but which are much less marked than increases in the overall stock rate.	20
16	Length of sentences imposed	Annual reports on prisons	As shown in Chapter 6 the number of offenders receiving longer-term sentences has dramatically increased.	30
17	Imprisonment rates using violent and property crime as a base	Annual reports on prisons/ Garda Síochána annual reports	Increases (60%) over the period 1976–94 are most pronounced in relation to violent crime rather than property crime. The decrease in relation to the use of imprisonment relative to violent crime in the period 2001–2006 should be treated with caution, moreover, given the sudden increase in crimes recorded in Ireland following the introduction of the PULSE recording system.	20

			OPS=21.7 The rapid expansion of the use of imprisonment at a time when crime was falling does appear to signal an increase in punitiveness.	
			Index D: Juvenile justice	
18	Age of criminal responsibility	Literature/ legislation	This was raised to 12 for most offences save murder, manslaughter and rape in the Children Act 2001 (as amended).	10
19	Compliance with human rights instruments	Literature	Kilkelly (2006) has mixed conclusions: she praises the Garda Diversion Programme and the Children Detention Centres. She voices reservations about the Children's Court and St. Patrick's Institution, although in relation to the latter plans are in train to comply with international standards by 2011.	20
20	Alternatives to prosecution and detention	Literature/ legislation	The Garda Diversion Programme appears to function relatively well and is on a statutory basis from 2002. After a considerable delay, community sentences provided for under the 2001 Act are beginning to be implemented.	10
21	Detention rates	Annual reports on prisons	Prison entry levels for under 21s and under 18s appear to be falling although data in relation to juvenile detention in Ireland are very limited. Ireland's detention rate appears to be midrange when compared with other jurisdictions.	10
			OPS=12.5 Steps have been taken with the 2001 Act to make progress in this area although much will depend on the Act's implementation.	
			Index E: Prison conditions	
22	Respect for human rights	Literature	The continued practice of 'slopping out' night waste in several old Irish prisons and the recent designation of a number of prisons by the CPT (2007a) as 'unsafe' due to prisoner-on-prisoner intimidation and violence are areas where concern is most warranted.	20
23	Size of institutions	Literature	Most institutions are small in size and CPT reports appear to suggest that relations between prisoners and staff are reasonably good and constructive.	10
24	Overcrowding	Literature	Despite an occupancy rate of 95.2% (ICPS 2008), this is severe in certain large Irish prisons such as Mountjoy and Cork.	30

Table 7.1 ***Concluded***

#	Variable name	Source	Result	Score
25	Medical services and food	Literature	Generally good. Deficits in psychiatric and psychological services have been made up in recent years (CPT 2003, 2007a). There is a high rate of transmission of HIV and Hepatitis C in Irish prisons (Allwright et al. 1999).	20
26	Prison deaths	Prison service reports/ Dáil debates	At the beginning of the period only one or two deaths per annum were common. There was a small increase in the late 1980s but since 2002 the number has ranged from 7 to 12 in 2006. This merits considerable concern.	30
27	Rehabilitation	Literature/ interviews	Rehabilitation remains part of the Irish Prison Service's mission statement, albeit after a commitment to maintain safe and secure custody for people sent to prison. The practical realisation of this goal is, however, questionable in an environment where overcrowding and poor physical conditions remain major problems. There is a humanitarianism within the Irish penal system that may not be present in larger systems. Prisoners do not wear a uniform and relations with staff are generally good.	20
			OPS=21.7 Poor physical conditions, overcrowding and high levels of inter-prisoner violence remain the worst features.	
			Index F: Post-release control	
28	Sex/drug offender notification schemes	Literature/ legislation	Sex offender notification scheme in operation since 1997; drugs offenders sentenced to over a year's imprisonment must also register with the Gardaí since 2006. Importantly, however, questions have been raised about the extent to which these provisions are enforced and offenders are actively monitored by Gardaí.	10
29	Shaming schemes	Literature	None exist in Ireland	10
30	Post-release supervision	Literature/ legislation	Post-release supervision orders are used frequently in relation to sex offenders (Sex Offender Act 2001) and these are implemented by the Probation Service.	20

31	Reintegration	Literature	There is a nominal commitment to reintegration in the community for offenders but this is given little practical effect. No disenfranchisement laws exist in Ireland. Prisoners have recently been provided with the practical means of voting in prison.	20
32	Expungement of criminal records	Literature/ legislation	Ireland remains the only country in the EU without such a scheme (save for provisions relating to juveniles in the Children Act 2001).	20
			OPS=16 While there are some legislative provisions aiming to increase control over ex-offenders, these are mitigated somewhat in practice.	
			Index G: Death penalty	
33	Date of abolition	Literature/ legislation	Death penalty for murder abolished in 1964; abolished for all offences in 1990. There has been a constitutional ban on the penalty since 2002.	10
34	Date of last execution	Literature	Noel and Marie Murray were sentenced to death for capital murder in 1974 but this was reversed on appeal; the last execution was in fact carried out in 1954.	10
			OPS=10	
OPS (All Indices)=15.8			*Overall Conclusions* The penal climate in Ireland remains relatively mild but significant advances in rates of imprisonment and police powers represent worrying manifestations of the 'culture of control' as understood in its intrinsic or historical sense.	

Scotland

As discussed in the previous chapter there is a curious reluctance on the part of criminal justice stakeholders in Scotland to characterise their country as 'punitive' despite it having one of the highest rates of imprisonment in Western Europe. This view is, however, supported by the data as Scotland achieved relatively low punitiveness scores on most of the indices. Both public and private policing practices cannot be characterised as overly punitive in Scotland. While the increase in police numbers and expenditure over the period appears to tally with Hinds's (2005) arguments concerning a concentration of control at the front end of the system, police *rates* have remained stable and police powers have been only incrementally enhanced. As Fyfe (2005) notes there is a preference for a crime prevention rather than 'sovereign state' policing strategy in Scotland. This is probably mirrored in the private sector: exclusionary tactics aimed at certain groups and behaviours are less in evidence in Scotland than in larger jurisdictions such as the US (Walker 1999). A relatively positive verdict may also be returned in relation to Index B. In contrast to England and Wales, reforms to the trial procedure have largely been resisted. For example, the English Criminal Justice Act 2003 which radically overhauled several of the well-established rules of evidence such as double jeopardy was not adopted in Scotland.

Similarly, evidence of a *new* punitiveness is difficult to find in relation to imprisonment. Viewed in a historical perspective, i.e. against 1976 standards, several variables such as convicted prisoner rates (+39 per cent), convicted prisoner entry rates (+13 per cent) and prisoners per violent crimes (–30 per cent) show only a slight increase or even a decline in punitiveness. Scotland has also remained relatively immune to the trend towards mandatory sentencing. The introduction of mandatory provisions in 1997 was strongly resisted and – while those provisions that have been introduced over the period have no doubt contributed to the rise in sentence length – these are mainly directed at very specific crimes and offences (Tombs 2004). Finally, physical conditions in prisons have improved: slopping out has been practically eradicated, electric power has been provided in all cells, the numbers of suicides have decreased and there remains a proliferation of programmes oriented around education and rehabilitation (Fairweather 2006). Overcrowding presents the main challenge to this more favourable environment (ibid.).

Despite the largely optimistic picture presented above, it would be misleading to suggest that change has not been visited on key institutional sites within the criminal justice system. Over the period the data show that longer sentences were more frequently handed down (the number of adult offenders receiving sentences of two years imprisonment or more 2006 figure is 3.4 times the number for 1976), and the use of imprisonment increased even as property crime rates fell in the last decade or so. Some years into devolution and in the aftermath of initiatives such as antisocial behaviour orders and youth courts for serious and persistent young offenders there was speculation that Scotland's youth justice system was being 'detartanised' (McAra 2006; Piacentini and Walters 2006). The more punitive rhetoric has not given rise to an increase in detention rates, however, and the commitment to welfarism within the Children's Hearings System has largely been preserved (McAra 2008). Finally, English polices (such as notification requirements and extended sentences) which aim to control the dangerous 'other' *qua* sexual and violent offender have been adopted in Scotland, often on account of the border shared by the two countries. Since devolution a new type of incapacitative order (Orders for Lifelong Restriction or OLRs) has continued the focus on the 'dangerous' offender. Policies in relation to less serious offenders reflect a more inclusionary approach, however: prison sentences of up to two and a half years are expunged after a certain period of time and local authorities in Scotland have a statutory responsibility to provide throughcare and aftercare services. Shaming schemes do not exist in Scotland.

Table 7.2 Summary of punitiveness in Scotland 1976–2006

#	Variable Name	Source	Result	Score
			Index A: Policing	
1	Zero-tolerance policing	Literature	Strathclyde police experimented with a ZTP type approach (Operation Spotlight) for a few years in the late 1990s although this has now been abandoned. Moreover, as Jones and Newburn (2007: 132) point out, there were significant differences between the Strathclyde and NYC operations (see further Chapter 4).	10
2	Law and order rhetoric which emphasises more police, more police powers	Literature/ interviews/ legislation	A law and order approach was advocated by Michael Forsyth during his period as Scottish Secretary (1995–97). Moreover, issues around police resources and powers have come in for considerably more attention since devolution (Donnelly and Scott 2005). Recent legislation has increased police powers regarding DNA and drug testing, establishing identity and dispersal orders, although the detention period of six hours remains short. Further, the police are often reluctant to use these new powers as demonstrated by the First Minister's criticism of the failure of the police to use dispersal orders in 2006.	20
3	Private security leading to the exclusion of marginalised groups	Literature/ interviews	Private security companies have flourished but there is a 'lesser salience in Scotland of a new urban underclass marginalized from mainstream political and economic institutions and practices' (Walker 1999: 103). The issue of spatial exclusion through the use of private security firms is therefore less relevant.	10
4	Strength of police	Scottish Executive	Despite the increased politicisation of the issue of police numbers, police rates have remained relatively stable, only showing a slight increase over the period.	10
5	Expenditure on police	Scottish Executive	As data in Chapter 6 demonstrate this has tripled over the period (in real terms). The Justice Committee report (2008) explains the need for increased resources in terms of increasing general demands created by both societal and legislative changes (e.g. demands of the night-time economy; management of sex offenders) and by new threats (e.g. terrorism).	20

6	Complaints about police	HM Inspector of the Constabulary	A steady increase in the number of complaints is discernible from the mid 1980s onward. This has intensified in recent years with a rise from 1,333 in 1996 to 3,122 in 2006. This is an unreliable indicator of police behaviour, however, on account of the variation in recording practices in place across the country until 2001. Police complaints since that date have seen only a modest increase (from 2,913 to 3,122 in 2006).	20
			OPS=15 Policing practices, both public and private, cannot be described as overly punitive in Scotland.	
			Index B: Procedural protections for defendants	
7	Right to silence	Literature/ interviews/ legislation	The right to silence continues to exist in the police station and, (to a much lesser degree), at trial. Since 1995 the prosecutor may comment upon the accused's failure to testify.	20
8	Double jeopardy rule	Literature/ interviews/ legislation	Rule has remained unchanged within the study period.	10
9	Evidential exclusionary rules	Literature/ interviews/ legislation	Changes have been very limited over the period so that the exclusionary rule remains substantially intact. Since 2002 evidence of an accused's previous convictions in sexual cases may be led at a trial for a sexual offence where s/he has put the complainer's character in issue.	10
10	Use of civil law to control criminal behaviour	Literature/ interviews/ legislation	Civil law has been used to seize the proceeds of crime, control antisocial behaviour, sex offenders and football hooliganism. Relatively few ASBOs have been used against children, however.	20
11	Right to bail	Literature/ legislation	No legal changes over the period save to the extent that provision was made in 2004 for electronic tagging to be made a condition of bail. The proportion of offenders on remand in the prison population has increased somewhat (from 15% in 1976 to 22% in 2006).	20
			OPS=16 To date reforms have been considerably more measured than in England and Wales.	

Table 7.2 ***Continued***

#	Variable Name	Source	Result	Score
			Index C: Use of imprisonment	
12	Use of mandatory/ presumptive sentences	Literature/ interviews/ legislation	Scotland has remained relatively immune to the trend towards mandatory sentencing over the 30-year period. Only two such provisions exist: one for three-time drug traffickers which has had little impact in practice and another concerning firearms which was part of a UK-wide Act. This may change with plans for a sentencing council.	10
13	Use of alternatives to custody	Literature/ interviews/ legislation	The range of alternatives to custody is well developed in Scotland and since the 1980s 'fiscal fines' have been used very successfully as an alternative to prosecution. The ratio of custody to community orders has steadily declined over time and it now appears that an equal number of people are received into prison than begin probation or community service (compared to four times as many 1976). The difficulty appears to be that the use of community penalties is increasing along with increases in prison population.	10
14	Imprisonment rates and convicted prisoner rates	Statistical bulletins: Scottish Executive	As the data in Chapter 6 illustrate Scotland has witnessed increases in its imprisonment rate and convicted prisoner rate in the order of 50% and 39% respectively over the period. While these are not negligible by any means, they are much less significant than increases in other jurisdictions.	20
14	Prison admission rates and convicted prisoners admission rates	Statistical bulletins: Scottish Executive	Data examined in the previous chapter show a remarkable stability in these variables over the period: the prison entry rate of offenders under sentence, for example, has increased by only 15%.	10
16	Length of sentences imposed	Statistical bulletins: Scottish Executive	Again, as shown in the previous chapter the number of offenders (excluding young offenders under 21) receiving longer-term sentences has increased by 233% since 1976 suggesting a 'new punitiveness' may be manifesting itself primarily through penal intensity rather than propensity to imprison.	20

17	Imprisonment rates using violent and property crime as a base	Statistical bulletins: Scottish Executive	Scottish punitiveness as measured by imprisonment per 1,000 violent crimes actually appears to be declining over the period; imprisonment rates per 1,000 burglaries have increased by nearly 200%, however, and imprisonment relative to thefts has increased by 30%.	20
			OPS=15 The best evidence for a 'new punitiveness' in Scotland lies in increases in sentence length and imprisonment related to property crimes; other variables suggest *relative* stability.	
			Index D: Juvenile justice	
18	Age of criminal responsibility	Literature	This is low (eight) but taking account of the CHS and other aspects of the juvenile justice system the *de facto* age is closer to 16 for minor offences.	10
19	Compliance with human rights instruments	Literature	Standards of compliance are generally good although there are concerns in relation to the prosecution and trial of 16- and 17-year-olds through the adult courts and in relation to conditions for young female offenders/young offenders in children's care homes (which house young offenders under 16).	20
20	Alternatives to prosecution and detention	Literature	In keeping with the diversionary and anti-custodial ethos of many international juvenile justice conventions the system has consistently strived towards maximum diversion and minimum use of custody. Cavadino and Dignan (2006) note the proportion of offences in which no action is taken in the hearings has risen from 39% in 1980 to 71% in 1999 and there has also been a fall in the proportion of cases referred to a Hearing from 48% to 20% (most referrals come from the police). Moreover, both the number of placements made by the panels and the proportion of those placements which involve residential care has steadily declined over this period (ibid.).	10
21	Detention rates	Statistical bulletins: Scottish Executive	Concerns have been voiced about the high proportion of young people (under 21s) in custody in Scotland (Cavadino and Dignan 2006). Prison entry levels for under 21s and under 18s appear to be steadily declining since 1978, however. Scotland's juvenile detention rate is mid range in comparative terms.	10
			OPS=12.5 In general terms the milder penal climate in Scotland in relation to youth offending has been preserved.	

Table 7.2 ***Continued***

#	Variable Name	Source	Result	Score
			Index E: Prison conditions	
22	Respect for human rights	Literature	Real progress has been made over the last 15 years in improving material conditions. New prisons have been built, old or unsuitable institutions have been closed and in cell sanitation has been fitted to cells in Barlinnie, Edinburgh, Perth and Polmont prisons, among others. Currently, the SPS has ended 'slopping out' practices in all prisons except HMP Peterhead and has provided electric power in all cells through a £16 million refurbishment programme (Audit Scotland 2008).	10
23	Size of institutions	Literature	With the exception of Barlinnie which holds upwards of 1,000 prisoners, most institutions hold fewer than 700 prisoners. Indeed, it is officially recognised that a capacity of 700 is the optimum size for future prisons and that prisons should be located near to the relevant population centres (Scottish Prison Service 2002).	20
24	Overcrowding	Literature	Overcrowding continues to blight many Scottish prisons, in particular local prisons and the sole facility for female prisoners at HMP Cornton Vale	30
25	Medical services and food	Literature	Generally good although Fairweather (2006) notes that low-cost prison food could be actually contributing to problem behaviour.	20
26	Prison deaths	Scottish Prison Service	There were significant increases in suicides and self-inflicted deaths in the mid–late 1990s peaking at 17 in 1999 (from 7 in 1992). The numbers have decreased somewhat since then (e.g. 10 in 2006).	20
27	Rehabilitation	Literature /interviews	Scottish prisons have traditionally shown a commitment to rehabilitation and there continues to be a genuine commitment to rehabilitation today with *inter alia* cognitive behavioural programmes, drug treatment programmes, etc. being rolled out in many prisons. Rehabilitation is necessarily hampered by severe overcrowding, however.	10
			OPS=18.3 Despite overcrowding, progress has been made in physical conditions over the period and a commitment to rehabilitation remains.	

		Index F: Post-release control		
28	Sex/drug offender notification schemes	Literature/ Legislation	Notification requirements can be imposed on sex offenders (Sex Offenders Act 1997; Criminal Justice and Courts Services Act 2000) and these offenders are actively policed within available resources.	30
29	Shaming schemes	Literature	These do not exist in Scotland.	10
30	Post-release supervision	Literature/ interviews/ legislation	Since 1998 extended sentences of up to 10 years can be imposed on serious sexual and violent offenders. Those convicted of football related offences can also be made subject to a football banning order instead of or in addition to their sentence. Similarly, sex offenders can be made subject to a sex offender order. Finally, since 2003 violent and sexual offenders may be made subject to a new type of incapacitative order called an Order for Lifelong Restriction (OLR). For the remainder of his/her life s/he will be subject to risk assessment and must abide by conditions designed to minimise his/her risk to the public.	30
31	Reintegration	Literature/ interviews/ legislation	In Scotland local authorities have a statutory responsibility to provide throughcare services to offenders sentenced to prison terms of over four years and aftercare to other prisoners in the first 12 months of their release from prison. Services vary, however, according to the prison/area from/ into which the offender is released.	10
32	Expungement of criminal records	Literature/ legislation	Scotland has the same spent convictions provisions in place as in the rest of the UK so prison sentences of up to two and a half years are deemed 'spent' after a defined 'rehabilitation period' has elapsed (Rehabilitation of Offenders Act 1974).	10
			OPS=18 Certain types of ex-offender *eg* sexual, violent are closely scrutinised post-release. In general, a good effort is made to reintegrate prisoners, however.	
		Index G: Death penalty		
33	Date of abolition	Literature/ legislation	1965 for all offences save treason; abolished for all offences in 1998	10

Table 7.2 ***Concluded***

#	Variable Name	Source	Result	Score
34	Date of last execution	Literature	The last execution was carried out in 1964.	10
			OPS=10	
OPS (All indices)=15			*Overall Conclusions*: Certain global trends such as an increased preoccupation with dangerousness and increased police presence/police powers are in evidence in Scotland in the last decade or so. Some evidence of a 'new punitiveness' may also be found in the tendency to impose longer sentences. However, core welfarist values continue to pervade the criminal justice system, particularly youth justice and prisons.	

New Zealand

As noted in Chapter 1, New Zealand is widely understood to have followed the putative Anglophone drift towards punitiveness (Pratt and Clark 2005; Cavadino and Dignan 2006). Certainly, of the three, it is the jurisdiction in which punitive rhetoric on criminal justice issues is most readily discernible since the mid 1990s. Several indices employed in the analysis bear out its more punitive reputation such as variables relating to policing (Index A). There are suggestions in the literature that Māori and Pacific Islanders may find themselves the focus of selective and discriminatory law enforcement at the hands of the New Zealand police (Quince 2007; Human Rights Commission 2009) as well as increasingly exclusionary private security practices. This should, however, be set against a background of stable police rates, (an increase of only 32 per cent between 1976 and 2006) as well as relatively limited police powers (importantly, there is no provision for detention for questioning: Newbold 2000).

These minority groups have also borne the brunt of the significant increases in the prison population (Index C). Māoris comprised 17 per cent of sentenced receptions in 1976, 32 per cent in 1986, 45 per cent in 1996 and 53 per cent in 2006. While, as with Scotland, New Zealand's use of imprisonment over time casts it in a more favourable light than cross-national comparison, the significance of a doubling of its rate of imprisonment over the period cannot be minimised (from 91 in 1976 to 183 in 2006). Further, clear signs of new punitiveness emerge when sentence lengths are examined: the number of offenders receiving long-term sentences of over two years in 2006 (1668) is over seven times the 1976 figure (224). On the other hand, continuities are also discernible. Considered in the light of its (already high) use of imprisonment in 1976, increases in its convicted prisoner rate to the order of 68 per cent over a 30 year period are not suggestive of radical change. The same may be said of its prison admission rates which have increased only by 54 per cent over the period. Further, despite the strong endorsement given to minimum sentences by the citizenry in 1999, none have been introduced over the study period.

An increasing preoccupation with dangerousness is evident in New Zealand across a number of indices. Prisons, although small in size and relatively liberal in the past with plentiful use of home and work leave, have become more security-minded and risk-averse (Newbold and Eskridge 2005; Workman 2008). The country's post-release policies in particular epitomise Garland's (2001: 180–1) proposition that in certain jurisdictions 'there is no such thing as an ex-offender'. Under the Sentencing Act 2002, the incapacitative sentence of preventive detention (likened by Vess (2005) to American civil commitment statutes) is now available for a wider range of offences and offenders. Further, the Parole (Extended Supervision) Amendment Act 2004 introduced extended supervision orders allowing the Department of Corrections to monitor medium- and high-risk child sex offenders for up to 10 years following release from prison. Expungement laws introduced in 2004 are highly restrictive allowing only those offenders who did not receive a sentence of imprisonment to benefit from the provisions. Informal practices such as shopkeepers placing pictures of ex-offenders in their windows also have a highly stigmatising effect (Pratt 2008c).

On the other side of the balance sheet, however, procedural protections such as the right to silence have remained relatively immune from populist attack (Index B). Its internationally renowned youth justice system (Index D) reflects many of the principles incorporated in the UNCRC and other international conventions and retains powerful protectors among the judiciary (Lynch 2008). A high rate of diversion of young offenders (70–80 per cent, Chong (2007)) and downward trend in terms of the number of juveniles committed to prison has also been maintained over the period (Maxwell et al. 2004).

Table 7.3 Summary of punitiveness in New Zealand 1976–2006

#	Variable Name	Source	Result	Score
			Index A: Policing	
1	Zero-tolerance policing	Literature	Although some far-right opposition parties such as ACT have promised to introduce a zero-tolerance policing strategy if elected, no moves in this direction have been taken over the study period. It should be noted, however, that it is not uncommon for police to distribute leaflets warning citizens about the imminent release of offenders into the community (Pratt 2008c).	20
2	Law and order rhetoric which emphasises more police, more police powers	Literature/ interviews/ legislation	Police powers are limited compared to other Western countries although recent legislation has increased their powers to some degree (Police Act 2008) and all officers have now (controversially) been issued with Taser guns. There is a widespread perception that more police are needed, owing to poor geographical distribution of resources and poor response times in some areas such as South Auckland. Recent elections have seen parties promise more police in a bid to gain seats (e.g. in 2005 New Zealand First made 1,000 new police part of their post-election deal with Labour).	20
3	Private security leading to the exclusion of marginalised groups	Literature/ interviews	There have been several developments here which have all increased the likelihood that undesirable 'others' may be increasingly excluded from private property and semi-public spaces such as malls. First of all, in frustration at the policing deficit, local communities have begun to hire private security firms to police their area and local authorities have recently started to follow suit, hiring private companies to patrol business districts, etc. Volunteer groups have also taken to organising patrols of their local areas acting as the eyes and ears of the police. There are suggestions in the literature (Pratt 2008c) and in the interviews that ex-offenders, Māori and Pacific Islanders may find themselves increasingly excluded from public/quasi-public spaces.	30
4	Strength of police	New Zealand statistics	Despite the increased politicisation of the issue of police numbers, police rates have remained relatively stable, only showing a slight increase over the period.	10
5	Expenditure on police	New Zealand Police annual reports/ interviews	This has more than doubled over the period (see data in Chapter 6). The suggestion in the interviews is that this has been spent on operations, upgrading equipment, keeping pace with technology and creating and maintaining specialist units within the service.	20

Table 7.3 ***Continued***

#	Variable Name	Source	Result	Score
6	Complaints about police	Police Complaints Authority annual reports	There has been a significant increase in the number of complaints going from 795 when the Police Complaints Authority (PCA) was established to 3,788 in 2006. However, the number of complain*ants* (which NZ PCA claim is the better measure) has remained fairly constant (2,066 in 1996 to 2,076 in 2006).	20
			OPS=20 There is some evidence of punitive policing practices in both the public and private sector in New Zealand.	
			Index B: Procedural protections for defendants	
7	Right to silence	Literature/ interviews/ legislation	The right to silence, both in the police station and at trial, remains intact although there has been some criticism of the right by a retiring defence counsel (*New Zealand Herald* 2006a).	10
8	Double jeopardy rule	Literature/ interviews/ legislation	No change within the period of the study.	10
9	Evidential exclusionary rules	Literature/ interviews/ legislation	Currently a predominantly exclusionary rule applies under the 2006 Evidence Act.	10
10	Use of civil law to control criminal behaviour	Literature/ interviews/ legislation	Civil orders of the kind found in the UK and Ireland are relatively unknown in New Zealand.	10
11	Right to Bail	Literature/ legislation	Bail is available ‘as of right’ for those offenders charged with an offence not punishable by imprisonment or less than three years imprisonment. The Bail Act 2000, however, reverses the burden of proof for those charged with specified serious offences against the person and drug dealing offences as well as those offenders with a long history of more minor offending. This has resulted in a significant increase in the number of offenders who are remanded in custody (from 5% in 1976 to 20% in 2006) (Tolmie 2007).	30

			OPS=14 To date (with the exception of bail), reforms in relation to procedural protections have been quite measured.	
			Index C: Use of imprisonment	
12	Use of mandatory/ presumptive sentences	Literature/ interviews	Despite the endorsement of minimum sentences in the 1999 referendum, no mandatory sentencing laws have been passed, although judges have come under increasing pressure to impose maximum sentences.	10
13	Use of alternatives to custody	Literature/ interviews/ legislation	There is a well-developed suite of alternatives to custody in New Zealand such that Newbold (2007: 257) describes the country as 'something of a leader in community corrections' The ratio of prison to community sentences has grown steadily in favour of the latter for most of the period: for every prison sentence handed down in 1980 1.9 community sentences were imposed and this improved to 3.8 in 1990 and 2000. This has failed to stem the rising prison population, however.	10
14	Imprison-ment rates and convicted prisoner rates	Ministry of Justice	Rates of imprisonment have doubled over the period while convicted prisoner rates have increased by approximately 50% (see previous chapter).	20
15	Prison admission rates and convicted prisoners admission rates	New Zealand Official Sourcebook; Dept of Corrections database	Data in Chapter 6 show that the prison entry rate has increased by 50% over the period.	20
16	Length of sentences imposed	Dept of Corrections database	The number of offenders receiving longer-term sentences has grown exponentially since 1985, and in 2006 was over five times the 1976 rate (see Chapter 6). There are clear signs of a 'new punitiveness' here.	30

Table 7.3 ***Continued***

#	Variable Name	Source	Result	Score
17	Imprison-ment rates using violent and property crime as a base	Ministry of Justice; New Zealand Police database	As with Scotland, punitiveness as measured by imprisonment per violent crimes actually appears to be declining over the period; imprisonment rates per property crimes have more than doubled, however.	20
			OPS=18.3 Given its already high imprisonment rate in 1976, a 'new punitiveness' is most clearly evident in the trend towards longer sentences.	
			Index D: Juvenile justice	
18	Age of criminal responsib-ility	Literature/ legislation	The age of criminal responsibility is 10 but this is only in homicide cases and for other crimes the age is 14. Lynch (2008) notes that 10–13-year-old offenders are dealt with in a way which promotes reintegration and recognises the child's needs in line with international standards.	10
19	Compliance with human rights instruments	Literature	New Zealand has implemented many of the principles incorporated in the UNCRC and other international conventions. There are serious difficulties, however, with the mixing of child prisoners with adults in adult correctional facilities, the exclusion of 17-year-olds from the youth justice system and the fact that children are frequently remanded to police cells owing to a shortage of places in residential units.	20
20	Alternatives to prosecution and detention	Literature	Diversionary mechanisms dispose of an impressive 70–80% of offenders aged 14–17 (Chong 2007). A smaller proportion of young offenders now appear in court in New Zealand than in any other country and the number of custodial outcomes resulting from court appearances has fallen dramatically (e.g. from approximately 300 in 1987 to just under 70 in 2001) (Maxwell 2007).	10
21	Detention rates	Dept of Corrections database	The downward trend in the number of under 18s committed to prison (since 1982) has continued in recent years despite the politicisation of youth justice issues. Juvenile custody rates per 1,000 under 18population are midrange at 0.09 (ICPS 2008; UNICEF 2009).	10
			OPS=12.5 New Zealand's progressive youth justice system has been maintained but faces a growing political challenge.	

			Index E: Prison conditions	
22	Respect for human rights	Literature	New Zealand has historically maintained relatively good prison conditions with home leave and good access to programmes (Newbold and Eskridge 2005). Cavadino and Dignan (2006) note there is no sense of 'penal crisis' in the country despite the record numbers in prison. However, with overcrowding many of the positive features have been undermined. The proportion of inmates in education or on work programmes has gradually declined over the last number of years with closures in prison education courses, library hours, horticulture, nurseries and other employment programmes (Newbold 2007; Office of the Ombudsman 2005). Access to families and release to work schemes has been increasingly restricted as prisons become more security-minded (Workman 2008: 10)	20
23	Size of institutions	Literature	New Zealand has a relatively progressive tradition in the prison system in that nearly half of all inmates are housed in small, modern prisons with open, minimum security conditions (Newbold 2007). Newer prisons seem to be larger in size, however, with a capacity of circa 600 places.	10
24	Overcrowding	Literature	'Prisons in NZ have regularly operated at full capacity over recent years. Muster increases have resulted in prisoners being moved to unsuitable cells in police stations and court houses' (Stanley 2009: 1). Double bunking has been introduced in some prisons since the government brokered a deal with prison staff in January 2006 to allow inmates to be housed two to a cell.	30
25	Medical services and food	Literature	Generally good, although Stanley (2009) writes that the right to health has been relegated as growing numbers cannot access therapy, drug/alcohol programmes or general health care in a timely manner (if, sometimes, at all).	20
26	Prison deaths	NZ Dept of Correct-ions annual reports	The numbers of unnatural deaths have remained fairly constant in recent years, averaging approximately 6–8 per annum.	20
27	Rehabilitation	Literature/ interviews	The Department of Corrections remains committed to rehabilitation and has implemented a range of programmes based on the Canadian 'what works' model. However, there has been criticism of the lack of meaningful activity for prisoners, the shortage of drug/alcohol programmes and restricted access to rehabilitative programmes in general (Office of the Ombudsman 2005).	20
			OPS=20 Overcrowding presents a serious challenge to the more progressive tradition in New Zealand's penal system and attitudes to prisoners have hardened in recent decades.	

Table 7.3 ***Concluded***

#	Variable Name	Source	Result	Score
			Index F: Post-release control	
28	Sex/drug offender notification schemes	Literature/ legislation	New Zealand does not have a sex offender register, although a private member's bill has been under consideration by Parliament since 2003 and unofficial versions are maintained by the Sensible Sentencing Trust (SST).	10
29	Shaming schemes	Literature/ legislation	Official schemes do not exist. However, rhetoric around the right of ex-offenders is harsh: offenders are not understood to have served their debt to society in prison. For example, the Prisoners and Victims Claims Act 2005 makes it clear that victims will continue to lay claim to restitution for a period of six years following release. Further, informal practices have a highly stigmatising effect, e.g. shopkeepers displaying pictures of local 'undesirables' in their windows and the distribution of flyers by the police warning local residents about the release of offenders into the community (Pratt 2008c).	20
30	Post-release supervision	Literature/ interviews/ legislation	The incapacitative sentence of preventive detention (PD) has undergone a major revival over the period (Meek 1995). In particular, the recent Sentencing Act 2002 significantly extended its scope to include a wider range of qualifying sexual and violent offending, such as conspiracy to murder, aggravated robbery, and kidnapping. A record of previous serious sexual or violent offending is no longer required. The 2002 changes have resulted in a significant increase in the number of sentences of preventive detention imposed (Hurd 2008). For child sex offenders not sentenced to PD, extended supervision orders (ESOs) are available to the courts since 2004. They provide for monitoring for up to 10 years following release from prison.	30
31	Reintegrat-ion	Literature/ interviews	Reintegration into the community has been the focus of renewed efforts by the Department of Corrections in recent years (Rethinking Crime and Punishment 2009) but has probably been neglected since the introduction of Integrated Offender Management in the mid 1990s (McCarthy 2006).	20

32	Expunge-ment of criminal records	Literature/ legislation	The Criminal Records (Clean Slate) Act 2004 allows only those offenders who did not receive a sentence of imprisonment to expunge their records. This can be compared to the Penal Review Group's recommendation in the 1980s that all offenders should be able to benefit from it (Kilcommins et al. 2004: 198).	30
			OPS=22 The jurisdiction's increasing emphasis on public safety at the 'back-end' of the criminal justice system is evident and this is clearly reflected in its stringent expungement laws.	
			Index G: Death penalty	
33	Date of abolition	Literature/ legislation	The death penalty was suspended from 1935 to 1950, restored again and then abolished for murder in 1961. It was removed for all offences in 1989.	10
34	Date of last execution	Literature	The last execution was carried out in 1957.	10
			OPS=10	
OPS (All Indices)=16.7			*Overall Conclusions*: A 'new punitiveness' is apparent in New Zealand in some respects, not just in relation increased imprisonment rates and longer sentences but in the tougher and increasingly exclusionary approach taken to prisoners and ex-offenders and the increasingly stringent post-release controls. However, this should be considered against progressive aspects of the system, such as the youth justice system and strong procedural protections afforded to defendants.	

Discussion: Is More Better?

It is notable that out of a maximum possible overall score of 30 all the countries obtained mean OPS scores below the moderate punitiveness level of 20. The results also clustered within a relatively narrow range: Scotland received the most favourable mean OPS at 15 points, Ireland scored 15.8 points and New Zealand 16.7 points. While the suggestion that Scotland may have resisted more punitive trends is far from new (McAra 1999, 2008) the homogeneity implied by the results is surprising given the suggestion in the research to date of a mild penal climate in Ireland (Kilcommins et al.2004) and an increasingly populist tone in New Zealand (Pratt and Clark 2005; Pratt 2007).

The key to understanding this is what Kutateladze (2009) refers to as the 'multi-level' and 'contradictory' nature of punitiveness or, more prosaically, the fact that all three countries possess both exacerbating and ameliorating features. These aggravating and mitigating features tend to cancel each other out as the level of aggregation increases. For example, New Zealand experienced significant increases in its prison population (Index C) and has introduced stringent measures to control serious offenders (Index F) although this can be considered against its progressive system of youth justice and strong procedural protections (Indices B and D). Indeed, on Index B New Zealand obtained the lowest scores of the three jurisdictions. This cancelling out effect is also observable in Ireland which attained its highest punitiveness scores in relation to two indices (C and E) and relatively low scores on the remainder. Scotland is more consistent in its scores across the six indices, although even in this jurisdiction scores for Indices E and F were higher than those for the other indices.

It is arguable that this finding *alone* highlights the importance of examining punitiveness multidimensionally. At least two of the states involved in the study may be regarded as relatively punitive on some indices of punitiveness and relatively lenient on certain others. However, the point may be further illustrated by comparing the results from the MDT with a multidimensional test with a more restricted number of variables. Tonry's (2007) multi-item test (discussed in Chapter 1) was selected for this purpose given that it currently represents one of the most sophisticated (if not holistic) instruments by which one can measure punitiveness. Using data from the MDT test provided in Tables 7.1–7.3 above, overall punitiveness scores (OPSs) for the three jurisdictions were obtained by totalling the scores obtained on the equivalent variable number in the MDT and dividing by the sum of the variables in Tonry's test (n=15). Counting variables more than once was avoided to prevent distortion of the score (Gordon, 1989). Also, for certain variables no data were available in the three jurisdictions and one variable (juvenile waiver to adult court) was difficult to apply outside North American jurisdictions such as the US and Canada. The results of the exercise are shown in Table 7.4.

Table 7.4 Punitiveness in Ireland, Scotland and New Zealand 2006 as measured by Tonry's (2007) indices (n=15)

Tonry's measures of punitiveness	Equivalent variable number of MDT	Score Ireland	Score Scotland	Score NZ
Policies:				
1. Capital punishment	33, 34	10, 10	10,10	10,10
2. Mandatory minimum sentence laws	12	20	10	10
3. Laws increasing sentence length	16	30	20	30
4. Pretrial/preventive detention	11	20	20	30
5. Prison alternatives	13, 20	10, 10	10, 10	10, 10
6. Juvenile waiver to adult courts	No equivalent	–	–	–
7. Weakened procedural protections	7–10	10, 10, 10, 20	20, 10, 10, 20	10, 10, 10, 10
Practices:				
1. Patterns of use of policies 1–7	Captured by above listed variables	–	–	–
2. Adult prison population and admission rates over time	14, 15	30, 20	20, 10	20, 20
a. Disaggregated for pretrial and sentenced prisoners	14	As above	As above	As above
b. Disaggregated by offence for sentence lengths and admission rates	Information not available for individual offences. Data available for violent and property crime in variable 17	20	20	20
3. Juvenile institutional population and admission rates over time	21 (population rates only)	10	10	10
a. Disaggregated for pretrial and sentenced juvenile offenders	Information not available	–	–	–
b. Disaggregated by offence for sentence lengths and admission rates	Information not available	–	–	–
Procedures: Patterns of use of procedural protections	Captured by 7–10	Already included	Already included	Already included
	OPS (14 variables)	**16**	**14**	**14.7**

Despite this test being significantly more refined than many of the current offerings, the results arguably underestimate New Zealand's punitiveness through the omission of certain important categories for the measurement of the concept. On Tonry's test Scotland retains its place as the least punitive state (score of 14) while New Zealand (14.7) is replaced by Ireland as the most punitive jurisdiction (16). Given that Tonry's test appears to map quite neatly onto Indices B (Procedural Protections), C (Imprisonment), D (Juvenile Justice) and G (Death Penalty), it is likely that differences in the overall scores obtained in the two tests can be attributed to the broader ambit of the MDT. The MDT test includes scores for Indices A (Policing), E (Prison Conditions) and F (Post-Release Controls), all incidentally indices on which New Zealand scored 20 or more (the score for moderate punitiveness). Contrariwise, Ireland's punitiveness is most likely overestimated in Tonry's test as it does not measure variables relating to Indices A and F, indices on which it obtained two of its lowest scores. Given the coexistence of policies which can be described as both punitive and lenient in the same jurisdiction and high levels of cross-sectoral variation, it would appear that the MDT is better at capturing this complexity.

Limitations of the MDT

It is also important to acknowledge the disadvantages associated with the multidimensional scale as applied above. First, as seen in its application to Ireland, Scotland and New Zealand an unexpected consequence of expanding the number of variables is that there is a 'cancelling out' effect as the level of aggregation increases. Researchers must remain alive to this issue both in determining the optimal number of variables and also in interpreting their results. Disaggregating the scores by index may go a long way towards identifying these effects and may also reveal some interesting nuances in the data. Thus, while the results at a certain level of aggregation suggest homogeneity, further analysis reveals that the three countries have pursued quite different criminal justice policies over the period. This is illustrated in Figure 7.1 which shows the number of indices in each of the countries with an OPS of 20 (moderate punitiveness) or above. (The maximum number of indices shown in the chart is six rather than seven as all states achieved the lowest possible score of 10 on Index G (death penalty)).

Despite the similar final scores achieved by Ireland and New Zealand in the multidimensional test (15.8 and 16.7 respectively), the differences in the distribution of moderate-high scores across the indices is suggestive of a more punitive approach gaining momentum across a number of different sectors of New Zealand's criminal justice system. This interpretation of the MDT scores paints a picture more in line with suggestions in the literature of a highly punitive climate in New Zealand over the period (Pratt and Clark 2005; Pratt 2006, 2007)

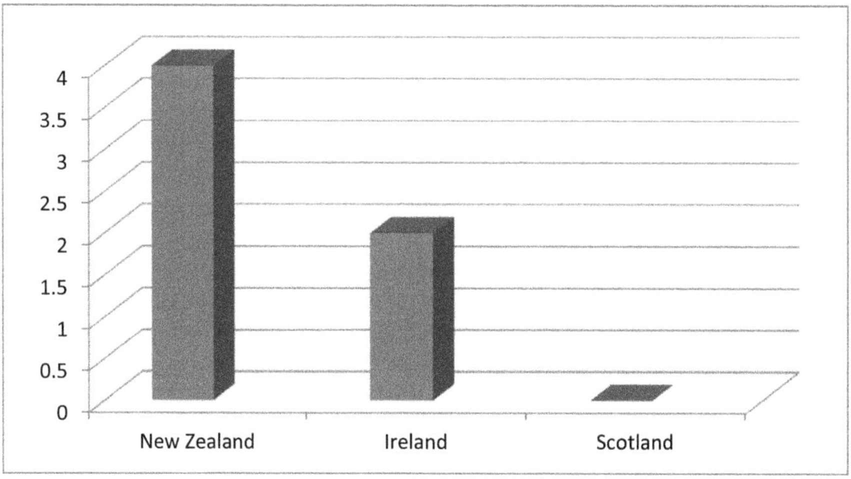

Figure 7.1 Number of indices with an OPS of 20 or above in Ireland, Scotland and New Zealand

and a more 'diluted' culture of control in Ireland (Kilcommins et al. 2004). Jurisdictions may ultimately reach similar endpoints by very different paths, displaying what Gordon (1989) has termed different 'national signatures'. On the other hand, the fact that Scotland failed to attain a score of above 20 in relation to any of the indices serves to reinforce its position as the least punitive state. The emphasis which researchers may choose to place on either interpretation (aggregated/disaggregated) in many ways returns us to questions already posed in Chapter 6 about the relative merits of aggregate scores versus measures which avoid such aggregation across dimensions. Can relatively moderate sentencing, for example, 'offset' heavy-handed policing practices? Can a lenient youth justice system 'compensate' for a more punitive adult system? The answer begs difficult theoretical questions relating to the nature of the underlying relationships between the variables. As discussed in previous chapters, it has been argued that to omit consideration of the experiences of the suspect/offender at the front end of the system would overlook the importance of procedures as *de facto* punishments, their symbolism and their attractiveness to policymakers. Leading on from this latter point, an additional consideration which certainly applies to the measurement of punitiveness is the policy implications attendant on a one-dimensional or multidimensional assessment. Given that legislative and policy measures are increasingly directed across the criminal justice system *as a whole* (e.g. Swedish Roadmap on Procedural Rights) it would appear imprudent to overlook such dimensions when testing punitiveness.

From a more technical perspective, it is of course possible to run statistical tests in order to test for relationships between the variables. In a study incorporating a bigger dataset (i.e. more jurisdictions)[1] the relationship between the variables can be tested using correlation analysis or factor analysis. In his research, Kutateladze (2009) used correlations testing to show the weak to moderate relationship between the variables, consistent with his argument that states vary in the ways in which they can be punitive. Gordon (1989), on the other hand, used factor analysis to determine which variables load onto a single factor, such as custody or symbolic punishment (e.g. death penalty), thus demonstrating the different preferences exhibited by individual states. In the instant case – reflecting once again the complex nature of the phenomenon under discussion–what may be said is that a more complete understanding of developments in the three jurisdictions can be achieved by approaching the issue from a variety of different perspectives. Important insights may be gained from *both* aggregated scores and disaggregated scores by index in order to capture the dynamic of differences across the indices.

A second limitation concerns the objectivity of selecting the criteria in an exercise such as this. This is a valid criticism and it is important for researchers to be as transparent as possible in providing the theoretical justification for the inclusion of each variable and the methods by which data were obtained. Clearly accounts of penal change can never illuminate 'the whole stage' (Daems 2008: 249) and variables will always be found which militate for and against the punitiveness of a particular state. This does not prevent a serious attempt being made at a more comprehensive delimitation of the punitiveness concept, however.

Another important limitation concerns the manner of determining the scores for each variable. In the instant research, scores were allocated to each jurisdiction based on the researcher's review of primary and secondary data sources at a given point in time (2006), having regard to the degree of change which had occurred over a 30-year period. Arguably this was the best method available given the restricted number of countries or observations involved and the aim of investigating a longitudinal or 'new' punitiveness rather than any pre-existing differences between nations. The inclusion of several more countries or states, however, opens up several possibilities in this regard. Kutateladze (2009), for example, was able to rank the 50 US states included in his study from least to most punitive according to the data relevant to each variable. He then scored each state from 0 to 4 by organising the states into quintiles (10 states per quintile) ranging from least (0) to most punitive (4). An alternative method which could be explored by researchers in this field is to attribute a punitiveness score to each jurisdiction *relative to* certain widely regarded punitive or non-punitive states (such as Texas or one of the Nordic states). This method may prove particularly useful in

1 Consideration was given in the instant research to carrying out inferential statistics testing to examine whether changes in penal trends in, for example, the 1990s and 2000s represent significant changes from previous decades. However, following advice from the Statistics Advice Unit in Dublin Institute of Technology relating to the inappropriateness of carrying out such tests on longitudinal whole population data I decided against this course of action.

conducting purely comparative rather than historical analyses of punitiveness in a given grouping of states, although it does pose the problem of identifying states which are uniformly punitive across all dimensions.

Conclusion

Despite the quantity of ink spilled on the punitive turn, issues concerning its definition and measurement remain largely under-examined in the mainstream literature to date (Matthews 2005). In light of the dearth of analytical work on this issue, this chapter has sought to refocus attention on the best ways in which to measure punitiveness and has argued for the application of both multidimensional tests and disaggregated scores by index. As discussed above, all three countries under examination return low-moderate scores on the multidimensional test, despite their very different depictions in the literature. This conclusion is, however, somewhat tempered by the differences revealed in the distribution of moderate-high punitiveness scores across the six indices. Viewed in this light, New Zealand looks considerably more punitive than the other two jurisdictions, Ireland more moderate and Scotland consistently mild across most of the sectors in its criminal justice system. The next chapter moves away from the *explananda* to consider the factors which may explain these differences.

Chapter 8
Explaining Differences

Introduction

The findings in the previous chapters raise important questions about the extent to which a *new* punitiveness or culture of control has in fact taken hold in the three jurisdictions in question. It has been seen that the overall punitiveness scores returned for each country on the application of the MDT indicate a surprising homogeneity, but also that New Zealand's moderate scores conceal increases in punitiveness across more sectors of the criminal justice system than the other jurisdictions. We have also seen in Chapters 5 and 6 that there is an important qualitative difference in the manner in which penal politics is conducted in New Zealand. Criminal justice has achieved a different level of embeddedness in New Zealand such that crime is regularly used as a wedge issue by politicians appealing to all sectors of the electorate. While the MDT scores suggest that punitive rhetoric has not become a reality in *all* of the sectors of New Zealand's criminal justice system (reasons behind the 'back-end' direction of crime control developments have been discussed in Chapter 6), the character of the penal discourse there nevertheless merits explanation. The particular 'ethnic toxicity' and punitive impact on indigenous communities of increases in imprisonment rates set it further apart from its two comparators.

Tensions in specifying the *explananda* are also evident within the other two jurisdictions. In many ways it is difficult to identify determinants which explain, for example, *both* the significant increases in imprisonment rates in Ireland *and* the lesser emphasis on risk and managerialism. Similar comments can also be made about paradoxical trends within the Scottish penal system (how does one explain a penal field which simultaneously veers towards convergence and divergence?), yet the findings in the previous two chapters suggest an overall more positive assessment of Scottish punitiveness than a simple comparative view affords. In the section below, explanatory factors identified by interviewees are discussed using Tonry's (2007) framework of risk, protective and non-factors (discussed in Chapter 2). In the final section, an attempt is made to draw together these different factors in a comprehensive model for future comparative research.

Risk Factors

It will be recalled that Tonry defined risk and protective factors as characteristics which made punitiveness more or less likely. These factors should not therefore be viewed as deterministic but rather as dynamic and probabilistic. The predominant risk factors emerging from the interviews fell into four main categories relating to (i) political structures and practices, (ii) the role of the expert and evidence-based policy, (iii) the history of race relations and (iv) national media characteristics. Other, less prominent risk factors (such as terrorism and its impact on front-end measures) have been discussed in Chapter 6.

Political Structures and Practices

We saw in Chapter 2 that the explanatory power which a country's political institutional arrangements hold for criminal justice policy is slowly gaining recognition in the criminological literature. In particular, recent work by Lacey (2008) and Green (2007, 2008, 2009) highlights Lijphart's dichotomy between 'consensus' and 'majoritarian' or 'conflict' democracies as a useful heuristic device in explaining a country's propensity to penal populism. The three countries in issue provide ample scope for testing theories concerning the effects of political culture on criminal justice policy given their different criminal justice profiles yet ostensibly homogeneous political systems. All three countries can be described as liberal market economies with minimal welfare states, both factors that have been linked with harsher penal policies in the comparative literature (Cavadino and Dignan 2006; Lacey 2008). Further, and most significantly for present purposes, all three can be characterised as traditional conflict democracies that have moved at some point in their history from a first-past-the-post system of voting to a system of proportional representation (PR) in which coalition government is now the norm.[1] Despite sharing certain structural (that is, electoral) features of the consensus model, however, the data revealed by the study below serve to problematise rather than confirm an understanding of political culture based solely on Lijphart's ideal types.

The limits of Lijphart's model In this regard, the first point to be noted is that Ireland does not fit comfortably within the ideal types identified by Lijphart. The unique feature of the Irish system of PR (proportional representation by single transferable vote) is that candidates of one party can be elected on the transfers of votes for other parties and this is believed to reduce partisanship and enhance the prospect of coalition government. Yet it was not until 1989 that the largest political party, Fianna Fáil, abandoned its traditional reluctance to form coalition governments. Even with this development, the high level of control wielded by Irish governments over

---

1 It should be noted that Ireland introduced proportional representation upon gaining independence in 1922, whereas Scotland and New Zealand have moved to PR electoral arrangements more recently, in 1998 and 1993 respectively. It is acknowledged that it may be difficult to definitively place the case studies into either the consensus or the majoritarian category. See, for example, Bulsara and Kissane (2009) on the difficulty of categorising Ireland. Indeed, Lappi-Seppälä (2008) treats all three as majoritarian democracies in his statistical analysis of imprisonment rates in consensus and majoritarian democracies.

parliamentary business (Döring and Hallerberg 2004) left little room for consensual politics because governments saw little need to negotiate with the opposition (MacCarthaigh 2007). This may be partly explained by the historical character of the parties: an adversarial 'Fianna Fáil versus the rest' dynamic has permeated Irish politics since independence (MacCarthaigh 2005: 62).

Brief comparison of the operation of the PR systems in New Zealand and Scotland, though strikingly similar in nature,[2] also yields very different results in terms of its impact on criminal justice policy. Only in Scotland has this brought about a more cooperative system of parliamentary politics, with the need to bring other parties along in the policymaking process sometimes acting as a brake on penal excess. Several Scottish interviewees referred to the composition of post-devolution governments as relevant in mitigating the effects of tougher policies pursued by the Scottish Labour Party. More specifically, one interviewee who had direct involvement with the policymaking process at the time noted that the Liberal Democrat party had managed to 'water down' Labour Party proposals relating to antisocial behaviour orders (ASBOs), the automatic retention of DNA from all crime suspects and the law on double jeopardy. In New Zealand, on the other hand, the new political arrangements have had the paradoxical effect of an increased politicisation of criminal justice issues (Pratt 2007, 2009). As discussed in Chapter 5, crime has been intensively politicised in the last decade and is now used as a 'wedge issue' by small political parties in New Zealand such as New Zealand First and ACT. Indeed, it is not uncommon for 'law and order' policies to form part of coalition agreements with larger parties.

In seeking to explain this, the influence of institutional structures clearly cannot be ignored. Several features of New Zealand's constitutional and political framework were highlighted by interviewees as relevant in this regard, including the unitary and centralised nature of the political system (the government and bureaucracy are all in Wellington), the three-year election cycle and the unicameral system of government. As one interviewee put it, 'there's no checks and balances around [legislation] so that is a sort of difference between some other larger democracies I suppose that have much more process' (NZ interviewee #7, p. 19). Though not mentioned by respondents, the absence of a written Constitution and a strong judiciary may also be added to this list (Barker and McLeay 2000).

In Scotland, one of the institutional factors that may have had a protective influence on the policymaking process is the committee system, which forms a central element of the Scottish legislative process and which is stronger than the equivalent systems in Ireland and New Zealand (Barker and McLeay 2000; MacCarthaigh 2005). Stronger parliamentary control of the political process is conducive to greater deliberation of justice policies and greater regard for evidence-led policy. Questioned on the role of evidence in Scottish justice policy, one

2 In Scotland, under the Scotland Act 1998 members of the Scottish Parliament are elected using a very similar system to the New Zealand system of mixed member proportional (MMP), which is known locally as the additional member system (AMS).

former policymaker described evidence-based legislation as 'one of the founding principles of the Parliament'; with legislation based on evidence 'expected' by the committees (Scottish interviewee #5, p. 16). Clearly, electoral arrangements such as PR may perform differently even in similar political cultures depending on their interaction with other institutional factors.

Political culture and trust While the institutional and parliamentary arrangements in place in the three countries seem to interact strongly with other structural factors such as national electoral arrangements, the interviews revealed another interesting aspect of New Zealand political culture which is suggestive of a more Weberian explanation. The absence amongst New Zealanders of what may be termed 'vertical' or 'institutional' trust in the state (Lappi-Seppälä 2008), revealed itself to be an important one in explaining the 'punitive turn' in New Zealand's penal policy. This strong cultural distrust of the state can be traced back to the radical changes in economic policy which were introduced by the Labour government in 1984. This radical policy shift (known as 'Rogernomics' after the Finance Minister at the time) took place, it should be stressed, without a mandate from the electorate. Pratt and Clark (2005) argue that the subsequent sense of disillusionment with the democratic process, combined with growing feelings of insecurity engendered by the economic and social reforms of the 1980s, are significant factors in explaining the formation of extra parliamentary groups such as the Sensible Sentencing Trust around the crime issue. While they also include in their analysis other characteristics usually associated with populist punitiveness, such as a decline in deference and the rise of the victims' movement, it is these local contingencies which they view as particularly important in the New Zealand context.

Data from the interviews bear out Pratt and Clark's (2005) analysis. As one respondent stated quite plainly, 'we don't trust in our bureaucracy' (NZ Interviewee #8, p. 12). An interview with one of the key victims' groups also revealed a deep suspicion of politicians and their motives and an even greater distrust of civil servants. This has manifested itself in routinised practices which bypass the state legislature. In common with populist measures in California and elsewhere, initiative processes such as referendums have served as critical statements against the state (Barker 2006). Most notably, one of the four Citizens Initiated Referendums (CIRs) introduced since 1996 sought to reduce the number of MPs from 120 to 99 with the stated purpose being to improve MPs parliamentary behaviour (Pratt and Clark 2005). The suggestion that public confidence in government plays an important role in shaping a country's political culture derives further support from social survey data on citizens' confidence and trust in political institutions collected in various sweeps of the World Values Survey (Lappi-Seppälä 2008). In the 1998/99 sweep the New Zealand results compared unfavourably with the two other jurisdictions as illustrated in Table 8.1 below (note: data specific to Scotland were not available so results for Great Britain are used as a proxy).

Table 8.1 Data on confidence in political institutions in New Zealand 1998/1999

	Ireland	Scotland (Great Britain)	New Zealand
Very little/no confidence in parliament	55	58	85
Very little/no confidence in civil service	42	54	71

Source: Four Wave World Values Survey/European Values Survey Official Integrated Dataset, www.worldvaluesurvey.org.

National culture and political culture The problems engendered by the binary categories in Lacey and Green's model are further compounded by the divorcing of political culture from underlying cultural values (Pratt 2009). In line with arguments advanced by several commentators discussed in Chapter 2 (Savelsberg 2002; Melossi 2001), it was to local differences that interviewees most often returned in their discussions. While policy transfer was clearly in evidence, the interview data presented below are suggestive of national and cultural differences remaining to the fore of the minds of the respondents.

Ireland. Interestingly, two of the Irish policymakers spoken with viewed the US and even recent criminal justice policies adopted in England and Wales as negative and extreme. This is evidenced by the following extract from an interview with a former senior policymaker who (while acknowledging the special influence of English criminal justice policy in Ireland) described the difficulties in implementing new managerialist techniques in an Irish context:

> The Blairite stuff of targets and quotas … maybe it's one way of doing it but it's repugnant to the Irish psyche … I mean the Irish media would be horrified if they saw a circular saying you are to catch, you are to increase your detection rate for burglars by 18% … they'd say what kind of nut decided that. (Irish interviewee #8, p. 8)

It is difficult to capture precisely the cultural values referred to by the interviewee but it is likely closely allied to the inherent conservativeness of politics in Ireland and, more generally, what O'Toole (2009: 215) describes as the 'anarchic attitude [of the Irish] to law and morality'. The less deferential approach taken by Irish people to authority, perhaps an overhang from colonial days, was cited by many interviewees as a critical factor in understanding the way in which criminal justice was done in Ireland. One referred to the cultural preference Irish people often exhibit for resolving matters informally, without the involvement of the formal criminal justice system; another suggested that it may speak to elements of a Catholic indulgentist tradition. Several respondents mentioned the tradition of Gardaí speaking up for criminal defendants at the sentencing stage or, in the past, withdrawing summary prosecutions in the District Court (this practice has since been discontinued). Even tacit acknowledgement from a Garda of the difficulties that a defendant has faced in his/her life to date lends an important ring of authenticity to a plea in mitigation, so this is not without practical significance. Moreover, Gardaí usually adopt a reasonable attitude in their dealings with defence solicitors and barristers and, as one interviewee noted, 'there isn't such a black and white approach to everything' (Irish interviewee #3, p. 4).

A note of caution must be sounded here lest we should fall prey to a one-dimensional, simplistic view of Irish informalism as something that is 'good', mitigating the effects of more punitive policies, which are 'bad' (see, further, Nelken 2006). It is perhaps the subject of another discussion whether this cultural willingness to bend the rules (even those which are not viewed as sensible or humane) can correctly be described as the country's 'saving grace' (Irish interviewee #4, p. 7). Suffice it to note for present purposes that this broader informality of approach operated on the minds of policymakers too.

Scotland. Cultural explanations also appeared to hold considerable purchase with Scottish interviewees. Strikingly, all of the respondents referenced Scottish civic culture, with its values of fairness, welfare and community support, at some point during the interview. Indeed, one former policymaker described it as something that united all Scots and transcends party loyalties (Scottish interviewee #5, p. 10). This culture holds important implications for criminal justice policy, in that more punitive, exclusionary policies (what Garland would term the 'criminologies of the other') may clash with deeply held Scottish traditions and beliefs. Rehabilitative policies that ultimately seek to reintegrate offenders into the community carry an instinctive attraction or elective affinity with Scottish civic culture in a manner that more punitive repertoires did not. This was eloquently explained by one senior policymaker in the following terms:

> [Social democracy]...isn't political in Scotland. It's as much based upon Presbyterianism or indeed Calvinism. It's part of the egalitarian interest of Scotland: 'we're all Jock Tamson's bairns'; these are our kids. These kids who are misbehaving, there's some right bad people who have to go to prison ... but the rest of them, they're our laddies ... they're our folk. We can't send them to the colonies, they don't come from somewhere else, they're our people. (Scottish interviewee #9, p. 3)

The same policymaker went on to explain how policies incorporating 'shaming techniques' were rejected in recent years as incompatible with Scottish cultural sensibilities. The roots of this culture, as with Ireland, are difficult to locate but may be related to the higher levels of poverty in certain Scottish cities such as Glasgow, its history of trade unionism and leftist politics or indeed democratic traditions within the Church. It may also be connected to the egalitarian tradition as reflected in the poetry of Robert Burns, supposedly the originator of the phrase cited by the interviewee above 'we're all Jock Tamson's bairns' – meaning we're all God's children.

Given the conservative nature of the Scottish criminal justice system (also strongly referenced by interviewees) there is small doubt that choices made by policymakers continue to be circumscribed by local cultural influences. As recently as 2003, Scotland had six Scottish Socialist Party MSPs, something which speaks to the distinctiveness of Scottish political values and which should not be discounted in any comparative exercise. This is not to suggest, however, that on other occasions 'harsher' policies do not win out against prevailing civic cultural values. Scotland remains particularly vulnerable to policy transfer from England given the shared border, media outlets, political parties and the fact that significant areas of criminal justice policy (terrorism, drugs and firearms) are reserved to Westminster. Interviewees acknowledged the special place occupied by England in this regard (as one interviewee put it, 'I think the international factor *is* England', Scottish interviewee #3, p. 8) but also viewed its influence as somewhat contingent upon the political party holding power. Elite networking between the Labour Party in Scotland and England was viewed as important in the transfer of policy north of the border in the early 2000s, whereas the Scottish National Party was now understood to be actively forging a different path in penal policy.

New Zealand. Turning now to New Zealand, a cultural strain to conformity was referenced in the interviews reflecting the arguments of Pratt (2006) and others on the 'perfect society' (see further Chapter 5). One respondent put this quite baldly: 'it's a hospitable, friendly place provided you conform … conformity is valued and nonconformity is not' (New Zealand interviewee #9, p. 2). There was a suggestion in the interviews that policymakers, together with other stakeholders, were not unaware of this cultural attachment to strict law enforcement, raising the possibility that this may (consciously or unconsciously) exert an influence on political decision-making. One former senior policymaker, for example, opined: 'New Zealanders are to some degree the Prussians of the South Pacific, you know; they do want to have law enforced, they take it very seriously' (New Zealand interviewee #3, p. 5).

Linked with this desire for conformity is an anti-intellectual strain to New Zealand culture, which was referred to by five of the nine respondents interviewed, including those within the administration itself. (None of the interviewees in Ireland and Scotland expressed a similar view concerning their own jurisdiction). In New Zealand, the idealised image of a New Zealander as someone who engages in manual labour and worships sports is sometimes encapsulated in the phrase 'Number 8 wire mentality', meaning that a New Zealander can make or fix anything with basic or everyday materials, such as Number 8 fencing wire. Debate and flowery language were therefore seen as demonstrations of elitism and as alien to the New Zealand tradition of egalitarianism (New Zealand interviewee #5, p. 2). It is interesting to note how this general suspicion of experts also appeared to extend to distrust of their own bureaucracy. Interviews with victims' groups that had been prominent in campaigning for harsher policies revealed a strong distrust of bureaucrats, who were seen as 'undermining' political successes in this area.

The data discussed above do little to disturb the argument advanced by Lacey and Green in relation to the key role played by political culture in the determination of criminal justice policy. In line with the analysis, however, questions may be raised as to the usefulness of political culture *as defined by Lijphart* (1999) and subsequently relied on by Lacey and others in explaining differences in a state's level of punitiveness. Ireland's proportional representation election system and strong executive do not fit easily into Lijphart's typology. Moreover, the palpably different effects that very similar political structures had in all three comparator countries call into question the explanatory value of the majoritarian-consensus distinction and are suggestive of a number of other factors at play, including constitutional and other institutional arrangements, local culture and national psyche. In particular, the close relationship between national culture and political culture suggested by the interview data mirrors research in Lijphart's own discipline of political science that seriously questions the applicability of Lijphart's models in different cultural settings (Bormann 2010; Fortin 2008; Spinner 2007).

The Role of Public versus Expert Opinion

Another critical aspect of political culture which may impact upon national criminal justice policies is the level of deference afforded expert views in terms of both policymaking and policy implementation. Garland (2001) (among others: Loader 2006; Ryan 2005) argues that criminal justice professionals, like welfare professionals, have increasingly had their expertise called into question as crime has become more politicised. While this may (broadly speaking) apply to England and Wales and the US, striking differences can be observed between these jurisdictions and the more expert-led approach adopted in many continental Western European states. Savelsberg's (1999) arguments concerning the role played by attitudes towards professional elites in explaining US and German differences will be recalled from Chapter 2. Similarly, Snacken (2007), Levy (2007), Roché (2007) and Lappi-Seppälä (2007) all view continued resort to independent expert advice in the media and politics in Belgium, France and the Scandinavian countries respectively as an important countervailing force in resisting the 'punitive turn'. As discussed in relation to the broader issue of political culture above, however, national specificities often defy precise categorisation. Resonances of Garland's arguments can be found in discussions with New Zealand policymakers but a distinct form of 'pragmatism' was in evidence in Scotland and Ireland which cannot be described as either 'elite' or 'populist'.

In New Zealand, it would appear that the influence wielded by civil servants has declined significantly in recent years and particularly since the 1999 referendum on crime. This appeared to be confirmed by the mandarins themselves when questioned about their role. Senior civil servants were emphatic that they did endeavour to base policy on analysis and evidence (the quality of which had improved over the years) but also acknowledged that the impetus for legislation was often a political desire to reassure the public. In this scenario, their role was often confined to 'damage limitation' of ostensibly weak and ill-informed policies:

> [First interviewee] Generally they [reforms] are politically driven and officials try and limit the damage; you try and make them as robust and limited as you can, as is politically acceptable.
>
> [Second interviewee] Yeah, I mean the reality is that there would be a political objective to create something, and our advice would be to say, well you don't want to do it like you said, this is how it would fit into the sentencing regime, here's the evidence which shows it should be shaped in this particular way and target these particular types of people or offences...
>
> [First interviewee] Ministers have generally been receptive to that.
>
> [...]
>
> [First interviewee] You don't start with going to the Minister saying this is our problem, this is our solution. The reality, it's ... they want to do something and ... you give them a proposal that will achieve what they are after. (NZ Interviewees #7 (group interview), p. 18)

If the New Zealand policymaking style has shifted in a more 'populist' direction then the more 'pragmatic' Irish political culture has remained fairly static. Unlike the situation which obtained in England in the post war decades, it is doubtful whether an elitist or even a research-led culture ever really held sway in the Department of Justice. Politicians preferred to reach their own 'common sense' conclusions on criminal justice matters without regard to evidence or even to the most rudimentary information about crime or imprisonment. As O'Donnell (2004) has written of the post-1996 decision to quadruple the number of prison cells in the state, this decision was made for purely political motives on the basis of a 'back of the envelope' calculation. Interviews with three persons who were currently or formerly involved in the policymaking process revealed that it would be most unusual to consult experts or commission research to guide policy development. Nor – importantly – did they see the need. One former senior policymaker candidly observed that his approach and, in his opinion, the approach taken by others, to criminal justice policymaking was 'most unintellectual'. He went on to describe the manner in which decisions were arrived at in the Department:

> This may sound shocking to you but there's an awful lot of *The Irish Times* level of blather on criminality. For example, to some extent you have to ask a simple question ... 'whether fingerprints should be destroyed after a year?'. Endless academics and lawyers could stand up and make speeches about the implications of doing or not doing it but to me it's just a matter of judgment.

> [CH: You take a more pragmatic approach?]
>
> Yes, not more reactive but I would look at it and say does that make sense …
>
> [CH: Would you say that is typical of the way most Minister of Justices have approached the issue?]
>
> I would yes.

Another former policymaker interviewed showed a similar impatience with the research and the consultative process, preferring instead to canvass the views of lawyer friends and colleagues within their political party. For them, criminal justice policy was a political matter, something to be determined by the 'the mood of society' (Irish interviewee #8, p. 3). The latter point is important in that these individuals showed a shrewd awareness of the *degree* of responsiveness necessary in order to maintain their legitimacy in the eyes of the public. Policymakers interviewed were keenly aware of the occasional need for 'symbol-driven' legislation which demonstrated to the public that the problem was being taken seriously. Speaking of the mandatory 10 year sentence for drugs, a piece of legislation which was pledged by Fianna Fáil in the wake of the Guerin and McCabe murders, one policymaker admitted it was unlikely to work on the basis that it had been presented to the electorate:

> One of the purposes of the legislation is to say, we the people think this is good, or this is bad, or this is more serious than that. So it's kind of a public affirmation that we think drug dealing is very bad and it's so bad we think it deserves a mandatory sentence. It is a kind of statement of things; it has a potential deterrent effect. But you don't deter people … most people involved, they are young, they are already on drugs, there is a good chance they'll get shot before they are 25. So the idea of sentencing and jail isn't a major deterrent… (Irish interviewee #3, p. 15)

The same 'pragmatism' is observable to a degree in post-devolutionary Scotland with MSPs quick to legislate in response to high profile cases. Unlike Ireland, , this represented a change in policymaking style in Scotland given the influence which was formerly wielded by elite policy networks (McAra 1999, 2008). One senior policymaker noted that since devolution there may be a greater tendency towards a knee jerk response in Scotland '[with] politically charged issues, governments tend to legislate … and again sometimes these new interventions have come on the back of very difficult and tragic cases' (Scottish interviewee #5, p. 8). Similarly, another interviewee felt strongly that politicians in the new institutional framework were quick to respond to criminal issues: 'I think that is one of things that has actually characterised things post devolution, is that mostly criminal justice changes have been about reacting to specific things' (Scottish interviewee #3, p. 5). On the other hand, it was also clear that there is a greater regard for evidence in this jurisdiction than in Ireland. For example, one policymaker noted that Ministers had in the past invited several academics into the department to deliver briefings on criminal justice matters and, as noted above, the committee system acts as an important filter for legislation. Further, as discussed in Chapter 6 in relation to both Ireland and Scotland, there is a clear difference between reacting to events as they occur and more cynical attempts to politicise crime (Caplow and Simon 1999). Most of the Scottish policymakers declined to characterise their approach as 'populist' although when pressed some of the interviewees agreed that Labour's antisocial behaviour agenda launched in 2003 represented a clear attempt to 'buy off' the public.

The History of Race Relations

Race features prominently in explanations of punitiveness in the US. Wacquant (2005, 2009), for example, has written extensively of the prisonisation of the ghetto in the US and the way in which American criminal justice practices operate as a mechanism of social control over ethnic minorities (they form approximately 50 per cent of the prison population there). Similarly, Tonry (2007) identifies the politics of race, particularly the status anxiety which the civil rights movement engendered in whites, as one of the key factors driving the 'new punitiveness' in America and Newburn (2007) argues that the absence of race as a focal point of policy in Britain has lessened the impact of populist punitive politics there. Demographic homogeneity is also linked with more moderate penal climates in the Scandinavian countries and the growth of multiculturalism via migration is often linked with growing punitiveness in Western Europe (Downes 2008). Yet, critically, Lappi-Seppälä (2008, 2011) cautions against conclusions that demographic factors act as simple predictors of punishment. Based on his quantitative analysis of 15 countries he found that associations are much stronger and more systematic between imprisonment rates, beliefs and attitudes than between imprisonment rates and demographic factors alone, a finding which perhaps lends support to Wacquant/Tonry's 'status anxiety' hypothesis.

Clearly, questions of race take on a different character in post-colonial societies. Recent comparative work has been (rightly) criticised by Cuneen (2010) for its underplaying of the issue of race and colonialism/post-colonialism in the production of imprisonment rates. The significance of these crucial factors is perhaps best appreciated by those living in post-colonial societies with high indigenous imprisonment rates. Responding to a paper which I delivered at the Australian and New Zealand Criminology conference in 2008, an overwhelming number of delegates argued that colonial history and racial politics formed a large part of the explanation for New Zealand's high rate of imprisonment and that this aspect clearly set it apart from its two comparators. Certainly, there is little to compare New Zealand's sizeable indigenous Māori population (15 per cent of the general population) with Scottish and Irish racial minorities (2[3] and 4[4] per cent of the population respectively according to censuses in 2001 and 2006). Further, in both jurisdictions it cannot be said that the politics of race has been a central feature of the criminal justice landscape over the last number of decades.

The striking racial imbalance in the New Zealand penal system will be recalled from Chapter 5. Māoris comprised 17 per cent of sentenced receptions in 1976 and this leapt to 53 per cent in 2006. Against this background it is unsurprising that interviewees agreed with their fellow Oceanians about the importance of Māori/non-Māori relations in understanding the country's high use of imprisonment. Indeed, following Cuneen (2010), some were critical of existing cultural accounts of New Zealand's punishment practices which did not take this into sufficient account. Several respondents identified it as *the* most important issue in explaining New Zealand punitiveness. One senior civil servant, for example, put it succinctly: 'Māori are 16 per cent and imprisonment rates in non-Māori, is it 80 per 100,000, that's low and it's about 500 for Māori. *That's the story. I don't think there is much more to it than that* ' (New Zealand interviewee #7, p. 7). The suggestion is clearly that the punitive shift in New Zealand is racism and intolerance in (thin) disguise. Others spoke of the need to understand the history of colonisation in New Zealand, the destruction of cultural links to land and the Māori economic basis (New Zealand interviewee #8, p. 1).

Yet the above to some degree still begs the question of New Zealand's more punitive approach. The fact that Māori are disproportionately affected by the increase in punitiveness in New Zealand doesn't explain why this occurred in the first place, particularly in a country which prides itself on its comparatively better race relations (Australia is generally cited as the example *not* to follow). In seeking to understand the role of race relations in the country in contributing to its punitiveness, one respondent put forward an interesting theory combining Pratt's (2006) arguments on the intolerant nature of New Zealand society (arising out of a desire to protect 'paradise', see Chapter 5) with the effects of urbanisation and laws which disproportionately affect Māori:

> Should this quote be indented? the urban migration of Māori in the 1950s … people were frightened, didn't quite know what to do with these people, these Māoris who were *all of a sudden quite visible*. You know prior to the 1950s, 80 per cent of Māoris lived in the country and now it's the other way around and I

---

3 This figure includes all those from a non-white background.

4 Ireland has admittedly become more ethnically and culturally diverse in recent years with the 2006 census figures showing that ten per cent of the population were foreign nationals. The country appears much more homogenous, however, in terms of *race* as a large proportion of the foreign national population is made up of people from a white background. The figure of 4 per cent (165,470) includes all those from a non-white background and also includes those from an Irish Traveller background (22,369). Significant numbers (72,303) did not state an ethnicity.

> was a policeman in the 60s and I am of Māori descent so I know, I saw first hand what was happening ... basically most families couldn't cope and were quite dysfunctional so we've seen rises in things like Māori mental health statistics and so on, educational achievement, social wellbeing and so on. And I think that's carried on in the way we deal with ... we've always imprisoned at a higher rate than the UK and Australia ... what we put people in prison for, you know vagrancy and drunkenness, you got three convictions for bring drunk and that was you in prison. And that was in the old days. They decriminalised some of that stuff but then they've introduced other stuff like ... and now with gangs, if you wear a gang patch you end up in prison, just for wearing an emblem. And being in a particular location... (New Zealand interviewee #9, p. 2)

While it is clearly difficult to be definitive about such a complex issue, it is at least arguable that a public culture that vilified criminals existed *prior to* the migration of Māori to the cities and that the crime issue subsequently became racialised. Risk factors more often than not do not operate in isolation but serve to reinforce one another. As Tonry (2009: 388) has written of the United States, 'patterns of racial insensitivity ... make sense in the light of the other ... [cultural] explanations. If crime and drugs are matters of good and evil, and criminals and drug users are evil, then there is little reason to expect sympathy or empathy toward them'. Thus, in the same way that the strong moralist streak in America associated with Protestant fundamentalism is critical to shoring up racial disproportionality in that jurisdiction, the strong cultural attachment to conformity and strict law enforcement in New Zealand ('the Prussians of the South Pacific', NZ Interviewee #3, p. 5) may also be pivotal to understanding the overrepresentation of Māori in the criminal justice statistics.

Mass Media Characteristics

The final risk factor distinguishing New Zealand from Scotland and Ireland is the quality of the media[5] there and the manner in which crime issues were reported. Several characteristics stand out in the New Zealand case. First, respondents identified the 'incredibly trivialised' (New Zealand interviewee #7, p. 10) nature of the media reporting on crime as detrimental to the debate on criminal justice issues. Unlike the print media in Scotland and Ireland, newspapers did not appoint specialised journalists such as legal or court correspondents who could form a depth of understanding about criminal justice issues. Reporters tended to attend the crime desk for six months and then move on to the next section of the newspaper with the result that populist statements by politicians and other interest groups largely escaped deeper inquiry. Indeed, one interviewee noted the symbiotic

5 By way of clarification it should be noted that what is being discussed here is the New Zealand 'quality press' (*The Dominion Post*, *New Zealand Herald*) rather than the tabloid press where there is little variation between the three jurisdictions.

relationship between newspaper columnists and self-styled 'experts' in criminal justice matters such as the leaders of the SST given their ready availability and appreciation of sound-bite politics (New Zealand interviewee #1).

A second issue was the absence of a left-wing press and investigative journalism which again impedes serious, critical debate. There is no New Zealand equivalent to *Panorama* in the UK or *Prime Time Investigates* in Ireland. Further, most of the newspapers take a centrist or right-wing political viewpoint. In contrast, left-leaning or centre-left broadsheets with a readership in Scotland and Ireland include *The Irish Times* (Ireland), *The Herald* (Scotland), *The Guardian* (Ireland and Scotland), *The Observer* (Ireland and Scotland) and *The Independent* (Ireland and Scotland) (admittedly, the latter three newspapers have only a limited readership in Ireland). In this regard, one New Zealand respondent commented:

> I mean there is no *Guardian, Telegraph, Times*, legal correspondent and there is never a serious talk about the law … we don't have investigative journalism in the way that perhaps Europeans do. I've got one … documentary coming out on one client of mine next year but that will be the first time it has happened to me… (New Zealand interviewee #4, p. 10)

These comments chime with views expressed by political commentators, such as Bruce Jesson (notably, a journalist himself) who have written on many occasions of the 'thinness' of the media. Following a brief period in politics acting as Chair of Auckland Regional Services Trust, Jesson wrote: 'perhaps the most disturbing aspect of the situation is the quality of the media scrutiny … we could feed whatever message we liked into the media with no critical evaluation of it' (Jesson 1999: 31). As with the issue of race relations, however, it is difficult to be fully satisfied with this level of explanation. It is clear that any newspaper that sought to run too far ahead of its readers would quickly find itself in difficulties. The lack of demand among the public for deeper analysis of such issues in the media again points towards the cultural characteristics of New Zealand society which fashion such proclivities.

Protective Factors

Legal Cultures

A country's legal culture forms another part of the complex tapestry of factors influencing penality in a particular jurisdiction. Both Tonry (2007) and Lappi-Seppälä (2007, 2012) acknowledge this through their identification of elected criminal justice officials (judges, prosecutors) in the American tradition as a risk factor for punitive policies while a custom of political neutrality in professional legal cultures exerts a protective effect. In a broader sense, however, a country's legal traditions and legal culture are also vital considerations. The influence of the

Utrecht School in the Netherlands in the 1950s provides a well-known example. In his seminal work on Dutch and English criminal justice policy, Downes (1988) argued that the culture and training of the legal profession (from which the judges were drawn) – and specifically the strong anti-penal influence exerted by the Utrecht School – was critical to the development of Dutch leniency in the 1960s and 1970s. He writes, '[in relation to sentencing] the manner of judicial training and socialisation, and the character and timing of the brief ascendancy of rehabilitative policies, seem to be crucial' (ibid.: 350).

More recently, in an example closer to home, two Irish criminologists (Vaughan and Kilcommins 2008) have argued that the Irish judicial *habitus* (Hutton 2006) acts as an important buffer against excessive securitisation on behalf of the Irish state. In their view, its constant affirmation of proportionality and due process values in individual cases sets up a 'legal dialectic' which continues to deliver significant protections to those accused of crime. The authors are correct to point to the continued force of liberal constitutionalism in Irish law and its influence in 'legal and judicial craft, if not in the public consciousness more generally' (Vaughan and Kilcommins 2008: 98). Active judicial interpretation of the due process provisions of the Irish Constitution in the 1960s and 1970s, most notably the development of the exclusionary rule where evidence has been obtained in an unconstitutional manner, *has* provided distinct advantages to an accused person in Ireland.

The embedded nature of liberal constitutionalism and the due process model in the Irish legal culture is something which emerged in a strong sense from the interviews as a significant protective influence. Respondents noted the jealous manner in which judges guarded their independence, the individualised nature of sentencing in Ireland and their more 'liberal instincts'. In line with Vaughan and Kilcommins's (2008) arguments, they argued the cultural disposition of the judiciary has had tangible effects for the way in which justice is administered in Ireland:

> because again Irish judges I think have a reasonable culture of fair play and even when the Oireachtas has attempted to maybe alter the pitch, judges either by the way they interpreted the legislation or the way they run a trial probably haven't given effect to it in quite the same way as the legislature might have always expected. The judges would have been in many cases practitioners from an early era and would still carry through the lot of the philosophy they were brought up with. (Irish interviewee #9, p. 2)

The argument can be carried further, moreover, in terms of its application to the legal profession as a whole. Several respondents noted that the legal profession constituted a powerful opposition lobby in Ireland to authoritarian legislation. Most interestingly, one senior legal practitioner spoke of the way in which lawyers, like the judiciary, could subvert the intentions of the Oireachtas where legislation conflicted with the legal culture:

> If you look at the Criminal Justice Act in 1984, there was this huge resistance to using the inferences [drawing inferences from a suspect's silence] provision in that and I think that a kind of consensus just grew that it was unconstitutional. And then there was the *Rock* case…
>
> [CH: which confirmed that it was in fact constitutional]
>
> Even after that, there was just no appetite for it. (Irish interviewee #5, p. 9)

While this failure on the part of prosecutors to apply legislation as enacted may also have a lot to do with the 'informalism' (discussed above) of the Irish criminal justice system, the extent to which judges and the legal profession generally are emboldened to challenge attempts by the executive to introduce harsher legislation marks an important point of distinction between Ireland and Scotland on the one hand and New Zealand on the other. Like due process and proportionality in Ireland, notions of fairness and individualised sentencing in Scotland have achieved a degree of embeddedness in the national legal system on account of its association with identity politics. As McAra (2005) has written of the country's legal system, it has come to be viewed as an important 'carrier' of Scottish identity, together with the education system and the Church. This has resulted in a strong pride in the Scottish legal system and a reluctance to change it; what O'Neill (2004) has described as the 'institutional conservatism' of Scottish legal culture or what one respondent more colloquially referred to as the 'canny, conservative approach' of the Scots to law reform (Scottish Interviewee #7, p. 6).

The double-edged nature of this conservatism has been discussed in Chapter 6 in terms of its ability to promote insular attitudes as well as resistance to punitiveness. However, its benefits as a prophylactic against more punitive policies are best illustrated by the responses received from one of the interviewees, a well-known 'penal hawk' in Scotland who has been outspoken on several justice issues. Several comments which he passed during the course of the interview fitted in well with this image: for example, he used politically incorrect terms such as 'neds'; was clearly a firm believer in deterrence and zero-tolerance policing; and was strongly opposed to the incorporation of the ECHR into Scottish law. However, he also believed strongly in due process ('I'm all for locking people up, I just require them to be guilty first' Scottish interviewee #6, p. 4); rejected mandatory sentencing as an affront to judicial independence ('I would hate to have the situation of mandatory sentencing' ibid., p. 5) and was ambivalent about the need for OLRs which he described as 'fairly draconian' (ibid., p. 7). Indeed, he thought there had been in general a lot of *unnecessary* tinkering with the Scottish criminal justice system (which he declared to be the 'best legal system in the world', ibid., p. 9) in the post-devolutionary period. Thus, the pride which he so clearly took in the various aspects of the Scottish criminal justice system ('we prefer to go our own way here and rightly so' ibid., p. 10) acted as an important moderating factor in his approach to criminal justice issues.

It is also highly significant that the Scottish criminal justice system is based on common law principles which have traditionally placed few restraints on sentencing discretion. There are no maximum penalties for common law offences save the jurisdictional limits of the sentencing court and the High Court of Justiciary has never developed any broad principles of sentencing. As noted in the interviews, over time an incredible affection has been built up within the legal system for the independence of the individual sentencer and this has been critical in resisting attempts to introduce mandatory sentences in the late 1990s (Scottish interviewees #2, #3, #5, #6 and #8). Consider for example the response of one interviewee when questioned about the relative absence of mandatory sentences in Scotland:

> until recently, a tenet of our system was that the judge is the sentencer, end of story. There is some leeway in allowing the accused to appeal against sentence but not much is made of that. Sometimes the Appeal Court say this is excessive and they knock off a few years but most them have never developed any broad principles of sentencing, never mind guidelines, never mind things like that, even broad principles of sentencing. It's always a matter for the discretion of the sentencing judge, the Appeal Court will rarely intervene, *that I think explains everything…* (Scottish interviewee #8, p. 3, emphasis added)

In contrast, in New Zealand some interviewees referred to an absence of criticism emanating from the legal professions and the judiciary in terms of the debate around criminal justice. While mandatory sentencing laws have not yet been introduced (despite political pledges to do so), recurrent amendments to legislation governing preventative detention and sentencing more broadly have been such that civil servants spoke of a 'constant tinkering' with the criminal justice system (see further Chapter 6). The legal culture in New Zealand appears less *embedded* than in Ireland and Scotland and therefore more susceptible to change. Part of the explanation may lie (as one respondent noted) in the absence (until recently) of a Supreme Court and a hierarchy of senior judges. Historically, this role was performed by the English Privy Council and this may have had a dampening effect on the development of a distinct judicial *habitus*.

Membership of the European Polity

Since this research was first conducted a range of publications have emerged concerning the putative role that human rights standards and cultural norms may play in protecting European countries from Anglo-American punitiveness. Following the work of Whitman (2003) and others (Salas 2005), respective authors have interrogated the significance of European culture and identity and their implications for penality (Snacken and Dumortier 2012; Daems et al. 2013; Body-Gendrot et al. 2013). The conception of Europe as an area which privileges particular normative values is also complemented by an institutional Europe, framed around two pan-European organisations, the Council of Europe and the

European Union. These institutions are increasingly involved in intergovernmental and supranational penal policymaking and penological standard setting. The leading body in this regard has long been the Council of Europe which has placed a strong emphasis on reductionism and minimum intervention in its sentencing recommendations (such as R 99(22) on prison overcrowding) (Snacken and Van Zyl Smit 2013). Principles of restraint in the use of custody are also endorsed to some degree in decisions of the European Court of Human Rights, such as the recent decision against the UK on life imprisonment without parole.[6] The EU too wields a great deal of power in matters of penological concern. While strong concerns may be expressed about the demands of securitisation placed on EU member states (Loader 2002; Baker 2010),[7] it also has a commitment, similar if not identical to that of the Council of Europe, to human rights values that impact on the penological sphere (Baker 2013).

Returning to the three case studies in issue, in Ireland the incorporation of the ECHR in 2003 has been met with some complacency, given the significant *de minimis* standards already provided by the Irish Constitution. Despite this, the influence of European human rights agreements on Irish and Scottish criminal law has been palpable in certain contexts. The case law of the ECHR has played a key role in the establishment of various accountability mechanisms for the Irish police (Vaughan and Kilcommins 2007), a development which was described by one respondent as a watershed moment in Irish criminal justice ('hugely significant in a positive sense', Irish interviewee #4, p. 1). Following the judgment of the European Court in *Hirst v. UK (No.2)*,[8] the Irish state also took the pre-emptive step of providing all prisoners with the practical means to vote in what may be understood as a process of 'controlled liberalisation' or tactical concession to forestall potential criticisms (Risse and Ropp 1999 cited in Vaughan and Kilcommins 2008). While Scotland did not follow suit (again testifying to the importance of viewing these factors in probabilistic rather than deterministic terms), the incorporation of the ECHR into Scottish law was viewed by a large number of respondents as a defining moment in Scottish criminal law. Indeed, despite initial hostility from some quarters, it has had significant practical effects on criminal justice in Scotland, not least in terms of the large sums paid out in compensation in the 'slopping out' cases and the improvements to the Scottish prison estate which followed.

---

6 *Vintner and others v. UK*, European Court of Human Rights, Grand Chamber, 9 July 2013.

7 Indeed, some commentators would actually go so far as to classify membership of the European polity as a risk rather than a protective factor. Lappi-Seppälä (2007), for example, notes that a large number of Nordic scholars remain hostile towards political attempts to harmonise criminal law on the basis that this development has diminished rather than enhanced the role of experts in the penal process.

8 (2006) 42 EHRR 41.

As observed previously New Zealand does not have a written Constitution containing fundamental rights (the Bill of Rights is a piece of legislation only and not a supreme instrument), nor is it a party to an international human rights agreement which either *requires* the national judiciary to enforce human rights or allows citizens to petition an international court for that purpose. This caused some respondents to cast a jealous eye on oversight organisations deriving from political affiliation with Europe:

> Well I do wonder if New Zealand was a small jurisdiction that bordered large jurisdictions and had exposure to the European Community ... Whereas we don't and I think that's another factor that I don't think anybody will articulate is the absence of the European Court. You know we have no international big brother saying look you've got it wrong and that's a great catalyst for change. (New Zealand interviewee #4, p. 13)

Relatedly, the country's geographical isolation and tendency to look inward rather than outward was identified by a number of interviewees as relevant to its harsher approach. Unlike Scotland and Ireland, New Zealand is not bound to the same degree by adherence to international norms and is therefore freer to respond to its internal anxieties through authoritarian measures.

Conclusion

It is worth reiterating that the above makes no claim to be a comprehensive account of the factors motivating the differences in penal policy between the three jurisdictions. Welfare policy, for example, is something which was not touched upon by respondents, yet compelling arguments have been advanced for associations between strong welfare states and more moderate penal policies (Downes and Hansen 2006; Lappi-Seppälä 2008; Snacken and Dumortier 2012). It is also important to leave room for historical contingency and the impact of unforeseen events on penal policy. Sensational incidents may clearly change the trajectory of criminal justice in a given jurisdiction, particularly in a smaller jurisdiction which may more easily facilitate dramatic changes in either direction. It seems difficult to deny, for instance, the impact of the Veronica Guerin murder on criminal justice in Ireland and the same can most probably be said of the radical economic restructuring of the early 1980s in New Zealand (see Chapters 3 and 5).

Caveats aside, however, it can be seen that the risk, protective and non-factors identified by the respondents bear a close resemblance to those outlined by Tonry (2007, 2009) and others (e.g. Lappi-Seppälä 2007, 2008; 2012; Lacey 2008; Green 2007, 2008, 2009). Political, legal and media elements all appeared to form parts of the jigsaw puzzle. Yet testing these ideas against the empirical situation in the three countries produced some important refinements and extensions of these concepts. Attention is drawn to the manner in which these explanatory factors reinforce, sustain, or weaken each other and – most significantly – interact with local cultural values and historical events.

Comparing political cultures in Scotland and New Zealand provides a good illustration. Despite political structures which were very similar and which are usually understood to facilitate a consensus style of politics (Lijphart 1999; Lacey 2008; Green 2007, 2008, 2009), crime has become deeply politicised in New Zealand. Factors which distinguish New Zealand from Scotland in this regard include: its weaker committee system; the decline in political legitimacy engendered by the new right economic restructuring of the 1980s; the shallow nature of crime reporting and the history of race relations in the country. All of these factors have no doubt contributed to a more conflictual political culture, even when refracted through similar institutional arrangements to Scotland. The Lijphartian model can also be criticised for its inattention to broader culture norms. Political cultures do not exist in isolation and are in turn supported by the national cultural context. On the basis of the interview data above, it is argued that these broader cultural values operate to shape policymakers' understanding of criminal justice problems and their solutions thereby militating in favour of more or less punitive political strategies. While useful, therefore, Lijphart's consensus-conflict dichotomy represents only one aspect of a country's political culture whose effects vary greatly depending on both national culture and the presence or absence of other risk and protective factors.

A further risk factor associated with political culture is the (non-)/involvement of experts in the policymaking process. Once again surface similarities across the three jurisdictions conceal more ambiguous processes, underlining the need to understand jurisdictions on their own terms. As Nelken (2005) has argued we should be wary of ethnocentric (Anglo-American) projections of punitiveness whereby the expectation is that the role of professional elites has been diminished. The Department of Justice in Ireland, for example, has never really had a tradition of research-led legislation, preferring instead to rely on the views of front-line practitioners or indeed, the personal views of Ministers themselves. This 'anti-intellectual', pragmatic approach to policymaking confounds those who seek to categorise jurisdictions neatly into those who follow the (public-led) Anglo-American or (expert-led) Western/northern European tradition. Its effects on criminal justice policy are also equivocal: a lack of a tradition of evidence-based policy in Ireland could clearly be viewed as a risk factor; yet there have also been suggestions that the absence of a body of research and data has been one of the main obstacles to the introduction of actuarial-style justice policies (O'Donnell 2010).

The critical mediating effects of local culture and national psyche are again revealed in examining the remainder of the risk and protective factors identified by the research. It would be imprudent, for example, to view the trivialised style of media reporting in isolation from the broader anti-intellectual and conformist current in that country's history (Jesson 1999; Easton 2005, 2007; Pratt 2006). Similarly, issues of race and colonialism need to be considered in interaction with broader cultural factors. Convincing arguments were made by interviewees

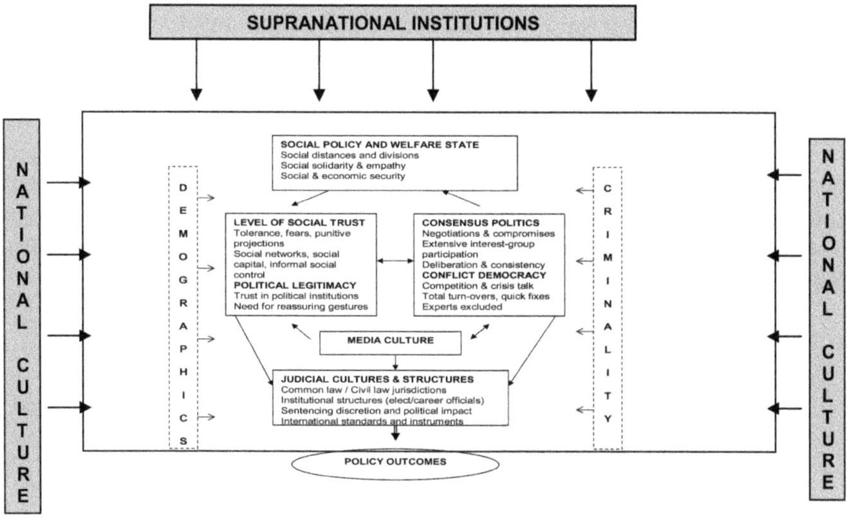

Figure 8.1 Model showing influences on penal policy

Source: Based on Lappi-Seppälä (2012).

that it was the *interrelationship* between the difficulties associated with Māori urbanisation and New Zealanders' strong cultural attachment to conformity which best explains Māori overrepresentation in the penal statistics.

Legal cultures too meet and mingle with extant traditions and sensibilities. The strong protective influences exerted by the Irish and Scottish legal cultures against populism form an important strand of the research but, again, one that is difficult to divorce from their surroundings. An interesting marriage of liberal constitutionalism and cultural informalism in Ireland, for example, resulted in prosecutors sometimes choosing to ignore legislative reforms. Indeed, its combined influence was such that one interviewee described it as the country's 'saving grace' (Interviewee #4). In Scotland, it was the association of the legal system with the country's identity politics which engendered such a strong resilience to change. Moreover, the penal welfarist values which continue to inform practices in the penal and juvenile justice systems have their roots in broader traditions of collectivism and fairness that permeate Scottish civic culture.

As noted, this is not a complete account of all the factors influencing penal policy outcomes. A more comprehensive model which sits comfortably with the findings highlighted by the research has been proposed by Lappi-Seppälä (2012: 63) and was discussed in greater detail in Chapter 2. As observed there, the strength of the model is its comprehensiveness and its sensitivity to the manner in which the various elements interact. The model reproduced again above with some suggested additional elements superimposed on the original image (these elements are highlighted in grey).

For the comparative researcher, it is submitted that this model serves as a useful working account of some of the key influences on penal policy. Additionally, based on the close relationship between national culture and the various factors identified above, it is argued that the more nebulous but crucial element of 'national culture/psyche' should also form part of any comprehensive understanding of penal policy. The original model was also one-dimensional: as previously noted, supranational institutions such as the European Union and Council of Europe add additional layers of complexity to the increasingly contested field of national politics (Vaughan and Kilcommins 2008, 2010).

Chapter 9
Reconceptualising Penality

Introduction

In addition to reaching conclusions about the punitiveness of the three states in question, it is submitted that the instant research holds some lessons for the broader criminological literature. The first lesson is a methodological one which has significant implications for how we interpret the messy field of contemporary crime control. It can be expressed simply: difficult questions of definition and measurement need to be addressed before states can be definitively categorised as 'punitive'. The story of escalating punitiveness described in Chapter 1 has been criticised for its totalising effects and generalising tendencies. As has hopefully been demonstrated in the foregoing chapters, some of these difficulties arise from insufficient attention to the problems surrounding the definition and operationalisation of the concept itself which allows other competing discourses and developments to be downplayed or ignored. It is argued here that a multidimensional tool for measuring punitiveness can act as an important heuristic device in understanding the complexities which inhere in contemporary penality. The second lesson is that while space should be made for grand theory concerning the conditions of late modernity or the rise of neo-liberalism, penal policies continue to take their colour from a combination of socio-political, legal, and media circumstances at local level. These two points are developed further below.

The Law of Requisite Variety

Issues relating to the definition and measurement of the 'punitive turn' have been under-examined in the mainstream literature to date (Matthews 2005). Indeed, analytic attention to the core components of the concept (Gordon 1989; Kutateladze 2009; Whitman 2003; Tonry 2007) appears in inverse proportion to its preponderance in the criminological literature (Bottoms 1995; Cavadino and Dignan 2006; Feeley and Simon 1992, 1994; Garland, 2001; Lacey 2008; Pratt et al. 2005; Pratt 2007; Simon 2007; Wacquant 2003, 2005, 2009). Many authors have satisfied themselves with commonly used but singular dependent variables such as imprisonment rates per 100,000 population, mandatory sentencing or the death penalty. While these are certainly convenient 'ready-reckoners' (Kilcommins et al. 2004: 250) they are limited in what they can reveal about state punitiveness and should not therefore be used as key metrics without justification and the attachment of adequate caveats.

The use of a singular index or indeed a select number of indices is unsatisfactory for a whole host of reasons, prime among them the inherent complexity of punishment. Some years ago, Garland (1983: 12) argued for a multidimensional sociology of punishment out of what he referred to as 'respect for the empirical object'. It is contended here that a similar rigour should be applied to the measurement of punitiveness. The 'law of requisite variety' (Ashby 1957) demands a richer, multilayered tool which is capable of understanding the level of complexity in the murky all-too-real world. An instrument which seeks to measure state punitiveness should therefore incorporate *at a minimum* variables measuring the use of imprisonment as well as those relating to: differences in police powers and policing practices (including post-release monitoring and restrictions); respect given to human rights instruments (including those relating to minors); the extent of procedural guarantees; and the quality of prison regimes. If data are available on prosecution practices, these too should form part of a multidimensional measure, particularly in jurisdictions where considerable power is held by prosecuting bodies. Second, the concentration on quantitative indices such as imprisonment rates has served to undermine the important qualitative dimension to punishment concerning policy intentions, system ethos (important in the Scottish context) and the 'weight' or oppressiveness of the system for the individual suspect/offender travelling through it (King and McDermott 1995). Simply 'reading off' punitiveness from penal statistics without (cautiously) talking to local actors fails to capture these vital elements and, worse still, risks confusing outcomes for intentions (Nelken 2006).

Third, this narrow definition of punitiveness has encouraged diagnoses which are at best premature or, at worst, simply incorrect. The surprising homogeneity revealed by the application of a multidimensional test to the three countries under analysis in the instant research is a case in point. Use of a multidimensional index of punitiveness in New Zealand over the study period serves to complicate the story which has to date been told about punishment in that country. A comparatively progressive tradition within the prison system (at least in terms of the size of the institutions and conditions for work and home leave) (Newbold and Eskridge 2005); strong procedural protections; a strongly diversionary youth justice system; and falling prison entry rates per 1,000 violent crimes evoke a less punitive society than that presented in the literature (Pratt and Clark 2005; Pratt 2007; Cavadino and Dignan 2006). A rethink may also be required of Irish exceptionalism, at least in so as far as the recent 'punitive turn' is concerned. With the singular (and dubious) exception of imprisonment rates correlated with property crime (theft and burglary) all other variables measuring the use of imprisonment show significant increases dating approximately from the mid 1990s. Moreover, highly critical reports from the CPT (2007) cast a critical eye on poor physical conditions within the prisons, overcrowding and high levels of inter-prisoner violence. Scottish punitiveness too was recast in a very different light by a relatively simple change in methodological approach. Viewed in a *historical* rather than *comparative* perspective, i.e. using 1976 as a base rate, several variables such as convicted prisoner rates, convicted prisoner entry rates and prisoners per 1,000 violent crimes show only a slight increase or even a decline in punitiveness. If – as is argued here – the growth in imprisonment relative to earlier levels provides the best empirical grounding for arguments relating to a *new* punitiveness then Scotland's position appears considerably ameliorated.

Given the importance of this issue for our ultimate assessment of the state of late modern penality, the dearth of attention in the literature to matters of definition and the formulation of clear-cut social scientific criteria to measure punitiveness is to be regretted. Many of the authors discussed in Chapter 2 who are critical of the 'new punitiveness' are at pains to emphasise the variability and complexity of punishment and thus the partiality of focus assumed by those advancing 'catastrophic criminologies'. Yet with the notable exception of Tonry (2007), Whitman (2003) and Kutateladze (2007a, 2009), few have actually taken steps to formulate a measure which would adequately capture some of the competing discourses and practices that they seek to highlight. This is problematic as it leaves these researchers equally open to charges of selectivity in the variables which they claim best represent the current *zeitgeist*. Matthews (2005: 181), for example, writes of the 'diversity and variability of penal developments' and 'variability and growing complexity of regulatory strategies'. He also points to improvements in prison conditions and the various ways in which the use of custody has been restricted to serious offenders in England and Wales. Similarly, Zedner (2002: 348) avers to the 'complex, differentiated and even progressive aspects of contemporary penal policy' and O'Malley (1999: 156) to the dangers associated with 'isolat[ing] prisons as definitive of penality and privileg[ing] them over many other developments in criminal justice that do not seem to match the criteria'. These points are all valid criticisms of generalising tendencies in the punitive turn literature. Nowhere in their writings, however, do these commentators adumbrate the ways in which this 'lack of empirical generality' (ibid.) can be addressed or indeed why *their* indices should be privileged. There is a lack of clarity about what criteria *can* be legitimately employed in the search to understand the current criminal justice terrain.

Certain criticism may also be reserved for those authors who have actually examined the empirical content of 'punitiveness'. Tonry (2007), for example, is to be commended for his efforts to operationalise the concept and, in line with what has been argued above, he incorporates variables relating to: penal policies and practices, imprisonment rates disaggregated by offence type, juvenile justice (waiver to adult courts) and procedural protections (see Chapter 2 for a detailed breakdown). Yet one still forms the impression that this exercise represents a mere prelude to the real discussion concerning the determinants of penal policies. Tonry (2007: 5) himself refers to his discussion on the dependent variable as 'ground clearing', a term which perhaps serves to reinforce its secondary status. Theoretical justification is not provided for inclusion of some variables and he omits important criteria relating to prison conditions and post-release practices. This creates difficulties for his arguments later on as he concludes that 'when multiple criteria are used, it becomes apparent that the United States and England are in a class by themselves in moving toward harsher penal systems across the board' (ibid.). This may perhaps be true when these jurisdictions are assessed according to the criteria selected by Tonry. As discussed below, however, it is open to some question when these other critical variables are taken into account.

In a comparative analysis of American, French, German and Russian punitiveness, Kutateladze (2005) rated US prison conditions above those in both Russia and France on the basis that Russian prisons are underfunded, overcrowded and plagued by tuberculosis. French prisons have also long had a reputation for overcrowding, poor hygiene, poor physical conditions and physical abuse; something which has drawn repeated criticism from the CPT (2007b). This is not deny that conditions in US prisons are bad, merely that issues of respectful treatment of offenders in American prisons must be considered against other major problems faced by the Russian and French correctional systems. English prisons too compare quite favourably with conditions in these countries, particularly in light of significant improvements in recent years (Matthews 2005). Post-release practices in both countries reveal further problems with Tonry's argument, specifically his tendency to equate punitive practices 'across the board' in the US with those in England. Despite the existence in England of a complex web of civil orders which may be used against ex-offenders, highly punitive practices such as community notification, civil commitment and disenfranchisement laws are mostly confined to certain states within the US, something which speaks to important differences between the US and England (Newburn 2007). Tonry's conclusions therefore appear somewhat premature, largely on account of the limited number of indicators which he employs for punitiveness.

To be fair to these authors, some have expressed serious doubts about the usefulness of the punitiveness concept itself. Matthews (2005), for example, suggests 'tolerance' as an alternative, but the point remains that if it is to be retained, (and it is argued that sufficient commonalities exist in criminal justice developments since the 1990s across the three jurisdictions to justify further empirical work into the 'punitive turn' e.g. the dramatic increase in sentence lengths), then much greater attention must be given to the wide variety of ways in which state punitiveness can be expressed, even within the criminal justice system itself. The issue holds great importance for comparative criminology in particular for, as Kutateladze (2009) observes, it prevents a comparison (on unidimensional measures) of the most punitive aspects of one system with the least punitive aspects of another system. As he suggests, it would be interesting to compare the most punitive region in the US (probably California or the American South) with those in Europe (probably one of the Eastern states) using a multidimensional measure. Perhaps the harsh prison conditions and weak procedural protections afforded inmates in the latter jurisdiction would cast the penal austerity of the Southern US states in a somewhat different light?

The above discussion raises the issue of the various indices to be employed in any test. In the current study a 34 variable test was applied incorporating indices relating to policing; procedural protections for defendants; the use of imprisonment; juvenile justice; prison conditions; post-release controls and the death penalty. It will be recalled that Kutateladze's (2007a, 2009) 44-variable test employed indices relating to: political and symbolic punishment; incarceration, punishing 'immorality'; conditions of confinement and juvenile justice. Clearly, both of the above tests, while an improvement on the status quo, do not represent a comprehensive measure of system punitiveness as experienced by the defendant/offender. Notable omissions concern data relating to stop and search, the number and proportion of police suspects arrested as well as important decisions at the prosecution stage. Ideally, as Pease (1994) argued nearly 20 years ago, we would be able to gauge system punitiveness by examining data relating to the various decision-making stages of the criminal process (suspects, people prosecuted; people convicted; people sentenced to imprisonment per 100,000 population), particularly rates of attrition. While this was not possible in relation to the three countries under examination, as further and better data become available for cross-national comparison future researchers may wish to refine or extend these models. They may also wish to consider the 10 indices of 'harshness' and 'mildness' formulated by Whitman (2003),[1] particularly indices (i)–(iv) which represent an important (and very rare) attempt at examining *criminalisation* as an aspect of criminal justice practice (see further discussion on Zedner (2010) below).

Punitiveness, Multidimensionality and Criminology

It is instructive to consider *why* such narrow, unidimensional conceptualisations of punitiveness have been (largely) uncritically accepted by criminologists to date. The strength of both Kutateladze's and Whitman's tests is that they incorporate 'legal' as well as 'criminological' criteria such as the number of criminal laws, the range of conduct prohibited (e.g. drug and sexual offences) and the ranges of offenders included (e.g. juveniles). This is important given that in all of the countries examined a toughening of the criminal and penal laws relating to sexual and violent offenders is discernible, particularly since the mid 1990s. Other countries such as Germany (Kury 2009; Sack and Schlepper 2013) have also found a rise in punitiveness that is most distinctly seen in the area of legislation. One troubling aspect of the proliferation and increasing complexity of criminal justice legislation, however, derives from its relative invisibility in *criminological* writing. With some important and notable exceptions (e.g. Ashworth and Zedner 2008; Hallsworth and Lea 2008), 'most criminologists ply their trade without recourse to a criminal law textbook … and other legal instruments…'(Zedner 2010: 279). This has left it up to criminal lawyers to lament critical developments such as the erosion of fundamental

1 These include (i) harshness in criminalising conduct, (ii) harshness in subjecting numerous classes of persons to potential criminal liability, (iii) harshness in grading criminal offences, (iv) harshness in inflexible doctrines of criminal liability, (v) harshness in enforcement, (vi) harshness in the law of punishment, (vii) harshness in the application of punishment, (viii) harshness in the inflexibility of punishment, (ix) the mildness of respectful treatment, and (x) the mildness of pardons.

procedural protections (e.g. Kennedy 2004; Walsh 2005a; Hamilton 2007), absent the important empirical insights criminologists can bring to the debate.

Invoking a broader definition of punitiveness thus indirectly challenges the established 'division of labour' between the disciplines. As Zedner (2010) astutely observes, criminal lawyers generally confine themselves to articulating principles on which given behaviours should be criminalised or not (or indeed the basis for criminal law protections to be restricted or not) while criminologists have tended to focus on questions of politics, enforcement and punishment. The tendency to remain within the limits of our comfortable disciplinary silos is unfortunate, if understandable, and one which carries implications beyond the conceptualisation of punitiveness (Murphy and Whitty 2013). As it relates to punitiveness, however, the failure of criminologists to adequately consider 'the legal' misses the strong symbolism associated with due process protections and police powers (Tonry 2001, 2004). Questions relating to the appropriate balance between state and citizen, particularly at the pretrial stages, are highly political issues, not simply the stuff of dusty legal doctrine.

The relationship of law with criminology has been the subject of some debate for several decades now. In 1961, for instance, Leon Radzinowicz (1961: 181) stated that criminal law must 'resolve its relationship with criminology', yet this process would still appear to be underway. Reviewing the state of opinion on this issue, Murphy and Whitty (2013) observe a 'stark polarity within contemporary criminology', veering from impatience with academic criminology's still reluctant relationship with the legal field (Zedner 2010) to calls for the criminological gaze to be directed *away* from the legal and the normative (Loader and Sparks 2010). Whatever the proper role of legal norms within the broader criminological academy, it is difficult to deny the ways in which law frames the discipline of criminology and thus too, questions of penality. 'Legal' criteria for testing punitiveness advocated by Gordon (1989), Whitman (2003) and Kutateladze (2009) thus add depth to the concept and serve to reinforce the importance of a *systems* approach.

A crucial point also relates to the potentially highly draconian nature of *criminal justice* procedures as they are experienced by the suspect/offender. As illuminated in the current debate over the use of the European arrest warrant (EAW) some of the more 'procedural' or 'black-letter' reforms may also represent some of the most coercive exercises of state power. Viewed from the perspective of the person sought, this instrument is 'grossly coercive, involving deprivation of liberty and forcible removal to another Member State, a country whose legal system they might not be familiar with or whose language they don't speak' (Haggenmüller 2013: 98). Despite strong criticism from the Council of Europe Commissioner for Human Rights and Fair Trial International for its disproportionate use against thousands of EU nationals, however, criminological analysis of these developments appears limited (but not entirely absent: see, for example, Baker 2010, 2013). It follows from the above that an interdisciplinary approach to the measurement of punitiveness is to be preferred. As recently observed elsewhere (Body-Gendrot et al. 2013: 6) there is a need to 'range across disciplinary boundaries in order to [adequately] analyse and understand the punitive turn'. Criminological studies aiming at a comprehensive assessment of cross-national punitiveness may therefore wish to take increasing cognisance of the legal parameters of their subject-matter, in much the same manner that Murphy and Whitty (2007) have argued for greater interdisciplinarity in the field of risk and human rights.

What of the other factors explaining the reliance on imprisonment rates? Practical considerations such as time and money no doubt play a part. The increasing demands placed on the time and budgets of researchers often mean that collating information from multiple data sources across several jurisdictions is impractical. Imprisonment rates, on the other hand, are the most readily available penal measure with Internet sites such as that hosted by International Centre for Prison Studies at King's College London providing invaluable single-point access to information from all over the world. Moreover, in some jurisdictions (such as New Zealand) it is costly as well as inconvenient for foreign nationals to obtain historical data on the criminal justice system which is not publicly available and this may well involve long delays. Added to this are the methodological considerations concerning cross-national comparison. These difficulties are substantial enough when dealing with one or two variables measuring the use of imprisonment and (particularly) crime. They become of an entirely different order, however, when adding additional quantitative variables such as police rates and expenditure. As discovered during the course of the research, recording and counting practices differ greatly in individual countries even in relation to these deceptively simple matters. Are special, temporary and part-time constables counted in overall police numbers? Do police budget figures include VAT/GST (New Zealand)? Increasing the number of variables clearly invites greater methodological complexity and increasingly fraught interpretation.

Moving away from the practical and towards the theoretic, there may be other reasons to explain the reliance on imprisonment rates. Hinds (2002: 189) has argued that the 'order' imposed by reliance on custody rates alone and the consensus as to growing punitiveness which this facilitates, allows academics to 'construct certainty from the range of contradictory and volatile crime control policies that characterise contemporary penality, and therefore reassures anxieties about the limits of the current knowledge systems of academics and criminal justice professionals'. Perhaps, after all, (as suggested in Chapter 2), we have succumbed as a discipline to the 'temptation of elegance' rather than confronting the untidy reality of modern-day crime control? Given the unprecedented diversity and complexity of current crime control measures (Zedner 2002), perhaps it is simply easier for researchers to resort to the shorthand of the imprisonment rate, issue the usual caveats and proceed regardless (see, e.g., Cavadino and Dignan 2006)? Pedagogical issues may also have some purchase in explaining the hegemony of pessimistic accounts in the criminological literature. As Zedner (2010) and others (Matthews 2009) observe, criminology has a long history of liberal pessimism and radicalism which has most likely influenced the way in which criminology has been and is being taught. Consequently, criminologists may be more receptive to dystopic accounts of ever-increasing punitiveness while ignoring 'good news stories' such as falling rates of crime.

Explaining National Differences

A tendency towards oversimplification can also be detected in the literature concerning the determinants of penal policies. Readers of theoretical criminology are by now familiar with the debate between, on the one hand, theorists who advance global arguments about the conditions of late modernity (Garland 2001) or the rise of neo-liberalism (Reiner 2007;Wacquant 2009) and, on the other, scholars advancing more particularistic accounts which see penal policy as the product of national and political cultures and contingencies (Melossi 2001; Nelken 2005, 2006; Tonry 2007). The evidence in the instant research suggests that there is room for both perspectives. It acknowledges the common problems faced by societies today such an increasing preoccupation with risk, victims and expressive policies (evident in all three case studies). Ultimately, however, it favours the particularistic side of the debate.

The case studies demonstrate in some detail that even in today's globalised society distinctive local conditions continue to exert a crucial effect on policy outcomes. In common with arguments made in the field of policy transfer (Jones and Newburn 2007), respondents drew attention to the continued salience of national legal and institutional factors. As these authors have also maintained, however, this is not at all to deny that influences may also be international. The normative framework and enforcement mechanisms of transnational institutions such as the European Union and the Council of Europe appear to exert a protective influence in terms of promoting human rights norms and a reductionist penal policy. At the same time, policymakers in all three jurisdictions observed that national interests act as important constraints on policy transfer from larger jurisdictions such as the US or England and Wales and the evidence suggests that even in New Zealand there has been little in the way of 'hard' or substantive policy transfer. There is a tension here between national divergences and moves towards increasing policy convergence (what Newburn and Sparks (2004) have termed the 'edges' and 'flows' of contemporary policymaking), which may perhaps be resolved by invoking the distinction between voluntary and coercive policy transfer (Newburn and Sparks 2004). Changes introduced in the penal sphere in both Ireland and Scotland came about either as the result of obligations arising under the ECHR (e.g. the 'slopping out' litigation in Scotland) or in a pre-emptive move to avoid litigation (e.g. prisoner voting in Ireland). Transfer of policies such as ZTP or 'three-strike' laws, on the other hand, seem to occur at the broadly voluntary end. In this type of transfer, local considerations have more scope to determine the shape and style of the transfer or indeed whether there is any transfer at all.

Turning now to the particular local factors suggested by the research, as observed in the previous chapter the risk, protective and non-factors identified by the respondents bear a close resemblance to those outlined by Tonry (2007, 2009) and others (e.g. Lappi-Seppälä 2007, 2008, 2012; Lacey 2008; Green 2007, 2008, 2009). Political institutions, trust and cultures, and the manner in which they interact with racial politics, the media and legal spheres proved the most critical determinants of criminal justice policy (see further Chapter 8 and Figure 8.1). As Tonry (2007) himself concedes, however, the complex field of penal policymaking is far from reducible to a checklist of risk or protective factors to be applied by future researchers. In the current research, elements of local culture and national psyche appeared to act as an important filter in limiting the options available to politicians and other decision-makers within the criminal justice system (Melossi 2001). The role played by this rather unquantifiable element thus urges caution in 'taking histories from one country as unambiguous lessons for another' (Lacey 2008: 104).

In light of the above, it barely needs stating that the instant study tends to side with those (discussed in Chapter 2) who criticise the 'criminologies of catastrophe' for *inter alia* their ethnocentrism (O'Malley 2000; Zedner 2002; Matthews 2005). Importantly, however, the research also serves as a corrective against generalisations of a different variety. As discussed in Chapter 2, one of the main strands of the arguments advanced by these authors concerns the complexity of the present and the persistence *contra* Garland of the correctional ethos. While this was certainly in evidence in the sample jurisdictions, albeit with a new managerialist bent, other key developments cited in support of a less dystopic vision of contemporary crime control such as restorative justice failed to ring true.

In both Ireland and Scotland respondents *unanimously* viewed restorative projects as operating on the margins of the 'mainstream' criminal justice system and, as such, as incapable of presenting a serious challenge to more punitive discourses. Where such schemes did operate respondents felt that they were confined to less serious offences and tended to feature in situations that will not affect custody rates anyway. Even in the home of restorative justice itself, New Zealand, interviewees were quick to point out that it was not widely practised with adult offenders (despite the best efforts of some) and that the youth justice system was very much a distinct system with its own particular champions. Many made the point that FGCs owed their origins to Māori dissatisfaction with the existing criminal justice system and are therefore best understood in light of the debate over the indigenisation of crime control policies. Interestingly for those who argue that the international restorative justice movement acts an important counterweight to punitiveness (Zedner 2002; Hutchinson 2006), interviewees noted that the restorative element in the 1989 Act was very much an *ex post facto* development inspired by Māori cultural values and beliefs which didn't form part of the original scheme of the Act.

It appears therefore that far from being a government sponsored project, influenced by 'the tireless promotional efforts of restorative justice advocates throughout the world' (Zedner 2002: 355–6), restorative justice in the New Zealand context was driven by predominantly local concerns. This calls into question the extent to which restorative justice can be seen 'as an attempt to revive rehabilitation for a new political era' (Zedner 2002, 256) or even the extent to which it can be said to be 'widely supported by various governments and politicians' (Hutchinson 2006: 450). Restorative justice may hold important potential for the future of criminal justice but at present it is mainly operated on a *de minimis* level (at least in the adult criminal justice arena) in a number of countries. Indeed, its continued growth and application to more serious offences is far from inevitable given the difficulties involved in its wider implementation (Zedner 2004; Hamilton 2004). There is a danger here of replacing one form of generalisation with another, including perhaps the potential to overlook national specifities.[2]

The Need for Analytical Pluralism

In the final result, the research suggests that we need to be wary of generalising about the 'punitive turn' across different societies, not least because of the inherent complexity of the phenomena under investigation. 'Analytical pluralism' (as advanced by Daems 2008) should be our starting point for a proper understanding of penal change *both* in relation to matters of measurement *and* those processes bearing on the determinants of penal policy. As Newburn and Sparks (2004) have observed in relation to crime policy, this is not to abdicate our responsibility as researchers to impose analytical order on the criminal justice field but rather to acknowledge the significant degree of disharmony and contradiction which often exists and to adjust our lens accordingly.

One question that has not been addressed thus far is why all this matters. Implicit within the use of the risk/protective factors framework discussed above is the undesirability of increased punitiveness as an outcome, something which may be the subject of strenuous debate among reasonable people (Tonry 2007). In particular, it may be said that greater punitiveness can be interpreted as greater responsiveness to public demands (Mattthews 2005) or the state simply becoming more democratic (Vaughan and Kilcommins 2007). Yet the pernicious effects of increased use of imprisonment (to the extent that it can be avoided) are widely recognised by criminologists. Fagan (2004: 41), for example, has shown that areas that experience high levels of incarceration can become locked into a vicious cycle, whereby: '[i]ncarceration begets more incarceration, and incarceration also begets more crime, which in turn invites more aggressive enforcement, which then resupplies incarceration'. Within the academy, harmful consequences are also widely believed to flow from policies which infringe offenders' human rights at both the front and back end of the criminal justice system (Ashworth 2002; Cavadino and Dignan 2007).

2 Zedner (2002: 355) for example underlines the significance of the restorative justice in *Britain* when this is clearly not the case in Scotland (Dignan 2007).

Given the huge social costs at stake, it is probably not an exaggeration to say that the lack of wide-ranging and sound criteria for the assessment of punitiveness has important implications for the wider discipline of criminology, particularly its public role. The interconnections between punitiveness and public criminology are thoroughly explored in a recent text on public criminology published by two well-known British criminologists, Ian Loader and Richard Sparks (2010). Described by Loader and Sparks as the increasingly 'hot' political climate in which criminologists operate, the authors convincingly link issues of populist punitiveness to broader questions relating to criminology's role in this changed climate. As they write, contemporary developments often classified under the broad rubric of 'punitiveness' (mass imprisonment, securitisation, etc.) bring criminologists ever closer to the *political*, to big debates in social and political theory. This naturally gives rise to questions about processes of knowledge selection and criminology's prospective role in a better politics of crime. For them, the answer lies principally in criminology's contribution to three main sites, namely, the production of criminological knowledge relating to crime and its control; the manner in which crime policy is understood and acted upon; and alternative ways of addressing crime.

A perhaps more prosaic issue not examined by the authors, however, was the question of the measurement of the penal temperature itself; or, to quote Jonathan Simon (2010: np): 'how hot is it?' What criminologists should do (if anything) in the face of contemporary developments is logically preceded (*inter alia*) by questions relating to what the punitive turn *looks like* and this issue, in turn, is largely determined by questions of methodology. Importantly, these methodological questions are no longer debated solely within the academy. In contemporary times, the range of groups and networks concerned with crime are acutely aware of the 'props of production' (Nelken 1994: 18) used by criminologists in assessing state punitiveness. Victims' groups and other more conservative voices spoken with during the course of the research surprised me with their sophisticated understanding of the concept of punitiveness and its dimensions. These groups rejected assertions that punitiveness had increased in the jurisdictions in question, pointing instead to the manner in which imprisonment was used relative to crime levels, particularly violent crime.

The issue is, of course, one of scientific legitimacy. While it would be naive to suggest that the legitimacy of academic work forms the only or indeed the main influence on the public impact of a scholar's findings (Mills 2010), it is nevertheless a vital means of distinguishing the 'criminologist' from just another 'common sense' contributor on the subject. In an oft-quoted paragraph, Roger Hood (2002: 159) rightly argued that what makes us different is that our claims-making derives from rigorous scientific research: 'criminologists will be heard only if they can speak in their "wide ranging role" from a firm base of empirical research and research that can make claims to be scientifically rigorous'. Hood's highly insightful comments unapologetically link legitimacy with methods: for him, criminologists can only promote and maintain their scientific credibility if they prioritise 'methodological integrity', eschewing work which they 'believe to be far less good than it should be' (2002: 168). Applying this to the study of punitiveness, the discussion in Chapters 6 to 8 raises important questions about the extent to which criminologists have pursued sufficiently methodologically rigorous approaches in the empirical inquiry into punitiveness. Take the issue of crime and imprisonment. Despite scholarship dating back several decades on the need to relate imprisonment rates to crime (Lynch 1988, 1995; Pease 1994), criminologists continue to look at imprisonment rates *simplicter* when measuring state harshness. This is unfortunate in light of concerns for accuracy and further, the fact that crime, as discussed above, remains focal to the concerns of other contributors to the debate. Yet other penal theorists have been accused of selectivity in the manner in which punitiveness is assessed, using it as an umbrella term for policies and practices which they simply consider undesirable while ignoring other more inconvenient truths (Daems 2008). As argued by both Hoods and Daems, this ultimately does damage to the public stock of criminology: criminologists must avoid at all costs accusations of adopting a position based more on ideological preferences than scholarship. A '*persuasive* public criminology' (Daems 2008) on this issue requires a multidimensional, multi-method and (ideally) multidisciplinary approach to complex issues concerning the 'penal temperature' in given jurisdictions. To continue with the medical metaphor, too often we have been seduced by diagnoses of a 'punitive turn' and their putative causes when perhaps further examination of the patient was required.

Thus, we should first of all recognise the value inherent in a multidimensional tool which facilitates *meaningful* discourse about a range of issues that are sometimes simplified almost to the point of meaninglessness through the use of imprisonment rates. Secondly, we should concede that the same complexity and diversity also characterise the determinants of penal policy. The answer *contra* Garland is unlikely to reside in global explanations invoking 'the conditions of late modernity' or arguments concerning the rise of neo-liberalism (Wacquant 2009). Surface similarities often belie the mediating influence of local politico-cultural environments. Indeed, the very different policy effects arising from similar political, legal and institutional arrangements in the three countries serve to underline the need for close attention to the empirical object (especially the mediating effect of domestic conditions) and the difficulty of drawing straightforward conclusions. To acknowledge this, however, is not to fall prey to relativism, 'the view that we will never ever really be able to grasp what others are doing, and that we can have no basis for evaluating whether what they do is right' (Nelken 2009: 292). Just as local factors are critical, a common understanding of concepts such as punitiveness can be achieved and evaluations can and should take place using cosmopolitan as well as local criteria. The challenge for comparative researchers is to hold these two interpretative frameworks simultaneously in focus. Finally, while the lessons learned here form only a beginning in response to Tonry's (2007: 38) timely appeal to 'learn more, do better', it is hoped they shed some light on the Byzantine complexities of penal affairs. Here, as in so many areas, there is a need to better understand the present before we begin to contemplate the future.

Bibliography

Aas, K. 2012. The Earth is one but the world is not: Criminological theory and its geopolitical divisions. *Theoretical Criminology*, 16(1), 5–20.

ACT New Zealand. 2002. Election Manifesto, in *Party Manifestos Project*, edited by P. Pennings and H. Keman [CD ROM]. Berlin: Gesis.

Action for Children and Youth Aotearoa ('ACYA'). 2003. *Children and Youth in Aotearoa 2003*. Wellington: Action for Children and Youth Aotearoa.

Adler, F. 1983. *Nations Not Obsessed with Crime*. Littleton, CO: Rothman.

Allwright, S., Barry, J., Bradley, F., Long, J. and Thornton, L. 1999. *Hepatitis B, Hepatitis C and HIV in Irish Prisoners: Prevalence and Risk*. Dublin: Stationery Office.

Anderson, S. and Leitch, S. 1996. *Main Findings from the 1993 Scottish Crime Survey*. Edinburgh: Scottish Office Central Research Unit.

Ashby, W. 1957. *An Introduction to Cybernetics*. London: Chapman and Hall.

Ashworth, A. 1998. *The Criminal Process: An Evaluative Study*. Oxford: Oxford University Press.

Ashworth, A. 2002. *Human Rights, Serious Crime and Criminal Procedure*. London: Sweet and Maxwell.

Ashworth, A. 2003. *Sentencing and Criminal Justice*. London: Butterworths.

Ashworth, A. 2004. Social control and 'anti social behaviour': The subversion of human rights? *Law Quarterly Review*,120(2), 263.

Ashworth, A. and Zedner, L. 2008. Defending the criminal law: Reflections on the changing character of crime, procedure and sanctions. *Crime, Law and Philosophy*, 2(1), 21–51.

Audit Scotland. 2008. *Managing Increasing Prisoner Numbers in Scotland.* Report prepared for the Auditor General of Scotland. Available at: www.audit-scotland.co.uk/.../2008/nr_080508_prisoner_numbers_km.pdf [Accessed 18 March 2009].

Baker, E. 2010. Governing through crime? The case of the European Union. *European Journal of Criminology*, 7(3), 187–213.

Baker, E. 2013. The Emerging Role of the EU as a Penal Actor, in *European Penology?*, edited by T. Daems et al. Oxford: Hart Publishing.

Balance in the Criminal Law Review Group. 2007. *Final Report*. Dublin: Department of Justice, Equality and Law Reform.

Barclay, G. and Tavares, C. 2003. *International Comparisons of Criminal Justice Statistics 2001*. London: Home Office.

Barker, V. 2006. The politics of punishing: Building a state governance theory of American imprisonment variation. *Punishment & Society*, 8(1), 5–33.

Barker, F and McLeay, E. 2000. How much change?: An analysis of the initial impact of proportional representation on the New Zealand parliamentary party system. *Party Politics*, 6(2), 131–54.

Bar Review. 1996. Editorial. *Bar Review*, 1(1),4.

BBC News. 2006. Drug courts' three year extension, 30 March.

Becroft, A. 2002. Police cell remands. *Court in the Act Newsletter*, December.

Behan, C. and O'Donnell, I. 2008. Prisoners, politics and the polls: Enfranchisement and the burden of responsibility. *British Journal of Criminology*, 48(3), 319–36.

Bell, E. 2011. *Criminal Justice and Neoliberalism*. New York: Palgrave Macmillan.

Bell, L. 2004. Police no place for youth – judge. *The Dominion Post*, 7 December.

Body-Gendrot, S., Hough, M., Kerezsi, K., Levy, R. and Snacken, S. 2013. *The Routledge Handbook of European Criminology*. Abingdon: Routledge.

Bormann, N-C. 2010. Patterns of Democracy and Its Critics. Living Reviews in Democracy, 2: np. Available at: http://democracy.livingreviews.org/index.php/lrd/article/viewArticle/lrd-2010–3/26. [Accessed various dates].

Bottoms, A. 1995. The Philosophy and Politics of Punishment and Sentencing, in *The Politics of Sentencing Reform*, edited by C. Clarkson and R. Morgan. Oxford: Clarendon Press.

Bowling, B. 1999. The rise and fall of New York murder: Zero tolerance or crack's decline?*British Journal of Criminology*, 39(4), 531–54.

Bradley, T., Tauri, J. and Walters, R. 2006. Demythologising Youth Justice in Aotearoa/New Zealand, in *Comparative Youth Justice*, edited by J. Muncie and B. Goldson. London: Sage.

Brash, D. 2005. *A New Government and a New Direction*. Official 2005 Campaign Opening, Sky City Convention Centre, Auckland, 21 August.

Brodeur, J. 2007. Comparative Penology in Perspective, in*Crime, Punishment and Politics in Comparative Perspective*, edited by M. Tonry, vol. 36 of *Crime and Justice: A Review of Research*, Chicago, IL: University of Chicago Press.

Brottsförebyggande rådet (brå). 1999. *Cross-National Comparison of Crime Statistics: An Empirical Study of the Effect of Different Statistical Rules*. Stockholm, Sweden: Brottsforebygganderadet. Available at: http://www.bra.se/extra/pod/?module_instance=11 [Accessed 9 September 2008].

Brown, D. 2005. Continuity, rupture or just more of the 'volatile and contradictory'? Glimpses of New South Wales penal practice behind and through the discursive, in *The New Punitiveness: Trends, Theories, Perspectives*, edited by J. Prattet al. Cullompton, Devon: Willan.

Brown, M. 2008. Risk, punishment and liberty, in *The Critical Criminology Companion*, edited by C. Cuneen and T. Anthony. Sydney: Hawkins Press.

Brown, M. and Young, W. 2000. Recent trends in sentencing and penal policy in New Zealand. *International Criminal Justice Review*,10, 1–31.

Campbell, L. 2008. The culture of control in Ireland: Theorising recent developments in criminal justice. *Web Journal of Current Legal Issues*, 1.[Online]. Available at: http://webjcli.ncl.ac.uk/2008/issue1/campbell1.html [Accessed 3 November 2008].

Canovan, M. 1999. Trust the people! Populism and the two faces of democracy. *Political Studies*, 47, 2–16.

Caplow, T. and Simon, J. 1999. Understanding prison policy and population trends, in *Prisons*, edited by M. Tonry and J. Petersilia, vol. 26 of *Crime and Justice: A Review of Research*. Chicago, IL: University of Chicago Press.

Carter, S. 2006. Policing in a wider context: Private sector and community views of cooperative domestic security, in *Securingthe Future: Networked Policing in NewZealand*, Wellington, New Zealand. 22 November. Available at: http://www.policeact.govt.nz/securing-the-future.html [Accessed 2 March 2009].

Castlerea Prison Visiting Committee. 2007. *Annual Report 2006*. Dublin: Department of Justice, Equality and Law Reform. Available at: www.justice.ie [Accessed 28 February 2008].

Cavadino, M. and Dignan, J. 2006. *Penal Systems: A Comparative Approach*. London: Sage.

Cavadino, M. and Dignan, J. 2007. *The Penal System: An Introduction*. London: Sage.

Central Statistics Office ('CSO'). 2008. *Irish Crime Classification System* ('ICSS'). Dublin: Stationery Office.

Chong, J. 2007. *Youth Justice Statistics in New Zealand: 1992 to 2006*. Wellington: Ministry of Justice.

Coleman, R. and Sim, J. 2005. Contemporary Statecraft and the 'Punitive Obsession': A Critique of the New Penology, in *The New Punitiveness: Trends, Theories, Perspectives*, edited by J. Pratt et al. Cullompton: Willan.

Council of Europe. 2008. *SPACE I (Annual Penal Statistics of the Council of Europe): 2006 Enquiry*. Strasbourg: Council of Europe. Available at: http://www.coe.int/T/E/legal_affairs/legal_cooperation/Prisons_and_alternatives/Statistics_SPACE_I/List_Space_I.asp [Accessed 2 March 2008].

Council of Europe.2009. *SPACE I (Annual Penal Statistics of the Council of Europe): Survey 2007*. Strasbourg: Council of Europe. Available at: http://www.coe.int/T/E/legal_affairs/legal_cooperation/Prisons_and_alternatives/Statistics_SPACE_I/List_Space_I.asp [Accessed 25 September 2008].

Comptroller and Auditor General 2004. *The Probation and Welfare Service: Report on Value for Money Examination*. Dublin: Stationery Office.

Consultative Group on the Private Security Industry 1998. *Report*. Dublin: Stationery Office.

Cork Prison Visiting Committee. 2007. *Annual Report 2006*. Dublin: Department of Justice, Equality and Law Reform. Available at: www.justice.ie [Accessed 28 February 2008].

Courts Service. 2004. *Annual Report of the Courts Service*. Dublin: Courts Service.

Croall, H. 2005. Criminal Justice in the Devolved Scotland, in *Exploring Social Policy in the 'New' Scotland*, edited by G. Mooney and G. Scott. Bristol: Policy Press.

Croall, H. 2006. Criminal justice in post-devolutionary Scotland. *Critical Social Policy*, 26, 587–607.

Cuneen, C. 2010. Postcolonial Perspectives for Criminology, in *What is Criminology?*, edited by M. Bosworth and C. Hoyle. Oxford: Oxford University Press.

Daems, T. 2007. Deconstructing punitiveness: Review: Natasha A. Frost (2006): *The Punitive State: Crime, Punishment and Imprisonment across the United States*, New York, LFB Scholarly Publishing. *Crime, Law and Social Change*, 47(2), 129–33.

Daems, T. 2008. *Making Sense of Penal Change*. Oxford: Oxford University Press.

Daems, T., van ZylSmit, D. and Snacken, S. (eds) 2013. *European Penology?* Oxford: Hart Publishing.

Dalziel, K. 2008. Should we name and shame? Disclosing personal information of child sex offenders, Privacy Issues Forum 2008, Intercontinental Hotel, Wellington, New Zealand, 27 August 2008.

Davis, M. 1992. *City of Quartz*. London: Vintage.

Department of Corrections, 2007. *Overrepresentation of Māori in the Criminal Justice System: An Exploratory Report*. Wellington: Department of Corrections.

Department of Justice. 1994. *The Management of Offenders: A Five Year Plan*. Dublin: Department of Justice, Equality and Law Reform.

Department of Justice. 1998. *Strategy Statement 1998–2000: Community Security and Equality*. Dublin: Stationery Office.

Department of Justice. 2002. *Strategy Statement 2001–2004: Community Security and Equality*. Dublin: Stationery Office.

Dignan, J. 2007. Juvenile Justice, Criminal Courts and Restorative Justice, in *Handbook of Restorative Justice*, edited byG. Johnstone and D. van Ness. Cullompton, Devon: Willan.

Donnelly, D. and Scott, K. 2005. Introduction, in *Policing Scotland*, edited by D. Donnelly and K. Scott. Cullompton, Devon: Willan.

Donoghue, J. 2007. *Antisocial Behaviour Orders (ASBOs): 'Evidence in, Order out?': A Critical Evaluation of the Evidence So Far*. Available at: www.cjscotland.org.uk/pdfs/asbos.pdf [Accessed 13 March 2009].

Döring, H. and Hallerberg, M. (eds) 2004. *Patterns of Parliamentary Behavior: Passage of Legislation across Western Europe*. Aldershot: Ashgate.

Downes, D. 1988. *Contrasts in Tolerance: Post War Penal Policies in the Netherlands and England and Wales*. Oxford: Clarendon.

Downes, D. 2007. Visions of Penal Control in the Netherlands, in *Crime, Punishment and Politics in Comparative Perspective*, edited by M. Tonry, vol. 36 of *Crime and Justice: A Review of Research*. Chicago, IL: University of Chicago Press.

Downes, D. 2008. Contrasts in tolerance: Twenty years on, VSR Conference, Ghent, Belgium, 11 and 12 December 2008.

Downes, D. 2011. Comparative Criminology, Globalization and the 'Punitive Turn', in *Comparative Criminal Justice and Globalization*, edited by D. Nelken. Farnham: Ashgate.

Downes, D. and Hansen, K. 2006. Welfare and Punishment in Comparative Perspective, in *Perspectives on Punishment: The Contours of Control*, edited by S. Armstrong and L. McAra. Oxford: Oxford University Press.
Downes, D. and Morgan, R. 1994. Hostages to Fortune: The Politics of Law and Order in Post-War Britain, in *Oxford Handbook of Criminology*, edited by M. Maguire et al. Oxford: Oxford University Press.
Downes, D. and Morgan, R. 2002. The Skeletons in the Cupboard: The Politics of Law and Order, in *Oxford Handbook of Criminology*, edited by M. Maguire et al. Oxford: Oxford University Press.
Duff, P. 2007. Disclosure in Scottish criminal procedure: Another step in an inquisitorial direction? *International Journal of Evidence and Proof*, 11(3), 153–80.
Duff, P. and Gibb, A. 2002. *Criminal Justice Systems in Europe and North America: Scotland*. Helsinki: HEUNI.
Duff, P. and Hutton, N. 1999. Introduction, in *Criminal Justice in Scotland*, edited by P. Duff and N. Hutton. Aldershot: Ashgate.
Easton, B. 2005. Dull, Philistine and Conforming? How have we changed over the years?. *Listener*, 1 January. Available at: http://www.eastonbh.ac.nz/?p=539 [Accessed 20 August 2009].
Easton, B. 2007. Interview, in *Speaking Truth to Power*, edited by L. Simmons. Auckland: Auckland University Press.
Edwards, L. 2001. *S v. Miller*: The end of the Children's Hearing System as we know it? *Scots Law Times*, 21, 187–93.
Ekblom, P. 2008. Let's face it: Crime prevention is complex. Australian and New Zealand Criminology Conference, National Convention Centre, Canberra, 26 November 2008.
European Committee for the Prevention of Torture and Inhuman or Degrading Treatment or Punishment ('CPT'). 1996. *Report to the Government of the United Kingdom on the visit to the United Kingdom carried out by the CPT from 15 to 31 May 1994*. CPT/Inf (1996) 11.
European Committee for the Prevention of Torture and Inhuman or Degrading Treatment or Punishment ('CPT').2003. *Report to the Irish Government on the visit to Ireland carried out by the CPT from 20 to 28 May 2002*. CPT/Inf (2003) 36.
European Committee for the Prevention of Torture and Inhuman or Degrading Treatment or Punishment ('CPT'). 2005. *Report to the Government of the United Kingdom on the visit to the United Kingdom and the Isle of Man carried out by the CPT from 12 to 23 May 2003*. CPT/Inf (2005) 1.
European Committee for the Prevention of Torture and Inhuman or Degrading Treatment or Punishment ('CPT').2007a. *Report to the Irish Government on the visit to Ireland carried out by the CPT from 2 to 13 October 2006*. CPT/Inf (2007) 41.
European Committee for the Prevention of Torture and Inhuman or Degrading Treatment or Punishment ('CPT'). 2007b. *Report to the French Government*

on the visit to France carried out by the CPT from 27 September to 9 October 2006. CPT/Inf (2007) 44.

Evening News. 2002. A week in Westminster: Blair's long game gives McConnell a free hand, 12 November.

Fagan, J. 2004. Crime, Law and the Community: Dynamics of Incarceration in New York City, in *The Future of Imprisonment*, edited by M. Tonry. New York: Oxford University Press.

Fairweather, C. 2002. The Scottish Example: No Longer a National Disgrace, Innocent until Proven Guilty. [Online] Available at: http://www.innocentuntilprovenguilty.com/scottishexample.html [Accessed 24 March 2009].

Fairweather, C. 2006. The need for reform in Scottish prisons, in *Whose Justice? The Law and the Left*, edited by C. Fox et al. Glasgow: Scottish Left Review Press.

Farrington, D., Langan, P. and Tonry, M. 2004. *Cross-National Studies in Crime and Justice*. Washington, DC: Bureau of Justice Statistics.

Feeley, M. 1979. *The Process is the Punishment*. New York: Russell Sage Foundation.

Feeley, M. and Simon, J. 1992. The new penology: Notes on the emerging strategy of corrections and its implications. *Criminology*, 30(4), 449–74.

Feeley, M. and Simon, J. 1994. Actuarial justice: The emerging new criminal law, in *The Futures of Criminology*, edited by D. Nelken. London: Sage.

Fennell, C. 1993. *Crime and Crisis in Ireland: Justice by Illusion*. Cork: Cork University Press.

FiannaFáil. 1997. *General Election Manifesto: The Choice before Ireland*. Dublin: Fianna Fáil.

Field, S. and Nelken, D. 2010. Reading and writing youth justice in Italy and (England and) Wales. *Punishment and Society*, 12(3), 287–308.

Fortin, J. 2008. Patterns of Democracy? Counter evidence from nineteen post-Communist countries. *Zeitschrift für Vergleichende Politikwissenschaft*, 2(2), 198–220.

Frost, N. 2005. *The Punitive State: Crime, Punishment and Imprisonment across the United States*. New York: LFB Scholarly Publishing.

Frost, N. 2008. The mismeasure of punishment: Alternative measures of punitiveness and their (substantial) consequences. *Punishment & Society*, 10, 277–300.

Fyfe, N. 2005. Policing crime and disorder in Scotland, in *Policing Scotland*, edited by D. Donnelly and K. Scott. Cullompton, Devon: Willan.

Fyfe, N. and Bannister, J. 1999. Privatisation, Policing and Crime Control: Tracing the Contours of the Public–Private Divide, in *Criminal Justice in Scotland*, edited by P. Duff and N. Hutton. Aldershot: Ashgate.

Garda Síochána. 2005. *Annual Report of AnGarda Síochána 2005*. Dublin: Stationery Office.

Garland, D. 1983. Durkheim's theory of punishment: A critique, in *The Power to Punish: Contemporary Penality and Social Analysis*, edited by D. Garland and P. Young. London: Heinemann.

Garland, D. 1996. The limits of the sovereign state: Strategies of crime control in contemporary society. *British Journal of Criminology*, 36(4), 445–71.

Garland, D.2001. *The Culture of Control: Crime and Social Order in Contemporary Society*. Oxford: Oxford University Press.

Garland, D. 2011. Concepts of Culture in the Sociology of Punishment, in *Travels of the Criminal Question: Cultural Embeddedness and Diffusion*, edited by D. Melossiet al. Oxford: Hart.

General Register Office for Scotland. 2002. *Scotland's Census 2001: 2001 Population Report Scotland.* Edinburgh: General Register Office for Scotland.

George, A. and Bennett, A. 2005. *Case Studies and Theory Development in the Social Sciences*. Cambridge, MA: MIT Press.

Goff, R. 1983. The Search for Principle. *Proc. Brit. Acad.* 69, 169–87.

Gordon, D. 1989. The topography of criminal justice: A factor analysis of the 'get tough' policy trend. *Criminal Justice Policy Review*, 3(2), 89.

Green, D. 2007. Comparing Penal Cultures, in *Crime, Punishment and Politics in Comparative Perspective*, edited by M. Tonry, vol. 36 of *Crime and Justice: A Review of Research.* Chicago, IL: University of Chicago Press.

Green, D. 2008. *When Children Kill Children: Penal Populism and Political Culture.* Oxford: Oxford University Press.

Green, D.2009. Feeding Wolves: Punitiveness and Culture. *European Journal of Criminology*, 6(6), 517–36.

Guardian, The. 2005. Scotland has second highest murder rate in Europe, 26 September.

Haggenmüller, S. 2013. The principle of proportionality and the European Arrest Warrant. *Oñati Socio-legal Series* 3 (1), 95–106. [online] Available at: http://ssrn.com/abstract=2200874. [Accessed various dates].

Hallsworth, S. and Lea, J. 2008. *Confronting the Criminology of Complacency: A Rejoinder to some recent critiques of the 'punitive turn'*.[Online] Available at: www.bunker8.pwp.blueyonder.co.uk/misc/complacency.html. [Accessed various dates].

Hamilton, C. 2004. Restorative justice in Ireland: A new way forward? *Irish Law Times*, 22(20), 315–20.

Hamilton, C. 2007. *The Presumption of Innocence and Irish Criminal Law: Whittling the Golden Thread.* Dublin: Irish Academic Press.

Hamilton C. and Kilkelly, U. 2008. Human rights in Irish prisons. *Judicial Studies Institute Journal*, 2, 58–85.

Hamilton, C. and Lines, R. 2009. The Campaign for Prisoner Voting Rights in Ireland, in *Criminal Disenfranchisement in an International Perspective*, edited by A. Ewald and B. Rottinghaus. New York: Cambridge University Press.

Havemann, P. and Havemann, J. 1995. Retrieving the 'Decent Society': Law and Order Politics in New Zealand 1984–1993, in *Perceptions of Justice*, edited by K. Hazlehurst. Aldershot, and Brookfield, VT: Avebury.

Hawke, G. 2006. Securing the future: Facing current and future realities, in *Securing the Future: Networked Policing in NewZealand*, Wellington, **New**

Zealand, 22 November. Available at: http://www.policeact.govt.nz/securing-the-future.html [Accessed 2 March 2009].

Herald, The (Glasgow). 1996a Law reforms criticised, sentences a charade, says judge, 28 March.

Herald, The (Glasgow). 1996b. Lord Hope warns that the Scottish Secretary is a threat to the nation's legal system; Forsyth accused of not listening, 1 October.

Herald, The (Glasgow).1996c. Crime and punishment in 69 pages, 18 June.

Herald, The (Glasgow). 1997. No consultation, no research, no study: This bill is a sham, 12 February.

Hinds, L. 2002. Law and order: The politics of get tough crime control. PhD thesis, Griffith University, Australia.

Hinds, L. 2005. Crime control in Western countries: 1970 to 2000, in *The New Punitiveness: Trends, Theories, Perspectives*, edited by J. Pratt et al. Cullompton, Devon: Willan.

Hogg, K. 1999. *Youth Crime in Scotland: A Scottish Executive Policy Unit Review*. Edinburgh: Scottish Executive.

Hood, R. 2002. Criminology And Penal Policy: The Vital Role of Empirical Research, in *Ideology, Crime and Criminal Justice*, edited by A. Bottoms and M. Tonry. Cullompton, Devon: Willan.

Howard League for Penal Reform. 2000. Remand on Bail and Remand in Custody. *Factsheet 14*, November.

Hughes, G. and Edwards, A. 2005. Comparing the governance of safety in Europe: A geo-historical approach. *Theoretical Criminology*, 9(3), 345–63.

Human Rights Commission. 2004. *Human Rights in New Zealand Today*. Wellington: Human Rights Commission.

Human Rights Commission. 2009. *Comments of the New Zealand Human Rights Commission on New Zealand's Implementation of the United Nations Convention Against Torture*. Wellington: Human Rights Commission.

Hurd, C. 2008. The changing face of preventive detention in New Zealand, Sentencing 2008 Conference, National Museum of Australia, Canberra, 8–10 February.

Hutchinson, S. **2006. Countering** catastrophic criminology: Reform, punishment and the modern liberal compromise. *Punishment & Society*, 8(4), 443–67.

Hutton, N. 2005. Beyond popular punitiveness. *Punishment & Society*, 7(3), 243–58.

Hutton, N. 2006. Sentencing as a Social Practice, in *Perspectives on Punishment: The Culture of Control*, edited by S. Armstrong and L. McAra. Oxford: Oxford University Press.

International Centre for Prison Studies (ICPS). 2006. *World Prison Brief*. Available at: http://www.kcl.ac.uk/schools/law/research/icps [Accessed various dates].

International Centre for Prison Studies (ICPS). 2008. *World Prison Brief*. Available at: http://www.kcl.ac.uk/schools/law/research/icps [Accessed various dates].

International Centre for Prison Studies (ICPS). (2009) *World Prison Brief*. Available at: http://www.kcl.ac.uk/schools/law/research/icps [Accessed various dates].

Inglis, T. 2003.*Truth, Power and Lies*. Dublin: UCD Press.

Inspector of Prisons and Places of Detention. 2003. *First Annual Report*, Dublin: Irish Prison Service.

Inspector of Prisons and Places of Detention. 2005. *Second Annual Report*. Dublin: Irish Prison Service.

Irish Prison Service.2005–2007. *Annual Reports 2004–2006*. Dublin: Irish Prison Service.

Irish Prison Service. 2007. *Annual Report 2006*. Dublin: Irish Prison Service.

Irish Times, The. 2001. Assault case raises issue of gardaí's night-club 'nixers', 5 July.

Irish Times, The. 2003. Should we extend the harmonisation of our criminal justice systems, 24 April.

Irish Times, The. 2006. Illegal firearms amnesty to follow Coolock murder, 6 March.

Irish Times, The. 2007. Prison deaths hit record high as 12 die in custody, 22 December.

Jesson, B. 1999. To build a nation. *New Zealand Political Review*, April 1999.

Jones, T. and Newburn, T. 2007. *Policy Transfer and Criminal Justice: Exploring US Influence over British Crime Control Policy*. Maidenhead: Open University Press.

Justice Committee. 2008. *Fourth Report 2008: Report into the Effective Use of Police Resources*. Available at: http://www.scottish.parliament.uk/s3/committees/justice/inquiries/policeRes/index.htm [Accessed 7 April 2009].

Kennedy, H. 2004. *Just Law: The Changing Face of Justice and Why it Matters to Us All*. London: Chatto & Windus.

Kilcommins, S. and O'Donnell, I. 2003. Wiping the slate clean: Rehabilitating offenders and protecting the public. *Administration*, 51(3), 73–89.

Kilcommins, S., O'Donnell, I., O'Sullivan, E. and Vaughan, B. 2004. *Crime, Punishment and the Search for Order in Ireland*. Dublin: Institute of Public Administration.

Kilkelly, U. 2006. *Youth Justice in Ireland: Tough Lives, Rough Justice*. Dublin: Irish Academic Press.

Kilkelly, U. 2008. Youth courts and children's rights: The Irish experience. *Youth Justice*, 8(1), 39–56.

King, R. and McDermott, K. 1995. *The State of Our Prisons*. Oxford: Clarendon Press.

Kommer, M. 1994. Punitiveness in Europe: A comparison. *European Journal of Criminal Policy and Research*, 2(1), 29–43.

Kommer, M. 2004. Punitiveness in Europe revisited. *Criminology in Europe*, 3(1), 8–12.

Kury, H. 2009. Dimensions of punitiveness in Germany. *European Journal of Criminal Policy and Research*, 15(2), 61–83.

Kutateladze, B. 2005. US v. Europe: Comparative analysis of American, French, German and Russian punitiveness. Unpublished MA thesis, John Jay College of Criminal Justice, New York.

Kutateladze, B. 2007a. How do we really know which country is more punitive? Introducing a 41-criteria measurement of state punitiveness, American Society of Criminology Annual Meeting, Atlanta, Georgia, 14–17 November.

Kutateladze, B. 2007b. Raising and addressing some methodological problems of an international comparison of punishment and sentencing law, American Society of Criminology Annual Meeting, Atlanta, Georgia, 14–17 November.

Kutateladze, B. 2009. *Is America Really so Punitive?: Exploring a Continuum of US State Criminal Justice Policies*. New York: LFB Scholarly Publishing.

Lacey, N. 2008. *The Prisoners' Dilemma: Political Economy and Punishment in Contemporary Democracies*. Cambridge: Cambridge University Press.

Lappi-Seppälä, T. 2007. Penal Policy in Scandinavia, in *Crime, Punishment and Politics in Comparative Perspective*, edited by M. Tonry, vol. 36 of *Crime and Justice: A Review of Research*. Chicago, IL: University of Chicago Press.

Lappi-Seppälä, T. 2008. Trust, Welfare, and Political Culture: Explaining Differences in National Penal Policies, in *Crime, Punishment and Politics in Comparative Perspective*, edited by M. Tonry, vol. 36 of *Crime and Justice: A Review of Research*. Chicago, IL: University of Chicago Press.

Lappi-Seppälä, T. 2011. Explaining imprisonment in Europe. *European Journal of Criminology*, 8(4), 303–28.

Lappi-Seppälä, T. 2012. Explaining National Differences in the Use of Imprisonment, in *Resisting Punitiveness in Europe?*, edited by S. Snacken and E. Dumortier. Abingdon and New York: Routledge.

Lash, B. and Luketina, F. 1990. *Offending While on Bail*. Wellington: Department of Justice.

Law Society of Scotland Joint Committee on Human Rights. 2009. *Children's Rights: A Call for Evidence*. Available at: www.lawscot.org.uk [Accessed 5 May 2009].

Lea, J. 2004. Hitting criminals where it hurts: Organised crime and the erosion of due process. *Cambrian Law Review*, 30, 81–96.

Leddy, J. and O'Connell, M. 2002. The prevalence, nature and psychological correlates of bullying in Irish prisons. *Legal and Criminological Psychology*, 7, 131–40.

Levy, R. 2007. Pardons and Amnesties as Policy Instruments in Contemporary France, in *Crime, Punishment and Politics in Comparative Perspective*, edited by M. Tonry, vol. 36 of *Crime and Justice: A Review of Research*. Chicago, IL: University of Chicago Press.

Lijphart, A. 1999. *Patterns of Democracy: Government Forms and Performance in Thirty-Six Countries*. New Haven, CT: Yale University Press.

Loader, I. 2002. Policing, securitisation and democratisation in Europe. *Criminal Justice*, 2(2), 125–53.

Loader. I. 2006. Fall of the 'platonic guardians: Liberalism, criminology and political responses to crime in England and Wales. *British Journal of Criminology*, 46(4), 561–86.

Loader. I. 2010. For penal moderation: Notes towards a public philosophy of punishment. *Theoretical Criminology*, 14(3), 349–67.

Loader, I. and Sparks, R. 2010. *Public Criminology?* Abingdon: Routledge.

Loucks, N. 1997. *HMPI Corton Vale: Research into Drugs and Alcohol, Violence and Bullying, Suicides and Self-Injury and Backgrounds of Abuse*. Scottish Prison Service Occasional Papers, Report No.1/98. Edinburgh: Scottish Prison Service.

Lynch, J. 1988. A comparison of prison use in England, Canada, West Germany and the United States: A limited test of the punitive hypothesis. *Journal of Criminal Law & Criminology*, 79(1), 180–217.

Lynch, J. 1995. Crime in International Perspective, in *Crime*, edited by J.Q. Wilson and J. Petersilia. San Francisco, CA: Institute for Comparative Studies Press.

Lynch, N. 2008. Youth justice in New Zealand: A children's rights perspective. *Youth Justice*, 8(3), 215–28.

McAra, L. 1999. The Politics of Penality: An Overview of the Development of Penal Policy, in *Criminal Justice in Scotland*, edited by P. Duff and N. Hutton. Aldershot: Ashgate.

McAra, L. 2002. The Scottish Juvenile Justice System: Policy and Practice, in *Juvenile Justice Systems: International Perspectives*, edited by J. Winterdyk. Toronto, ON: Canadian Scholars Press.

McAra, L. 2004. The cultural and institutional dynamics of transformation: Youth justice in Scotland and England and Wales. *Cambrian Law Review*, 35, 23–54.

McAra, L. 2005. Modelling penal transformation. *Punishment & Society*, 7(3), 277–302.

McAra, L. 2006. Criminal justice in these islands: Scotland, Encounter/RSE conference on Alternatives to Prison, Edinburgh, Scotland, 7–9 December 2006.

McAra, L. 2008. Crime, criminology and criminal justice in Scotland. *European Journal of Criminology*, 5(4), 481–504.

McAra, L.2011. Global politics and local culture: A response to Nicola Lacey. *Punishment & Society*, 13(1), 96–104.

MacCarthaigh, M. 2005. *Accountability in Irish Parliamentary Politics*. Dublin: Institute of Public Administration.

MacCarthaigh, M. 2007. The Recycling of Political Accountability, in *Recycling the State: The Politics of Adaptation in Ireland*, edited by M. MacCarthaigh and K. Hayward. Dublin: Irish Academic Press.

McCarthy, P. 2006. Prisoner reintegration: Looking forward, Prison Fellowship New Zealand Conference, Beyond Retribution- Advancing the Law and Order Debate, Upper Hutt, New Zealand, 14 May 2006.

McCullagh, C. 1999. Rural Crime in the Republic of Ireland, in *Crime and Conflict in the Countryside*, edited by G. Dingwall and S.R. Moody. Cardiff: University of Wales Press.

McCutcheon, J.P. and Walsh, D. 1999. Seizure of criminal assets: An overview. *Irish Criminal Law Journal*,9(2), 127–32.

McDonald, S. 2003. The nature of the Anti-Social Behaviour Order – *R (McCann & Others) v. Crown Court at Manchester*. *Modern Law Review*, 66(4), 630–39.

McIvor, G. and Williams, B. 1999. Community-Based Disposals, in *Criminal Justice in Scotland*, edited by P. Duff and N. Hutton. Aldershot: Ashgate.

MacLeod, G. 2002. From urban entrepreneurialism to a revanchist city?On the spatial injustices of Glasgow's renaissance. *Antipode*, 34, 602–24.

McManus, J. 1999. Imprisonment and Other Custodial Sentences, in *Criminal Justice in Scotland*, edited by P. Duff and N. Hutton. Aldershot: Ashgate.

McNeill, F. 2005. Offender Management in Scotland: The First Hundred Years. [Online] Available at: www.cjscotland.org.uk/ee.php/articles/offender_management/index.php [Accessed 6 March 2009].

Matthews, R. 2005. The myth of punitiveness. *Theoretical Criminology*, 9(2), 175–201.

Matthews, R. 2009. Beyond "so what" criminology: Rediscovering realism. *Theoretical Criminology*, 13(3), 341–62.

Maxwell, G. 2007. The Youth Justice System in New Zealand: Restorative Justice Delivered through the Family Group Conference, in *Restorative Justice and Practices in New Zealand: Towards a Restorative Society*, edited by G. Maxwell and J. Liu. Wellington: Institute of Policy Studies, Victoria University of Wellington.

Maxwell, G. and Popplewell, E. 2003. *Youth Court Offending Rates: Final Report*. Wellington: Crime and Justice Research Centre, Victoria University of Wellington.

Maxwell, G., Kingi, V., Robertson, J., Morris, A. and Cunningham, C. 2004. *Achieving Effective Outcomes in Youth Justice: Final Report*. Wellington: Ministry of Social Development.

Meade, J. 2000. The disguise of civility: Civil forfeiture of the proceeds of crime and the presumption of innocence in Irish law. *Hibernian Law Journal*, 1, 1.

Meek, J. 1995. The revival of preventive detention in New Zealand 1986–1993. *Australian and New Zealand Journal of Criminology*. 28(3), 225–57.

Melossi, D. 2001. The cultural embeddedness of social control: Reflections on the comparison of Italian and North American cultures concerning punishment. *Theoretical Criminology*, 5(4), 403–24.

Melossi, D. 2011. Neoliberalism's Elective Affinities: Penality, Political Economy and International Relations, in *Travels of the Criminal Question: Cultural Embeddedness and Diffusion*, edited by D. Melossiet al. Oxford: Hart.

Mills, L.J. 2010. Have I Got News for You? Media, Research and Popular Audiences, in *What is Criminology?*, edited by M. Bosworthand C. Hoyle. Oxford: Oxford University Press.

Ministry of Justice. 1998. *The Use of Imprisonment in New Zealand*. Wellington: Ministry of Justice.

Ministry of Justice 2002. *International Comparisons of Recorded Violent Crime Rates for 2000*. Wellington: Ministry of Justice.

Moody, S. and Tombs, J. 1993. Alternatives to prosecution: The public interest redefined. *Criminal Law Review*, May, 357–67.

Mooney, G. and Poole, L. 2004. A land of milk and honey?: Social policy in Scotland after devolution. *Critical Social Policy*, 24(4), 458–83.

Mooney, G. and Scott, G. (eds) 2005. *Exploring Social Policy in the 'New' Scotland*. Bristol: The Policy Press.

Morris, A. and Maxwell, G. 1993. Juvenile justice in New Zealand: A new paradigm. *Australian and New Zealand Journal of Criminology*, 26(1), 72–90.

Mulcahy, A. 2002. The Impact of the Northern Troubles on Criminal Justice in the Irish Republic, in *Criminal Justice in Ireland*, edited by P. O'Mahony. Dublin: Institute of Public Administration.

Mulcahy, A. and O'Mahony, E. 2005. *Policing and Social Marginalisation in Ireland*. Dublin: Combat Poverty Agency.

Muncie, J. 2008. The 'punitive turn' in juvenile justice: Cultures of control and rights compliance in Western Europe and the USA. *Youth Justice*, 8(2), 107–21.

Muncie, J. 2011. On Globalisation and Exceptionalism, in *Comparative Criminal Justice and Globalization*, edited by D. Nelken. Farnham: Ashgate.

Murphy, T. and Whitty, N. 2007. Risk and human rights in UK prison governance. *British Journal of Criminology*, 47(5), 798–816.

Murphy. T. and Whitty, N. 2013. Making history: Academic criminology and human rights, *British Journal of Criminology*, 53(4), 568–87.

National Crime Council and Institute of Criminology, University College Dublin. 2003. *Public Order Offences in Ireland*. Dublin: National Crime Council.

National Crime Forum. 1998. *Report*. Dublin: Institute of Public Administration.

National Economic and Social Forum. 2002. *Reintegration of Prisoners*. Report No. 22. Dublin: Stationery Office.

National Party of New Zealand.1987. Election Manifesto, in *Party Manifestos Project*, edited by P. Pennings and H. Keman [CD ROM]. Berlin: Gesis.

Neapolitan, J. 1997. *Cross National Crime: A Research Review and Sourcebook*. Westport, CT: Greenwood Press.

Neapolitan, J. 2001. An examination of cross-national variation in punitiveness. *International Journal of Offender Therapy and Comparative Criminology*, 45(6), 691–710.

Nelken, D. 1994. Reflexive Criminology?, in *The Futures of Criminology*, edited by D. Nelken. London: Sage.

Nelken, D. 2005. When is a Society Non-Punitive?: The Italian Case, in *The New Punitiveness: Trends, Theories, Perspectives*, edited by J. Pratt et al. Cullompton, Devon: Willan.

Nelken, D. 2006. Patterns of punitiveness. *Modern Law Review*, 69(2), 262–77.

Nelken, D. 2008. The punitive obsession and the obsession with punishment, European Society of Criminology Conference, Edinburgh, Scotland, 5 September 2008.

Nelken, D. 2009. Comparative criminal justice: Beyond ethnocentrism and relativism. *European Journal of Criminology*, 6(4), 291–311.

Nelken, D. 2011. Making Sense of Punitiveness, in *Comparative Criminal Justice and Globalization*, edited by D. Nelken. Farnham: Ashgate.

New Zealand Herald. 2004. Goon squad inquiry condemns prison culture, 17 December.

New Zealand Herald. 2005. Do nothing plan defended, 5 November.

New Zealand Herald 2006a. Crimefightinggroup looks to set up in West Auckland, 11 January.

New Zealand Herald 2006b. End the right to silence says QC, 20 October.

New Zealand Herald on Sunday. 2006. The price of home security, 9 April.

New Zealand Police. 1984. *Digest of Statistics 1984*. Wellington: New Zealand Police.

New Zealand Police. 2006. *Consultation Document for the Police Act Review*. Available at: www.policeact.govt.nz [Accessed 14 April 2009].

Newbold, G. 1992. *Crime and Deviance*. Auckland: Oxford University Press.

Newbold, G. 2000. *Crime in New Zealand*. Palmerstown North: Dunmore Publishing.

Newbold, G. 2007. *The Problem of Prisons: Corrections Reform in New Zealand since 1984*. Wellington: Dunmore Publishing.

Newbold, G. and Eskridge, C. 2005. History and Development of Modern Correctional Practices in New Zealand, in *Comparative and International Criminal Justice*, edited by C. Fields and R. Moore.Prospect Heights, IL: Waveland Press.

Newburn, T. 2007. 'Tough on Crime': Penal Policy in England and Wales, in *Crime, Punishment and Politics in Comparative Perspective*, edited by M. Tonry, vol. 36 of *Crime and Justice: A Review of Research*. Chicago, IL: University of Chicago Press.

Newburn, T. and Sparks, R. 2004. Criminal Justice and Political Cultures, in *Criminal Justice and Political Cultures*, edited by T. Newburn and R. Sparks. Cullompton, Devon: Willan.

O'Connell, M. 1998. Stop this madness: And tone down the headlines too. *Magill*, 1 January.

O'Connor, G. 2006. Response to keynote address, Securing the future: Networked policing in New Zealand, Wellington, New Zealand, 22 November. Available at: http://www.policeact.govt.nz/securing-the-future.html [Accessed 2 March 2009].

O'Donnell, I. 2001. Prison matters. *Irish Jurist*, 26, 153–73.

O'Donnell, I. 2002. Interpreting Crime Trends. *Irish Criminal Law Journal*, 12(1), 10–16.

O'Donnell, I. 2004. Imprisonment and penal policy in Ireland. *Howard Journal of Criminal Justice*, 43(3), 253–66.

O'Donnell, I. 2005. Putting prison in its place. *Judicial Studies Institute Journal*, 5(2), 54–68.

O'Donnell, I. 2008. Stagnation and change in Irish penal policy. *Howard Journal of Criminal Justice*, 47(2), 121–33.

O'Donnell, I. 2010. Criminology, Bureaucracy and Unfinished Business, in *What Is Criminology?*, edited by M. Bosworth and C. Hoyle. Oxford: Oxford University Press.

O'Donnell, I. and O'Sullivan, E. 2001. *Crime Control in Ireland: The Politics of Intolerance*. Cork: Cork University Press.

O'Donnell, I. and O'Sullivan, E. 2003. The politics of intolerance – Irish style. *British Journal of Criminology*, 43(1), 41–62.

O'Donnell, I., O'Sullivan, E. and Healy, D. (eds) 2005. *Crime and Punishment in Ireland 1922–2003: A Statistical Sourcebook*. Dublin: Institute of Public Administration.

O'Dwyer, K. 2002. Juvenile Crime and Justice in Ireland, in *Juvenile Justice Systems: An International Comparison of Problems and Solutions*, edited by N. Bala et al. Toronto, ON: Thompson Educational Publishing.

O'Mahony, P. 1996. *Criminal Chaos: Seven Crises in Irish Criminal Justice*. Dublin: Round Hall Sweet and Maxwell.

O'Mahony, P. 1998. Losing the plot. *Magill*, 1 January.

O'Mahony, P. 2002. The Psychology of Police Interrogation: The Kerry Babies Case, in *Criminal Justice in Ireland*, edited by P. O'Mahony. Dublin: Institute of Public Administration.

O'Malley, P. 1992. Risk, power and crime prevention. *Economy and Society*, 21(3), 251–68.

O'Malley, P. 1999. Volatile and contradictory punishment. *Theoretical Criminology*, 3(2), 175–96.

O'Malley, P. 2000. Criminologies of catastrophe? Understanding criminal justice on the edge of the new millennium. *Australian and New Zealand Journal of Criminology*, 33(2), 153–67.

O'Malley, T. 2006. *Sentencing Law and Practice*. 2nd edn. Dublin: Thomson Round Hall.

O'Neill, A. 2004. Judging democracy: The devolutionary settlement and the Scottish Constitution. *Edinburgh Law Review*, 8(2), 177–205.

O'Sullivan, E. and O'Donnell, I. 2007. Coercive confinement in the Republic of Ireland: The waning of a culture of control. *Punishment & Society*, 9(1), 27–48.

O'Sullivan, E. and O'Donnell, I. 2012. *Coercive Confinement in Ireland: Patients, Prisoners and Penitents*. Manchester: Manchester University Press.

O'Toole, F. 2009. *Ship of Fools: How Stupidity and Corruption Sank the Celtic Tiger*. London: Faber and Faber.

Office of the Ombudsman. 2005. *Ombudsman's Investigation of the Department of Corrections in relation to the Detention and Treatment of Prisoners*. Wellington: Office of the Ombudsman.

Optican, S. 2007. Criminal Procedure, in *Criminal Justice in New Zealand*, edited by J. Tolmie and W. Brookbanks. Wellington: Lexis.

Orr, J. 1997. Strathclyde's Spotlight Initiative, in *Zero Tolerance: Policing a Free Society*, edited by N. Dennis. London: Institute for Economic Affairs.

Packer, H. 1968. *The Limits of the Criminal Sanction*. New York: Stanford University Press.

Pease, K. 1994. Cross-national imprisonment rates: Limitations of method and possible conclusions. *British Journal of Criminology*, 34(5), 116–30.

Penal Policy Review Committee. 1981. *Report*. Wellington: Department of Justice.

Piacentini, L. and Walters, R. 2006. The politicisation of youth crime in Scotland and the rise of the 'Burberry Court'. *Youth Justice*, 6(1), 43–59.

Pratt, J. 1988. Law and order politics in New Zealand 1986: A comparison with the United Kingdom 1974–79. *International Journal of the Sociology of Law*, 16, 103–26.

Pratt, J. 1995. Dangerousness, risk and the technologies of power. *Australian and New Zealand Journal of Criminology*, 28(1), 3–31.

Pratt, J. 1996. Governmentality, neo-liberalism and dangerousness: Reflections on recent trends towards the punishment of persistence. Unpublished paper. Victoria University, Wellington.

Pratt, J. 2002. *Punishment and Civilization*. London: Sage.

Pratt, J. 2005. Elias, punishment and decivilization, in *The New Punitiveness: Trends, Theories, Perspectives*, edited by J. Pratt et al. Cullompton, Devon: Willan.

Pratt, J. 2006. The dark side of paradise. *British Journal of Criminology*, 46(4), 541–60.

Pratt, J. 2007. *Penal Populism*. London: Routledge.

Pratt, J. 2008a. Scandinavian exceptionalism in an era of penal excess. Part 1: The Nature and roots of Scandinavian exceptionalism. *British Journal of Criminology*,48(2), 119–37.

Pratt, J. 2008b. Scandinavian exceptionalism in an era of penal excess. Part 2: Does Scandinavian exceptionalism have a future?. *British Journal of Criminology*, 48(3), 275–92.

Pratt, J. 2008c. Penal Populism and the Contemporary Role of Punishment, in *The Critical Criminology Companion*, edited by C. Cuneen and T. Anthony. Sydney: Hawkins Press.

Pratt, J. 2009. Book Review: *When Children Kill Children: Penal Populism and Political Culture*. *Punishment & Society*: 11(1), 134–6.

Pratt, J. and Clark, M. 2005. Penal populism in New Zealand. *Punishment & Society*, 7(3), 303–22.

Pratt, J. and Treacher, P. 1988. Law and order and the 1987 New Zealand election. *Australian and New Zealand Journal of Criminology*, 21(3), 253–68.

Pratt, J., Brown, D., Brown, M., Hallsworth, S. and Morrison, W. (eds) 2005. *The New Punitiveness: Trends, Theories, Perspectives*. Cullompton, Devon: Willan.

Prisons Hygiene Policy Group. 1997. *Report*. Dublin: Stationery Office.

Private Security Authority (PSA) 2006. *Annual Report 2005*. Dublin: Stationery Office.

Quince, K. 2007. Māori and the Criminal Justice in New Zealand, in *Criminal Justice in New Zealand*, edited byJ. Tolmie and W. Brookbanks. Wellington: Lexis-Nexis.

Radzinowicz, L. 1961. *In Search of Criminology*. London: Heinemann.

Reiner, R. 2007. *Law and Order: An Honest Citizen's Guide to Crime and Control*. Cambridge, and Malden, MA: Polity Press.

Rethinking Crime and Punishment. 2009. *Let's End the Law and Order Auction*. Press release, issued 8 January 2009. Available at: www.scoop.co.nz/stories/PO0901/S00036.htm [Accessed 4 April 2009].

Rifkind, M. 1989. Penal policy: The way ahead. *Howard Journal of Criminal Justice*, 28(2), 81–90.

Roberts, J. 2003. Sentencing reform in New Zealand: An analysis of the Sentencing Act 2002. *Australian and New Zealand Journal of Criminology*, 36(3), 249–71.
Robinson, G. and McNeill, F. 2004. Purposes Matter: Examining the Ends of Probation, in *What Matters in Probation Work*, edited by G. Mair. Cullompton, Devon: Willan.
Roché, S. 2007. Criminal Justice Policy in France: Illusions of Severity, in *Crime, Punishment and Politics in Comparative Perspective*, edited by M. Tonry, vol. 36 of *Crime and Justice: A Review of Research*. Chicago, IL: University of Chicago Press.
Roper, C. 1989. *Prison Review: Te Ara Hou – The New Way: Report of the Ministerial Committee of Inquiry into the Prisons System*. Wellington: Government Printer.
Ross, G. 2006. *Conditions in Scottish Prisons Updated.* SPICe Briefing 3 May 2006, 06/41. Available at: www.scottishparliament.uk [Accessed 17 March 2009].
Rottman, D.B. 1980. *Crime in the Republic of Ireland: Statistical Trends and their Interpretation*. General Research Series No. 102. Dublin: Economic and Social Research Institute.
Rottman, D.B. 1984. *The Criminal Justice System: Policy and Performance*. Report No. 77. Dublin: National Economic and Social Council.
Ryan, M. 2003. *Penal Policy and Political Culture in England and Wales*. Winchester: Waterside Press.
Sack, F. and Schlepper, C. 2013. Changes in Criminal Law in German Late Modernity, in *The Routledge Handbook of European Criminology*, edited by S. Body-Gendrot et al. Abingdon: Routledge.
Salas, D. 2005. *La volunté de punir: Essai sur le populisme pénal*. Paris: Hachette.
Sankoff, P. 2007. Constituents in the Trial Process: The Evolution of the Common Law Criminal Trial in New Zealand, in *Criminal Justice in New Zealand*, edited by J. Tolmie and W. Brookbanks. Wellington: Lexis Nexis.
Savelsberg, J. 1999. Cultures of punishment: USA-Germany, American Society of Criminology Annual Meeting, Toronto, Canada. 17–21 November.
Savelsberg, J. 2002. Cultures of control in modern societies. *Law and Social Inquiry*, 27(3), 685–710.
Savelsberg, J. 2004. Religion, historical contingencies and cultures of punishment: The German case and beyond. *Law and Social Inquiry*, 29(2), 373–401.
Savelsberg, J. 2011. Globalization and States of Punishment, in *Comparative Criminal Justice and Globalization*, edited by D. Nelken. Farnham: Ashgate.
Scotsman, The. 1994. New curbs on bail for killers and rapists, 28 June.
Scotsman, The. 1995. Forsyth's juggling act on crime and punishment, 7 September.
Scotsman, The. 1996a. Do-gooders derided by Forsyth, 25 April.
Scotsman, The. 1996b. Planned crime legislation attacked, 24 October.
Scotsman, The. 1996c. Criminal justice complexities, 18 June.
Scotsman, The. 1997. Lib Dems rip heart out of flagship Crime Bill, 19 March.
Scotsman, The. 2004. Prison ruling paves the way for costly claims, 27 April.

Scotsman, The. 2006. Senior policeman hits back at ministers over ASBO use, 8 July.

Scotsman, The. 2007. Scottish children's homes in crisis, 13 March.

Scottish Consortium of Crime and Criminal Justice. 2008. *Crime and Justice in Scotland 2006/7: A Third Review of Progress*. Edinburgh: Scottish Consortium of Crime and Criminal Justice. Available at: www.sccj.org.uk [Accessed various dates].

Scottish Executive. 1999. *Statistical Bulletin: Prison Statistics Scotland*. Edinburgh: Scottish Executive.

Scottish Executive. 2000. *It's a Criminal Waste: Stop Youth Crime Now: The Report of the Advisory Group on Youth Crime*. Edinburgh: Scottish Executive.

Scottish Executive. 2001. *Regulation of the Private Security Industry in Scotland: A Consultation Document*. Edinburgh: Scottish Executive.

Scottish Executive. 2002. *Scotland's Action Programme to Reduce Youth Crime*. Edinburgh: Scottish Executive.

Scottish Executive. 2004. *Re:duce, Re:habilitate, Re:form: A Consultation on Reducing Reoffending in Scotland*. Edinburgh: Scottish Executive.

Scottish Executive. 2006a. *Statistical Bulletin: Prison Statistics Scotland 2005/06*. Edinburgh: Scottish Executive.

Scottish Executive. 2006b. *Statistical Bulletin: Recorded Crime in Scotland 2005/06*. Edinburgh: Scottish Executive.

Scottish Executive. 2007a. *Statistical Bulletin: Prison Statistics Scotland 2006/07*. Edinburgh: Scottish Executive.

Scottish Executive. 2007b. *Criminal Justice Series: Homicide in Scotland 2006/07*. Edinburgh: Scottish Executive.

Scottish Home and Health Department. 1985. *Report of the Review of Suicide Preventions at HM Detention Centre and HM Youth Offenders Institution, Glenochil*. Edinburgh: HMSO.

Scottish Office. 1994a. *Firm and Fair: Improving the Delivery of Justice in Scotland*. Edinburgh: HMSO.

Scottish Office. 1994b. *Juries and Verdicts*. Edinburgh: HMSO.

Scottish Office. 1996a. *Making the Punishment Fit the Crime*. Edinburgh: HMSO.

Scottish Office. 1996b. *Crime and Punishment*. Edinburgh: HMSO.

Scottish Office. 1998. *Community Sentencing: The Tough Option: Review of Criminal Justice Social Work Services*. Edinburgh: HMSO.

Scottish Prisons Commission. 2008. *Scotland's Choice*. Edinburgh: Scottish Prisons Commission.

Scottish Prison Service. 1990. *Opportunity and Responsibility*. Edinburgh: HMSO.

Scottish Prison Service. 2002. *Estates Review*. Edinburgh: Scottish Prison Service.

Scraton, P., Sim, J. and Skidmore, P. 1988. Through the barricades: Prisoner protest and penal policy in Scotland. *Journal of Law and Society*, 15(3), 247–62.

Security Industry Authority. 2006. *Update Scotland*. Available at: http://www.the-sia.org.uk/NR/rdonlyres/AC0C5E14-0189-4534-B7AA-F3C320551415/0/sia_update_scotland.pdf [Accessed 1 March 2009].

Selmini, R. 2011. The Governance of Crime in Italy: Global Tendencies and Local Peculiarities, in *Travels of the Criminal Question: Cultural Embeddedness and Diffusion*, edited by D. Melossiet al. Oxford: Hart.

Seymour, M. 2006. Transition and Reform: Juvenile Justice in the Republic of Ireland, in *International Handbook of Juvenile Justice*, edited by J. Junger-Tas, and S.H. Decker. Dordrecht: Springer.

Simon, J. 1995. They died with their boots on: The boot camp and the limits of modern penality. *Social Justice*, 22(2), 25–48.

Simon, J. 1997. Governing through Crime, in *The Crime Conundrum: Essays under Criminal Justice*, edited by L. Friedman and G. Fisher. Boulder, CO: Westview Press.

Simon, J. 2007. *Governing through Crime: How the War on Crime has Transformed American Democracy*. Oxford: Oxford University Press.

Simon, J. 2010. Governing through crime: A cool read on a hot topic. [online]. Available at: http://governingthroughcrime.blogspot.ie/2010/08/public-criminology-cool-read-on-hot.html [Accessed various dates].

Smith, D. and Young, P. 1999. Crime Trends in Scotland since 1950, in *Criminal Justice in Scotland*, edited by P. Duff and N. Hutton. Aldershot: Ashgate.

Snacken, S. 2007. Penal Policy and Practice in Belgium, in *Crime, Punishment and Politics in Comparative Perspective*, edited by M. Tonry, vol. 36 of *Crime and Justice: A Review of Research*. Chicago, IL: University of Chicago Press.

Snacken, S. and Dumortier, E. 2012. *Resisting Punitiveness in Europe?* Abingdonand New York: Routledge.

Snacken, S. and Van ZylSmit, D. 2013. Distinctive Features of European Penology and Penal Policy-Making, in *European Penology?*, edited by T. Daemset al. Oxford: Hart Publishing.

Soboleva, N., Kazakova, N. and Chong, J. 2006. *Conviction and Sentencing of Offenders in New Zealand 1996–2006*. New Zealand: Ministry of Justice.

Social Work Services and Prisons Inspectorates for Scotland. 1998. *Women Offenders: A Safer Way*. Edinburgh: HMSO.

Sozzo, M. 2011. Cultural Travels and Crime Prevention in Argentina, in *Travels of the Criminal Question: Cultural Embeddedness and Diffusion*, edited by D. Melossiet al. Oxford: Hart.

Sparks, R. 2000. Perspectives on Risk and Penal Politics, in *Crime, Risk and Insecurity*, edited by T. Hope and R. Sparks. London: Routledge.

Sparks, R. 2001. Degrees of estrangement: The cultural theory of risk and comparative criminology. *Theoretical Criminology*, 5(2), 159–76.

Sparks, R. 2011. Preface toReview Symposium on Nicola Lacey, *The Prisoners' Dilemma: Political Economy and Punishment in Contemporary Democracies*. *Punishment & Society*, 13(1), 93–5.

Spier, P. 1997. *Conviction and Sentencing of Offenders in New Zealand 1987–1996*. Wellington: Ministry of Justice.

Spier, P. 2002. *Conviction and Sentencing of Offenders in New Zealand 1992–2001*. Wellington: Ministry of Justice.

Spier, P. and Lash, B. 2004. *Conviction and Sentencing of Offenders in New Zealand 1994–2003*. Wellington: Ministry of Justice.
Spinner, M. 2007. Compulsory consensus? The sources of elite political culture and the consolidation of central and East European democracies. PhD thesis, Central European University. Available at: http://web.ceu.hu/polsci/dissertations/Max_Spinner.pdf [Accessed various dates].
Stanley, E. 2009. Human rights in prisons: Evaluating the current situation, Addressing the Underlying Causes of Offending: What is the Evidence?, Institute of Policy Studies, Victoria University Wellington, New Zealand, 27 February 2009.
Stenning, P. and Shearing, C. 1980. The quiet revolution: The nature, development and general legal implications of private security in Canada. *Criminal Law Quarterly*, 22(2), 220–48.
Stenning, P. 2006. Principles/foundations of policing, **Securing** the **future:** Networked policing in **New Zealand**, Wellington, **New Zealand,** 22 November. Available at: http://www.policeact.govt.nz/securing-the-future.html [Accessed 2 March 2009].
Stewart Committee. 1980. *The Motorist and Fixed Penalties*. Edinburgh: HMSO.
Stewart Committee. 1983. *Keeping Offenders Out of Court: Further Alternatives to Prosecution*. Edinburgh: HMSO.
Sunday Star Times. 2009. The vigilantes,3 March.
Sunday Tribune. 2007. Life after losing: What ex-PD Michael McDowell did next, 18 November.
Te Whaiti, P. and Roguski, M. 1998. *Māori Perceptions of the Police*. Parekereke: Victoria Link Ltd.
Tolmie, J. 2007. Crime in New Zealand over the Last Ten Years, in *Criminal Justice in New Zealand*, edited by J. Tolmie and W.J. Brookbanks. Wellington: Lexis.
Tombs, J. 2004. *A Unique Punishment: Sentencing and the Prison Population in Scotland*. Edinburgh: Rethinking Crime and Punishment/Scottish Consortium on Crime and Criminal Justice. Available at: www.sccj.org.uk [Accessed 4 January 2009].
Tonry, M. 1996. *Sentencing Matters*. Oxford: Oxford University Press.
Tonry, M. 2001. Symbol, substance and severity in western penal policies. *Punishment & Society*, 3(4), 517–36.
Tonry, M. 2004. *Punishment and Politics: Evidence and Emulation in the Making of English Crime Control Policy*. Cullompton, Devon: Willan.
Tonry, M. (ed.) 2007. *Crime, Punishment and Politics in Comparative Perspective*, vol. 36 of *Crime and Justice: A Review of Research*. Chicago, IL: University of Chicago Press.
Tonry, M. 2009. Explaining American penal policies. *Punishment & Society*, 11(3), 377–94.
Tonry, M. 2012. Foreword, in *Resisting Punitiveness in Europe?*, edited by S. Snackenand E. Dumortier. Abingdon and New York: Routledge.
Torrance, D. 2006. *The Scottish Secretaries*. Edinburgh: Birlinn Ltd.

TV3 Nightly News with Vincent Brown. 2008. TV3, 14 January 2008.

United Kingdom Children's Rights Commissioners. 2008. *Report to the UN Committee on the Rights of the Child*. Available at: www.sccyp.org.uk/UK_Childrens_Commissioners_UN_Report.pdf [Accessed 10 March 2009].

UN Committee Against Torture. 2009. *Committee Against Torture Hears Response of New Zealand*. Press release, issued 4 May 2009. Available at: http://www.hrea.org/lists2/display.php?language_id=1&id=12553 [Accessed various dates].

UN Committee on the Rights of the Child. 2002. *Concluding Observations on the United Kingdom and Northern Ireland*. CRC/C/15/Add.188.

UN Committee on the Rights of the Child.2007. *General Comment No. 10: Children's Rights in Juvenile Justice*. CRC/C/GC/10.

UN Committee on the Rights of the Child. 2008. *Concluding Observations on the United Kingdom of Great Britain and Northern Ireland*. CCR/C/GBR/CO/4.

UNICEF. 2009. *Information by Country: At a Glance: New Zealand*. Available at: http://www.unicef.org/infobycountry/newzealand_statistics.html [Accessed 25 April 2009].

US Department of State.1994–2008. *Country Reports on Human Rights Practices: Ireland*. Washington, DC: Government Printing Office.

Van Dijk, J. and Mayhew, P. 1992. *Criminal Victimization in the Industrialized World: Key Findings of the 1989 and 1992 International Crime Surveys*. The Hague: Ministry of Justice, Department of Crime Prevention.

Van Dijk, J., Manchin, R., van Kesteren, J., Nevala, S. and Hideg, G. 2007. *The Burden of Crime in the EU. Research Report: A Comparative Analysis of the European Crime and Safety Survey (EU ICS) 2005*. Brussels: EUICS Consortium.

Van Dijk, J., van Kesteren, J. and Smit, P. 2008. *Criminal Victimisation in International Perspective: Key findings from the 2004–2005 ICVS and EU ICS*. The Hague: Boom Legal Publishers.

Vaughan, B. and Kilcommins, S. 2007. The Europeanisation of human rights and the limits of authoritarian policing in Ireland. *European Journal of Criminology*, 4(4), 437–59.

Vaughan, B. and Kilcommins, S. 2008. *Terrorism, Rights and the Rule of Law: Negotiating Justice in Ireland*. Cullompton, Devon: Willan.

Vaughan, B. and Kilcommins, S. 2010. The governance of crime and the negotiation of justice. *Criminology and Criminal Justice*, 10(1), 59–75.

Vess, J. 2005. Preventive detention versus civil commitment: Alternative policies for public protection in New Zealand and California. *Psychiatry, Psychology and the Law*, 12(2), 357–66.

Vowles, J. and Aimer, P. 1993. *Voters' Vengeance: The 1990 Election in New Zealand and the Fate of the Fourth Labour Government*. Auckland: Auckland University Press.

Wacquant, L. 2003. The penalisation of poverty and the rise of neo-liberalism. *Capítulo Criminológico*, 31(1), 7–22.

Wacquant, L. 2005. The Great Penal Leap Backward: Incarceration in America from Nixon to Clinton, in *The New Punitiveness: Trends, Theories, Perspective*, edited by J. Pratt et al. Cullompton, Devon: Willan.

Wacquant, L. 2009. *Punishing the Poor: The Neoliberal Government of Social Insecurity*. Durham, NC: Duke University Press.

Walker, N. 1999. Situating Scottish Policing, in *Criminal Justice in Scotland*, edited by P. Duff and N. Hutton. Aldershot: Ashgate.

Walker, D. 2004. *A Legal History of Scotland, Vol. 8: The Twentieth Century*. Edinburgh: Lexis-Nexis.

Walsh, D. 2002. *Criminal Procedure*. Dublin: Thomson Round Hall.

Walsh, D. 2005a. The Criminal Justice Bill: Completing a crime control model of criminal justice?, Criminal Justice Bill 2004: Implications for Human Rights and Legal Practice, Trinity College Dublin, Ireland, 20 April 2005.

Walsh, D. 2005b. *Juvenile Justice*. Dublin: Thomson Round Hall.

Walsh, D. 2009. *Human Rights and Policing in Ireland*. Dublin: Clarus Press.

Whitman, J. 2003. *Harsh Justice: Criminal Punishment and the Widening Divide between America and Europe*. New York: Oxford University Press.

Workman, K. 2008. Politics and punitiveness: Overcoming the criminal justice dilemma, Lunchtime Series: Election 2008, School of Government and Institute of Policy Studies, Victoria University of Wellington, New Zealand, 20 October 2008.

Workman, K. 2009. Back to Churchill: An old vision for prisoner reintegration, Addressing the Underlying Causes of Offending: What is the Evidence?, School of Government and Institute of Policy Studies, Victoria University Wellington, New Zealand, 27 February 2009.

Whyte, B. 2007. *Social Work in Criminal Justice in Scotland*. [Online] Criminal Justice Social Work Development Centre for Scotland. Available at: http://www.cjsw.ac.uk/cjsw/files/CJSW%20READER%2007%20DOC.doc [Accessed 12 March 2009].

Wilson, J.Q. and Kelling, G.L. 1982. Broken windows. *Atlantic Monthly*, 249(3), 29–38.

Young, P. 1996/7. The peculiarities of the Scots. *Criminal Justice Matters*, 26, 22–4.

Young, P. 1997. *Crime and Criminal Justice in Scotland*. Edinburgh: The Stationery Office.

Young, W. and Brown, M. 1993. Cross-National Comparisons of Imprisonment, in *Crime and Justice: A Review of Research*, vol. 17, edited by M. Tonry, Chicago, IL: University of Chicago Press.

Zedner, L. 2002. Dangers of dystopias in penal theory. *Oxford Journal of Legal Studies*, 22(2), 341–66.

Zedner, L. 2010. Putting Crime Back on the Criminological Agenda, in *What is Criminology?*, edited by M. Bosworth and C. Hoyle. Oxford: Oxford University Press.

Index

Bold page numbers refer to figures, *italic* numbers refer to tables.

For Product Safety Concerns and Information please contact our EU
representative GPSR@taylorandfrancis.com
Taylor & Francis Verlag GmbH, Kaufingerstraße 24, 80331 München, Germany

www.ingramcontent.com/pod-product-compliance
Ingram Content Group UK Ltd.
Pitfield, Milton Keynes, MK11 3LW, UK
UKHW021722240926
475702UK00029BA/1786

* 9 7 8 0 3 6 7 6 0 0 5 0 1 *